SAP PRESS e-books

Print or e-book, Kindle or iPad, workplace or airplane: Choose where and how to read your SAP PRESS books! You can now get all our titles as e-books, too:

▶ By download and online access
▶ For all popular devices
▶ And, of course, DRM-free

Convinced? Then go to **www.sap-press.com** and get your e-book today.

Using SAP®

 **PRESS**

SAP PRESS is a joint initiative of SAP and Rheinwerk Publishing. The know-how offered by SAP specialists combined with the expertise of Rheinwerk Publishing offers the reader expert books in the field. SAP PRESS features first-hand information and expert advice, and provides useful skills for professional decision-making.

SAP PRESS offers a variety of books on technical and business-related topics for the SAP user. For further information, please visit our website: www.sap-press.com.

Venki Krishnamoorthy, Alexandra Carvalho
Discover SAP (3rd edition)
2015, 535 pages, paperback and e-book
www.sap-press.com/3586

Jens Krüger
SAP S/4HANA Finance: An Introduction (2nd edition)
2016, 411 pages, hardcover and e-book
www.sap-press.com/4122

Silvia, Frye, Berg
SAP HANA: An Introduction (4th edition)
2017, 549 pages, hardcover and e-book
www.sap-press.com/4160

Baumgartl, Chaadaev, Choi, Dudgeon, Lahiri, Meijerink, and Worsley-Tonks
SAP S/4HANA: An Introduction
2017, 449 pages, hardcover and e-book
www.sap-press.com/4153

Olaf Schulz

Using SAP®

An Introduction for Beginners and Business Users

Bonn • Boston

Editor Will Jobst
Acquisitions Editor Emily Nicholls
German Edition Editor Eva Tripp
Translation Lemoine International, Inc., Salt Lake City, UT
Copyeditor Julie McNamee
Cover Design Graham Geary
Photo Credit Shutterstock.com/376834639/© g-stockstudio
Layout Design Vera Brauner
Production Kelly O'Callaghan
Typesetting SatzPro, Krefeld (Germany)
Printed and bound in the United States of America, on paper from sustainable sources

ISBN 978-1-4932-1404-4
© 2017 by Rheinwerk Publishing, Inc., Boston (MA)
3rd edition 2017
3rd German edition published 2016 by Rheinwerk Verlag, Bonn, Germany

Library of Congress Cataloging-in-Publication Data
Names: Schulz, Olaf, author.
Title: Using SAP : An introduction for beginners and business users / Olaf Schulz.
Other titles: SAP-Grundkurs für Einsteiger und Anwender. English
Description: 3rd edition. | Bonn ; Boston : Rheinwerk Publishing, 2016. |
Translation of: SAP-Grundkurs für Einsteiger und Anwender.
Identifiers: LCCN 2016051694 | ISBN 9781493214044 (alk. paper)
Subjects: LCSH: SAP ERP. | Integrated software. | Business--Data processing.
Classification: LCC QA76.76.I57 S3813 20164 | DDC 650.0285--dc23
LC record available at https://lccn.loc.gov/2016051694

Contents at a Glance

Dear Reader,

The SAP landscape is broad and vast, and each successful go-live and employment offer letter creates new beginning SAP users. So if you've ever felt tired of opaque, confusing instructions, or wondered whether technical literature is *actually* written in secret code, you're not alone.

This book is your easy-to-follow guide to using SAP, from log-on to log-off. You can leave your decoder ring and cipher at home, and instead rely on SAP codebreaker Olaf Schulz for the tools you need to navigate otherwise puzzling SAP systems. His simple explanations and screenshots will provide you with the smoothest software guidance you've ever had, so you can move from feeling like an SAP newbie to operating like an SAP pro.

As always, we appreciate your feedback. What did you think about *Using SAP*? Your comments and suggestions are the most useful tools to help us make our books the best they can be. Please feel free to contact me and share any praise or criticism you may have.

Thank you for purchasing a book from SAP PRESS!

Will Jobst
Editor, SAP PRESS

Rheinwerk Publishing
Boston, MA

willj@rheinwerk-publishing.com
www.sap-press.com

Contents

Part II   Basic Principles of System Operation

Appendices

About This Book

This book is aimed at anyone who wants to become familiar with the SAP system or get an overview of the most important functions and components. We'll describe the software, how you navigate in the SAP system, and which central functions are available for the various business areas—logistics, accounting, and human resources.

If you're already familiar with the SAP system and want to specialize in one of the various SAP components, or if you're looking for detailed information, this book is probably not the best resource for you. In this case, you should refer to a book that deals with your specific field of interest at *www.sap-press.com*.

Structure of the Book

The book is divided into 3 parts and 20 chapters:

Part I outlines the history of the SAP enterprise and provides an overview of its products and special features.

Chapter 1, Brief History of the SAP Enterprise, describes the history of SAP SE from its foundation to the present.

In **Chapter 2**, How Does SAP Software Work?, you learn how to adapt the software to the requirements and needs of enterprises.

Chapter 3, Overview of the Most Critical SAP Products, provides an overview of the products of SAP Business Suite—that is, SAP ERP, SAP Supply Chain Management (SAP SCM), SAP Product Lifecycle Management (SAP PLM), and SAP Supplier Relationship Management (SAP SRM).

Part II forms the centerpiece of this book. It explains step by step how you operate the SAP system.

Chapter 4, Organizational Structures and Master Data, illustrates the significance of master data for all business processes and how you can map the enterprise structure in SAP systems using organizational units.

Chapter 5, Logging On to the SAP System, describes how you establish a connection from a workplace computer to an SAP system.

Chapter 6, Navigating in the SAP System, discusses the navigation in the program interface.

Chapter 7, Maintaining the System Layout and User Data, shows you how to adapt the SAP system to your requirements.

Chapter 8, Creating Evaluations and Reports, deals with evaluating and reporting processes. The data stored in the SAP system are often used for evaluations, which then form the basis for the decision-making process in the enterprise.

Chapter 9, Printing, describes the print process in the SAP system, how to print documents, and the creation of screenshots from the SAP system.

Chapter 10, Automating Tasks, teaches you how to have the SAP system work for you by automating tasks via batch jobs.

Chapter 11, Working with Messages and Business Workplace, shows you how to use the SAP system to perform different office administration tasks. The Business Workplace enables you to send messages, manage documents, and deploy workflows.

Chapter 12, Electronic Data Exchange, explains how you can use Electronic Data Interchange (EDI) to transfer data to other systems seamlessly.

Chapter 13, Using Help Functions, describes the different help functions: the SAP online help, the F1 and F4 help, and many more.

Chapter 14, The Role and Authorization Concept, provides general information on authorization control and the role concept in SAP ERP.

Part III of this book provides an overview of the most critical business processes in the SAP system.

In **Chapter 15**, Materials Management, you learn how purchasing processes are mapped in the Materials Management (MM) component in the SAP ERP system. The chapter provides information on the required master data, the organizational structures, and the procurement process, including purchase order, goods receipt, and invoice verification.

Chapter 16, Sales and Distribution, discusses sales processes and illustrates the sales process with the Sales and Distribution (SD) component in the SAP

ERP system. It introduces master data and organizational structures, as well as sales order, goods issue, and invoicing.

Chapter 17, SAP ERP Financials, gives you an overview of the central functions of the Financials (FI) component in SAP ERP. It discusses the SAP General Ledger, as well as accounts receivable and accounts payable.

Chapter 18, Controlling, describes the basic principles and functions of the Controlling (CO) component in SAP ERP. This includes controlling tasks, overhead cost controlling, product cost controlling, and profitability analysis.

Chapter 19, Human Resources, deals with the tasks and processes of human resources (HR) in the SAP system, for example, organizational management, recruitment, personnel administration, and time management.

The case study in **Chapter 20** reinforces your understanding of the basic SAP processes by reproducing a continuous process in the SAP system.

The **Appendix** of this book provides critical information for quick reference: abbreviations, a glossary with the most important SAP concepts, and an overview of transaction codes, menu paths, key combinations, buttons, and function keys.

More content is available on the book's catalog page. There you can download solution notes for the exercises, additional information, and the overviews from the appendix for printing. You can find documents for download under *https://www.sap-press.com/using-sap_4155/* in the **Product Supplements** area.

Working with This Book

You can use this book both as a general introduction and as a reference book. Each chapter of Part II contains exercises in which you can apply what you've learned. You can also carry out the exercises directly in an Internet Demonstration and Evaluation System (IDES) training system. Allow yourself plenty of time, and make sure that you understand all of the steps. This way, you become acquainted with the SAP system. Remember: Never carry out the exercises in a live SAP system; if you're unsure, ask your supervisor or administrator.

Reading this book doesn't require previous knowledge of SAP, just basic PC knowledge and an understanding of the processes in business enterprises.

Beginners should read the book from the beginning because the individual chapters build on each other. Each topic provides background information about concepts and processes. Finally, the processes in the system are described click by click and with numerous screenshots.

SAP's Training System

You can maximize your success with this book if you have access to an SAP ERP test or training system. All the examples in this book are based on the IDES system, which means that you don't have to implement Customizing settings to reproduce examples or carry out exercises.

IDES is the SAP ERP training system where you navigate in a virtual enterprise. It maps an entire enterprise structure and provides master data for all areas. SAP customers have free access to IDES.

Preparing for User Certification

You can also use this book to prepare for the SAP user certification, *Foundation Level – System Handling*. Although it can't completely replace classroom training with trainer and training system, it still provides useful tips in preparation for the test. The author has prepared courses for SAP certifications and provides you with the information necessary to help you prepare. You can find more information about the user certification on the book's catalog page at *https://www.sap-press.com/using-sap_4155/*.

SAP offers different certifications for users and consultants. This book covers the knowledge that you need for the *Foundation Level – System Handling* user certification. You can find up-to-date information on this certification on the SAP website at *https://training.sap.com/shop/certification/*.

Acknowledgments

It's not easy to write a book on this kind of subject, especially because it covers such a wide range of topics, all of which are useful to readers.

While writing this book, I received support from many people. First of all, I want to thank my wife, Nicole, for her support, and Eva Tripp, editor at SAP PRESS, for the excellent cooperation and infinite patience. My thanks also go to Ana Carla Psenner and Anja Marxsen for their constructive reviews of the chapters on Financial Accounting, Controlling, and Human Resources. Thank you to my employer ABISCON GmbH in Nuremberg for letting me use the SAP test system.

Part I

The SAP Enterprise

1 Brief History of the SAP Enterprise

SAP produces software to support the processes of businesses from different industries and of various sizes. Since it was founded in the 1970s, SAP has become the largest European and fourth-largest global software manufacturer. This chapter outlines the most critical milestones in the development of SAP from the early stages up to today.

This chapter discusses the following:

- Where SAP began
- How SAP became the enterprise it is today
- What the SAP R/3 and SAP ERP products are made of

1.1 Getting Started: From Realtime Financials to SAP R/3

SAP's history begins in Weinheim, Germany, in the early 1970s. In 1972, five former IBM employees—Hans-Werner Hektor, Dietmar Hopp, Hasso Plattner, Klaus Tschira, and Claus Wellenreuther—founded the enterprise *Systemanalyse und Programmentwicklung* (System Analysis and Program Development), which was later renamed *Systeme, Anwendungen und Produkte in der Datenverarbeitung* (Systems, Applications, and Products in Data Processing). In the early stages, they programmed at their customers' data centers because they didn't have their own systems yet. The very first product was created on computers that belonged to their first customer, Imperial Chemical Industries (ICI).

The Realtime Financials (RF) system was the first SAP product that supported financial business processes. The computers of the time can't even be compared with today's IT systems. The software was operated on large computer systems, punch cards were used as data carriers (Figure 1.1), and memory capacities were limited to only a few kilobytes.

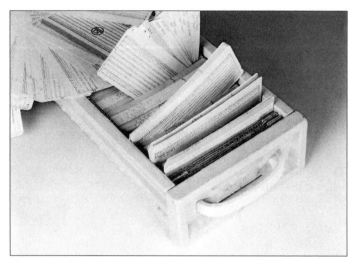

Figure 1.1 *Former Data Carriers: Punch Cards*

RF formed the basis of further software parts, called modules (components today). Later, RF was also referred to as SAP R/1. The letter "R" stands for real time, and even decades later, this letter is still included in the names of SAP's core products.

> **INFO**
>
> **Real-Time Processing**
> Real-time processing means that actions (e.g., creating or changing data records) are immediately executed in the system and have immediate effect on the processes concerned.

SAP's software had the following three features from the outset:

- **Real-time processing**
  The processing was supposed to be made in real time; that is, an input is immediately available in the entire system.

- **Standard software**
  The software was supposed to be standardized to a large extent. In other words, every enterprise obtains the same software, which is then customized during the implementation project.

- **Integration**
  The various modules or components are supposed to be integrated, which means that the data from one application are also available to other applications.

You can find more information on these properties in Chapter 3.

> **Integration**
>
> The settlement for a completed procurement process (the Materials Management (MM) component in SAP ERP) is implemented in financial accounting (the SAP ERP Financials [FI] component in SAP). In this process, the relevant departments use the documents that were created or stored in the SAP system during the operation.

Two years after SAP was founded, it established itself for more than 40 additional customers from different industries. *SAP GmbH* was founded in 1976. In the following year, SAP relocated its headquarters from Weinheim to Walldorf, Germany.

In 1979, SAP redesigned its applications and revised the technologies in system and database development; these were included in the SAP R/2 system (the successor of SAP R/1). The next leap in SAP development was the initial public offering; in 1988, SAP GmbH became SAP AG. In 2014, it became SAP SE.

In 1991, SAP AG presented the first applications of the SAP R/3 system at the CeBIT trade fair in Hanover, Germany. SAP R/3 is a system with new client-server architecture and a graphical user interface. The three layers of this client-server architecture (database layer, application layer, and presentation layer) are represented by the figure "3" in the product name. Relational databases are used internally, and the system can be used in different platforms. Chapter 2 and Chapter 3 provide additional information about this.

> **Relational Databases**
>
> Information is stored as tables for relational databases. The tables are linked with one another so that the information doesn't need to be stored multiple times in the system. Connections—or relations—emerge between the tables. Relational databases that are well-known today include SAP MaxDB, Microsoft SQL Server, mySQL, Oracle, and DB2 from IBM.

The client-server architecture is based on a three-layer concept that describes the system's technical task allocation: The presentation layer is a user PC (frontend) in the network, on which the screens are displayed. If one user PC fails, it won't affect the other users because the applications are "only" presented. The system's programs and the user's inputs are processed at the application layer. Various user PCs are connected with a server. One or more servers access the databases, which can be installed on separate machines. Chapter 3 discusses the client-server principle in more detail.

The SAP R/3 system was extremely successful. The hardware required by a client-server system was more efficient and less expensive; at the same time, a greater number of users could work with the system. SAP R/3 consisted of a technical basis, SAP's "operating system" so to speak, and the applications, which were broken down into various modules for the different enterprise areas.

From the functional perspective, SAP R/3 provided software for all steps in the value chain of an enterprise. The SAP software mapped these steps (i.e., purchase, dispatch, and invoicing) so that all essential departments of an enterprise were now able to use the SAP system for their work: accounting, controlling, sales and distribution, purchasing, production, stockholding, and human resources.

> **Enterprise Resource Planning**
> An IT system that supports enterprise processes is referred to as an enterprise resource planning (ERP) system. The goal is to use these resources as efficiently as possible and effectively control the enterprise.

1.2   SAP from the Turn of the Millennium to the Present

In 2000, there were more than 10 million SAP users around the world. The software, which covers the classic enterprise areas, is still available. In addition to that, however, the Internet era that dawned in the 1990s brought new technologies, which involved new options for communication between customers and enterprises, such as web sales. In addition, the cooperation of businesses changed, and they increasingly communicated via web technologies.

1

SAP R/3 Enterprise (Release 4.7) was the last SAP system to include the real time "R" in its name. In 2003, the product name SAP R/3 was replaced with mySAP ERP and then SAP ERP. A stronger emphasis was placed on the purpose of SAP software—enterprise resource planning.

SAP ERP 6.0 is the current release that is used in 2016 and as the basis of this book. New functions are imported via enhancement packages (EHP). The core of the system, however, is still composed of the applications from R/3 times; the range of products, however, contain more solutions that further refine the functional scope of SAP ERP or offer support for processes that aren't covered in SAP ERP. Chapter 3 provides a more detailed description of these solutions.

An important innovation was the implementation of SAP NetWeaver as a technology platform. Among other things, SAP NetWeaver includes those functions that were previously located in SAP Basis. The keyword for SAP NetWeaver is *integration*—there is the option to access the SAP system via the Internet to support processes using different software applications and to gather information. You'll find a brief overview of SAP NetWeaver in Chapter 3.

In past years, SAP has focused on expanding into new markets. Various software products are directed toward the target group of small and medium businesses (SMB). In addition, SAP's acquisitions (e.g. BusinessObjects in 2007 and Sybase in 2010) have attracted attention. In this context, SAP has focused on cloud computing, mobile business applications, and so-called in-memory technology (described in more detail in the two subsequent chapters).

INFO

SAP Figures

To illustrate SAP's market success, let's talk numbers: As of 2016, SAP has a workforce of approximately 78,000 employees located in Germany, the United States, and India. SAP is a global enterprise with more than 310,000 customers in more than 190 countries. Its headquarters are still located in Walldorf, Germany (Figure 1.2).

Figure 1.2 *SAP Main Building at the Enterprise's Headquarters in Walldorf*

In this chapter, you've learned about the history of the SAP enterprise and its most essential product, SAP ERP. Some important characteristics of the SAP software were also discussed, including the separation of client, server, and database, as well as integration. The following chapters discuss how the SAP system functions in more detail.

2   How Does SAP Software Work?

Chapter 1 already introduced you to some characteristics of SAP systems. In addition to features such as standardization, real-time processing, and integration, these also include adaptability and extensibility.

This chapter discusses the following:
- Basic principles of SAP software
- Characteristics of standard software
- How you can adapt the SAP system to your enterprise
- Characteristics of client-server architecture
- How business processes are mapped and integrated continuously
- What real-time processing is

2.1   What Is Standard Software?

SAP provides standard software. This means that the basic functions without modifications can map many business processes in various industries. Using standard software has a lot of advantages. The customer can benefit from continuous optimizations, enhancements, and new technologies. Because the developers work closely with their customers, other users' requirements are considered for new versions.

The opposite of standard software is individual software, which is developed for one customer and is supposed to meet only one customer's specific requirements. In this case, this single customer has to pay the development costs and all subsequent costs.

SAP provides predefined packages, called industry solutions, for use in specific industries. Currently (in 2016), about 24 industry solutions are available, for example, SAP for Utilities (IS-U), SAP for Automotive (IS-A), and SAP for Defense & Security (DFPS). See Chapter 3 for more information on these. Industry solutions are standard software with an extended functional scope to map the processes of an enterprise from a specific industry.

2.2   Adapting the SAP System to an Enterprise

The previous section referred to SAP as standard software. Of course, the requirements and processes vary from business to business. SAP products can be adapted to each customer's requirements and business processes. SAP software consists of modules or components with different functions; the customer can select those that suit his needs. The SAP system is adapted during the implementation project.

This adaptation of the system is enabled by *Customizing*, which allows you to set up the system without programming (called *configuring*). For example, when you implement a new system, the system maps the structure of the business—called the organizational structure—including clients, company codes, and so on. (You can find more information on organizational structures in Chapter 4.) In the SAP ERP Financials (FI) component, for example, you as the customer define how taxes on your business are determined because SAP products are used in countries where tax rates vary and taxes are determined differently.

The adaptation of the SAP system in Customizing is also the reason why the screens in your system may not be identical to those shown in this book.

You can implement Customizing in the SAP system via the Implementation Guide (IMG), which maps the setting options in a tree structure sorted by areas. The next two figures show screens from Customizing of the SAP system.

Customizing maps the structure of the enterprise and its individual areas and departments in the SAP system through the organizational structure. Figure 2.1 shows how the organizational structure of an enterprise is set up in the SAP system and which organizational units are linked together. Customizing of the organizational structures provides a Customizing table you can use to assign plants to a purchasing organization within the organizational structure, for example.

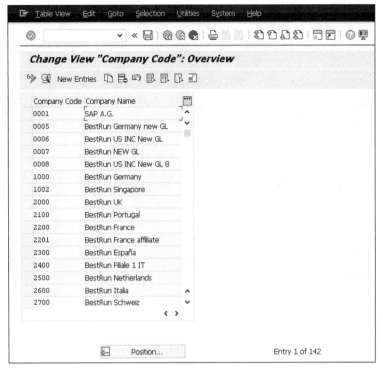

Figure 2.1 *Customizing of Organizational Structures (Example Purchasing Organization: Plant)*

Customizing also sets the business's processes. Figure 2.2 shows how you can make various settings in the SAP system via the IMG. In this example from the organizational structure area, a plant is assigned to a company code.

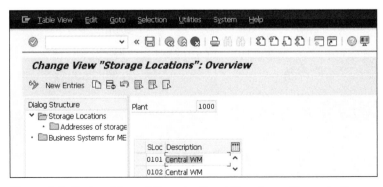

Figure 2.2 *Customizing of Organizational Structures (Example Company Code: Plant)*

EXAMPLE

Customizing Activities

- Creating organizational structures
- Mapping business processes
- Implementing basic system settings
- Adding selection lists
- Creating material types that aren't included in the standard version
- Defining approval procedures
- Defining whether fields are supposed to be hidden
- Configuring areas for automatic number assignments

With Customizing, settings are made in the system without writing a single line of program code. However, programming may be necessary if the requirements can't be met with Customizing. In the SAP system, you can implement developments using the ABAP and Java programming languages, as described in the next section.

2.3   What If the Standard Isn't Sufficient?

If the standard system and the Customizing options aren't sufficient to meet your business requirements, you can extend the system with custom developments or products by SAP partners. You can integrate these non-SAP products by SAP partners via the technical platform SAP NetWeaver (see Chapter 3).

NOTE

Programming for the SAP System

Programming requirements can be implemented using the development environment that is provided in the SAP system, using ABAP, or using Java. ABAP programmers use the ABAP Workbench, a development environment from SAP NetWeaver.

2.4   Orientation toward the Process

Business processes are defined sequences of steps in the enterprise. When you order goods, you trigger a process, for example, a purchase requisition is implemented, the incoming goods posted, and, finally, the invoice verified.

The SAP system focuses on the business process because it needs to be mapped continuously within the system.

It's critical that you as the user visualize the process when working in the system. Make sure you understand what the process is supposed to achieve, where it starts, and where it ends before you begin.

Figure 2.3 shows the sales process from the perspective of the SAP system and makes it easy for you to understand the individual substeps: The customer inquires about the availability and price of a specific product. He then places an order with your enterprise. Your enterprise executes the order and creates and posts the invoice.

Figure 2.3 *Sales Process as Mapped in the SAP System*

For enterprises that use SAP software, it's common that multiple departments are involved in a business process. For example, the sales process involves the sales department, the warehouse, and invoice verification (which is usually integrated with accounts receivable accounting as a part of financial accounting). The SAP system ensures that the individual processes integrate seamlessly and can be processed.

The system records all processes, steps, and user activities so that they are continuous, transparent, and reproducible at any time. The basic principle of "Don't post without documentation" also applies to IT systems because business processes have to be effective and auditors must be able to trace all processing steps and documents.

2.5   Real Time

Because the SAP system is highly integrated, changes must be accessible to everyone involved. Otherwise, a colleague from another department may work with inaccurate or obsolete information. That's where the real time principle comes into play. *Real time* is the amount of time that is required to complete a system activity, and it means that changes are immediately available to all users across the system.

Real Time

You add a contact partner to the vendor master record in the SAP system. After this information has been saved, the change is immediately effected in the entire SAP system. Every user who has the respective authorization can access the master record and thus view the new entry.

The result is that all pieces of information are kept up to date in the business, and completed process steps can be directly used as a basis for others.

In-Memory Computing

When using the new SAP HANA product, which makes it possible to work in "real" real time by leveraging in-memory technology, you can now process even extensive data volumes within seconds. Because data are kept in-memory, access to this information is accelerated significantly. A great variety of SAP applications can now be used on SAP HANA.

2.6   Central Data: Decentralized Processing

In most businesses, data aren't stored on the employees' PCs but instead on a central computer. This client-server architecture lets you access a central computer (server = provider) from your workplace computer (client = customer).

SAP uses a three-layer client-server architecture, which has the following layers (Figure 2.4):

❶   Client (presentation layer, e.g., your workplace computer)

❷   Server (application layer)

❸   Database (database layer)

If, for example, you use the SAP system on your workplace computer and call customer data, this request is transferred from your computer to the server. The database server then processes this data (by editing, deleting, or requesting the data). The result of the task is finally transferred from the server back to the client so that you can view and process the data on your screen.

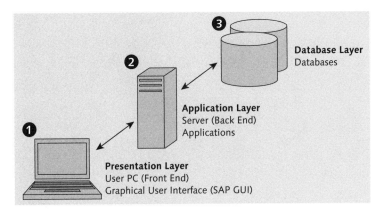

Figure 2.4 *The Three-Layer Client-Server Architecture*

This concept is central to many professional business applications (ERP systems) that are used by more than one person. Using a client-server architecture has numerous advantages:

- You can use different hardware and operating systems on the server and on the client.
- If one client fails, the other users can continue working.
- Central data backups are possible.
- The data retention can be centralized.

However, client-server architectures also have disadvantages:

- If the server fails, none of the clients can work.
- The network infrastructure must be stable and secure.

With client-server architecture, it doesn't matter whether the client accesses the server applications via a local area network (LAN) or via an Internet connection.

This chapter introduced the most important basic principles of SAP systems and described the characteristics of standard software. When a business purchases a complete software package, the package is then adapted to its requirements and specific processes using Customizing. Custom solutions can be programmed if the Customizing options aren't sufficient. You also learned about the most critical basic principles of SAP systems. Chapter 3 provides an overview of the SAP products.

3 Overview of the Most Critical SAP Products

SAP offers software for different sized enterprises and business requirements. Before you get to know the practical parts of the SAP system in upcoming chapters, first you need to understand SAP's most critical products. Many software solutions are available for special requirements beyond those presented here, but this chapter covers the largest and most important.

This chapter discusses the following:
- SAP software for financial accounting, human resources, and logistics
- SAP Business Suite applications
- Technology support for these solutions
- SAP NetWeaver

3.1 Complete Package: SAP Business Suite

Since the early years, SAP has extended and diversified its software offerings to cover different business requirements. Rather than a single application, the SAP Business Suite is SAP's core product and consists of various solutions. You can purchase (or license) these solutions individually or as a complete package.

The SAP Business Suite consists of the following parts (Figure 3.1):

- SAP ERP
- SAP Customer Relationship Management (SAP CRM)
- SAP Supplier Relationship Management (SAP SRM)
- SAP Product Lifecycle Management (SAP PLM)
- SAP Supply Chain Management (SAP SCM)

SAP NetWeaver is the technical basis for all of these products.

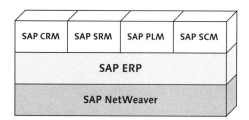

Figure 3.1 *Parts of the SAP Business Suite*

The following sections discuss these individual parts and their most important functions.

3.2   The Central Component: SAP ERP

SAP ERP forms the core component of the SAP Business Suite. You can use SAP ERP to map operative and administrative business processes across departments.

SAP ERP contains the following applications:

- Accounting (SAP ERP Financials)
- Human resources (SAP ERP Human Capital Management)
- Logistics (SAP ERP Operations and SAP ERP Corporate Services)

Within these applications, you can find the components (formerly known as modules) that you already know from SAP R/3. Table 3.1 shows some of these components; the most essential are detailed in Part III of this book.

Application	Function	Component (acronym)
Accounting	SAP ERP Financials/External Accounting	FI
	Controlling/Managerial Accounting	CO
	Financial Supply Chain Management	FSCM
	Treasury	TR

Table 3.1 *Essential SAP ERP Components*

Application	Function	Component (acronym)
	Enterprise Controlling	EC
	Strategic Enterprise Management	SEM
	Project System	PS
Human resources	Personnel Administration	PA
	Recruitment	RC
	Personnel Development	PD
	Payroll	PY
	Training and Event Management	PE
	Time Management	PT
	Organizational Management	OM
	Travel Management	TM
Logistics	Purchasing	MM-PUR
	Production Planning and Control	PP
	Sales and Distribution	SD
	Customer Service	CS
	Warehouse Management	WM
	Transportation and Distribution	TD
	QM	QM
	Real Estate Management	RE
	Plant Maintenance	PM (subset of SAP EAM)
	Environment, Health, and Safety Management	EHS

Table 3.1 *Essential SAP ERP Components (Cont.)*

Figure 3.2 shows the Graphical User Interface of the SAP system (SAP GUI) directly after logon. Here, you can clearly identify the application areas covered by SAP ERP.

Figure 3.2 SAP GUI

The following sections briefly discuss the processes that can be mapped in SAP ERP and the associated SAP components. Keep in mind that you typically can't consider each area of a business separately because many functions are linked together.

Accounting

SAP ERP Financials (FI) contains software for both financial accounting and controlling. New tools (e.g., cash flow management) have been added since the early versions of SAP R/3 were released. In addition, SAP has completely revised general ledger accounting in the system (new SAP General Ledger [new G/L]).

You can use the financial accounting component (FI) to map financial reporting requirements that are applicable in many countries, languages, and currencies. Important areas of accounting include the following:

- Financial accounting (external accounting)
- Controlling (managerial accounting)

- Corporate governance
- Treasury
- Receivables management

The tasks of financial accounting, which are supported by FI, center on business accounting. All business transactions are entered, documented, and allocated to accounts. Based on this data, you can create the legal balance and the profit and loss statement (P&L) at the end of the fiscal year.

The SAP component for managerial accounting or Controlling (CO) focuses on business success. Business processes need to be optimized for profit maximization. Cost accounting, performance accounting, and investment are utilities in CO. The information gained from these processes forms the basis for important business decisions and the business's orientation. Legal provisions aren't binding for the business in managerial accounting, as they are in financial accounting.

Beyond that, you can use SAP to meet further financial requirements: SAP ERP contains functions that help businesses comply with national and international rules and regulations. Here you must distinguish between legally binding and voluntary measures. These measures are summarized under the concept of *corporate governance*, which entails responsible business management and control.

Functions are also available in the Treasury area to create and plan financial means and to ensure payments. Another increasingly important task of financial accounting is the safeguarding of liquidity (i.e., the solvency of the business).

> **NOTE**
>
> **Receivables Management**
> Receivables management plays a critical role in ensuring liquidity. Tasks required for this goal range from credit standing check of customers and processing of clarification cases to electronic invoicing and online payment transactions.

Human Resources

Another important area in which the SAP system is used involves human resources. SAP ERP Human Capital Management (SAP ERP HCM) has replaced Human Resources (HR) in SAP R/3.

SAP ERP HCM enables enterprises to do the following:

- Manage employees (personnel administration)
- Create payrolls
- Plan qualification measures and trainings
- Record and settle working times
- Manage applicant data

Personnel Administration involves the management of employees. Data are presented in the form of infotype records, such as organizational assignments, personal data, addresses, planned working time, basic pay, and bank details.

With the Payroll tool, you can create salary certificates for employees and transfer the results to accounting.

Personnel Development helps you plan and implement education and training measures for employees. The development requirement of the employee is derived by comparing the current qualification with the job profile. Training and Event Management is an integrative part of SAP ERP HCM, which allows you to plan, implement, and manage trainings and other business events.

Time Management is the management of attendance times, flextime, annual leave, and absences. The information is entered online in the system by those employees responsible in Employee Self-Service (ESS) applications or time-recording systems.

The system supports the entire recruitment process, from entering applicant data to final staffing assignments. Applicant data can be entered either by the applicants themselves (via an Internet portal) or by employees of personnel management.

In Organizational Management, employees are then assigned to their corresponding positions in the business. The system provides organizational units to map organization structures in the system.

Logistics

The SAP system supports all business areas that belong to the supply chain, which includes all business processes that concern suppliers and customers, as well as the production of products (as illustrated in Figure 3.3):

- Purchasing (materials management)
- Production and product development
- Sales and customer service

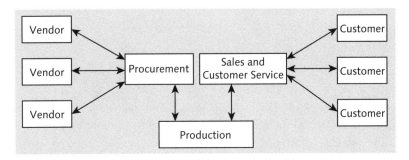

Figure 3.3 *Supply Chain*

Materials Management (MM) involves goods or services that must be procured (purchased) and then managed and paid. The process starts with the processing of the purchase requisitions, which are sent to Purchasing from various departments of the business and then trigger the purchase order itself. MM is also responsible for inventory management of materials with material valuation for the financial statements. Information about the material that is still in stock must be gathered in inventories. Another important task within MM is invoice verification, where invoices for purchased goods or services are checked for correctness. MM is also responsible for the maintenance of material master data. You'll find more details on MM in Chapter 15.

The materials procured in MM can be used for production, for example. Production Planning (PP) in the SAP system includes SAP Sales and Operations Planning (S&OP) as well as PP itself (both for discrete manufacturing—i.e., manufacturing of general goods—and for process manufacturing, which is the manufacturing of uncountable units, e.g., fluids in the chemicals industry). This process includes capacity and requirements planning, production orders, Kanban (a method of production flow control that works according to the pull principle), make-to-order production, repetitive manufacturing, and assembly processing.

In Sales and Distribution (SD), the SAP system supports all processes associated with the sale of goods or services. In this context, employees must process quotations and sales orders, determine the availability of goods, and create scheduling agreements. SD includes the check of credit limits in sales, determination of prices and conditions, and invoicing. If a business exports a high volume of goods, then foreign trade and customs processing becomes important.

Supply Chain

The processes in Purchasing, Product Development, and SD can be mapped using SAP. In this example, a mechanical engineering business manufactures different types of pumps. Because the storage costs need to be kept as low as possible, only customer inquiries with quantities of up to 10 pieces can be handled immediately. Larger quantities are produced in separate production plants. A safety stock of 3 pieces is kept in stock for each pump type for guarantee cases.

In line with the incoming sales orders, materials are procured from the suppliers and further processed in the in-house production plants to produce the end products. The ordered pumps are delivered to the customer and invoiced. All business processes described here between the suppliers and the customers of the mechanical engineering business belong to the Logistics area. Data can be automatically transferred from Logistics to FI through integration.

The logistics process concludes with the Customer Service area (CS), which is used for customer care. It includes the management and processing of customer service orders, such as warranty, maintenance, and repair.

Beyond the core business processes described here, SAP ERP also includes other components, which SAP summarizes in SAP ERP Corporate Services. These include, among others, Quality Management (QM) and Environment, Health, and Safety (EHS), which aren't further discussed in this book.

3.3   Maintaining Customer Relationships: SAP Customer Relationship Management

SAP Customer Relationship Management (SAP CRM) is the active management of customer relationships. SAP CRM supports all phases in which employees of a business communicate and contact customers:

- Marketing
- Sales and distribution
- Service

The functions of SAP CRM cover a wider scope and are used to map more complex processes than the components of SAP ERP.

Information on customers, which is usually only available to sales employees with direct customer contacts, is stored in the system. This information is also relevant for employees from the marketing and product development areas for use as the basis for promotions or to help product development better cater to customer requests. Without an IT system, important information gets lost (e.g., if an employee with close customer contact leaves the business). The sales, marketing, and service areas can access central information on current customers and potential customers to respond to their needs. You can also use SAP CRM for scheduling and resource control. In SAP CRM, reporting and analytical functions increase in importance because they are required to gain insight on customer behavior that can be used for future promotions.

> **Mobile Application**
>
> Customer relationship management applications have been used more and more in the past few years on mobile devices such as tablet PCs or smartphones.
>
> This trend is not limited to customer relation management. In other areas (e.g., sales, maintenance, services, etc.), employees increasingly use their own mobile devices or mobile devices provided by the company as well. When using mobile devices, stricter security guidelines might have to be followed to avoid unauthorized users from accessing confidential data.

3.4   Optimizing Supplier Relationships: SAP Supplier Relationship Management

The purchasing department of a business is invested in collaborating with good suppliers for a long time. Of course, it's always best to procure the required goods or services as cost-effectively as possible. However, there may be reasons not to decide on the supplier who offers the lowest prices. This may be the case if, for example, a more expensive supplier offers a better delivery service that can ensure fast and easy delivery despite possible bottlenecks.

The purpose of SAP Supplier Relationship Management (SAP SRM) is to optimize business relationships with existing and potential suppliers. It lets you strategically plan and control relationships with these suppliers by integrating them closely with the purchasing processes. SAP SRM supports contract and supplier management, supplier selection, supplier qualification, creation of purchase orders, source determination, creation of invoices, and credit memos.

3.5   The Entire Lifecycle of a Product: SAP Product Lifecycle Management

SAP Product Lifecycle Management (SAP PLM) supports the "lifecycle" of a product, from the initial product idea, to drafts and alignment of production, to customer service.

SAP PLM consists of all functions associated with these tasks, such as the management of plants, equipment, and product documentations. With product development projects, for example, it's important to keep an overview of all product master data and product structures, recipes, and specifications. The component also supports quality control and project and resource management. If you deploy product portfolio management, you can control various projects.

With regard to the cooperation with colleagues and development partners, SAP PLM lets you exchange information such as project plans, technical drawings, product structures, product documentations, maintenance instructions, and so on.

EXAMPLE

Using SAP PLM

SAP PLM is frequently used in the automotive industry. Consider the following example:

A car manufacturer designs the successor Type 2 of a compact car because the current model, Type 1, has good sales figures. Prototypes are tested and optimized until the new model, Type 2, is ready for

3

series production. At the same time, provisions are made for the production and market launch. Type 2 then replaces its predecessor, Type 1, and the demand among the customers of this brand is high.

After several years, the demand for the current Type 2 has decreased. To make this model more attractive for potential customers, minor changes are made to this model, and special promotions are started. Prototypes of the successor model, Type 3, already exist.

Type 3 replaces Type 2, but the buyers of Type 2 still receive services and replacement parts from their car dealers. The product lifecycle ends when the production of replacement parts for Type 2 ceases.

3.6 For all Supply Chain Elements: SAP Supply Chain Management

SAP Supply Chain Management (SAP SCM) includes functions for the entire supply chain, from the supplier to the customer. The software offers advanced functions for complex business processes in logistics (Figure 3.4).

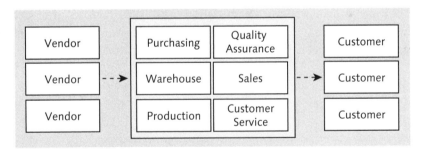

Figure 3.4 *Advanced Supply Chain*

SAP SCM is an extremely powerful software solution with diverse individual components. Due to its wide functional scope, the following list only provides a short overview of SAP SCM (illustrated in Figure 3.5):

- **Warehouse management**
  SAP Extended Warehouse Management (SAP EWM) is the SAP SCM solution for warehouse management, and it has options that go far beyond the Warehouse Management component (WM) in SAP ERP. SAP EWM is deployed for all processes in warehouse management.

- **Transportation management**
  SAP SCM provides a separate solution in the transportation area called SAP Transportation Management (SAP TM). In contrast to SAP Logistics Execution System (SAP LES) in SAP ERP, this solution was also developed for transport service providers.

- **Tracking of logistics processes**
  SAP Event Management (SAP EM) was designed for tracking and status management tasks.

- **Support of RFID processes**
  Radio Frequency Identification (RFID) allows for the noncontact identification and localization of objects (which are provided with an RFID label) using RFID readers. This facilitates data entry. In this context, the SAP component, SAP Auto-ID Infrastructure (AII), represents a link between the RFID reader and the SAP system.

- **Supplier collaboration**
  By means of SAP Supply Network Collaboration (SAP SNC), you can achieve closer cooperation of external suppliers by letting them respond to customer stocks and requirements independently.

- **Planning and optimization of the supply chain**
  SAP Advanced Planning and Optimization (SAP APO) consists of a very widespread task area with functions for production planning, sales planning, availability checks, transportation planning, and so on.

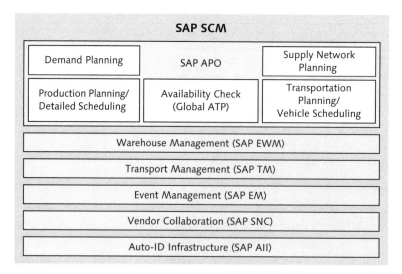

Figure 3.5 *Overview of SAP SCM Components*

If you take a close look at the usage areas of SAP SCM, you may notice some overlap of SAP ERP components. For example, there is a component for warehouse management within SAP ERP (i.e., WM) and SAP SCM (i.e., SAP EWM), respectively; the latter, however, has more refined options than the former.

3.7 Industry Solutions

Besides the standard solutions, SAP also offers solutions for different industries. This is because the processes that an energy supplier needs to map are different from those of a mechanical engineering business. Industry solutions combine standard processes with special requirements and functions. SAP offers packages for the following industries, among others:

- Manufacturing industry
  - SAP for Automotive
  - SAP for Aerospace and Defense
  - ...
- Processing industry
  - SAP for Oil & Gas
  - SAP for Chemicals
  - ...
- Financial service providers and public administration
  - SAP for Banking
  - SAP for Healthcare
  - SAP for Defense & Security
  - ...
- Services industry
  - SAP for Utilities
  - SAP for Retail
  - SAP for Consumer Products
  - ...

In total, 24 industry solutions are currently available at the time of publishing (2016).

3.8 Special Software for Medium-Sized Enterprises

In addition to the solutions for large businesses—such as the SAP Business Suite—SAP also offers solutions for small- and medium-sized businesses, which are briefly discussed in the following sections.

SAP Business One

With SAP Business One, SAP addresses customers for whom SAP ERP or the software products of SAP Business Suite are too complex or too expensive. SAP Business One can be used to map core functions such as financials, human resources, and materials management. This product can "grow" together with the enterprise and can be implemented at relatively low costs within a couple of days.

SAP Business All-in-One

SAP Business All-in-One is a solution for medium-sized businesses that offers different industry-specific features. Different solutions from SAP Business Suite are used as required. SAP NetWeaver is the technological platform for SAP Business All-in-One.

SAP Business ByDesign

SAP Business ByDesign is an on-demand solution, which means that the business that uses the solution only selects the functions it actually requires. The application server, which the customers use, is hosted by SAP and is available via a secured Internet connection. The server on which the applications are located is supported and managed at SAP's data centers. The user can access the required functions via an Internet browser. The users' access to the servers is provided via a virtual private network (VPN) connection that is secured in multiple levels (Figure 3.6).

> **INFO**
>
> **Virtual Private Network**
> A VPN is a secure connection via the Internet. The data packages are transferred in encrypted form between sender and receiver.

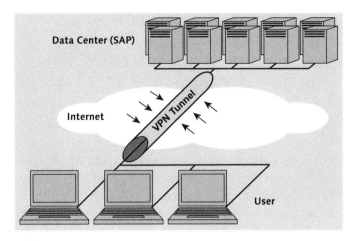

Figure 3.6 *SAP Business ByDesign: System Infrastructure*

SAP Business ByDesign covers all business processes mentioned in this chapter: financials and accounting, logistics, human resources, customer relationship management, and so on.

> **INFO**
>
> **Cloud Computing**
>
> An increasing number of companies decide to outsource their IT (hardware, software, data) to external providers whose services are "leased" for a certain period. Applications and data are no longer located within the company's data center but are provisioned via the Internet. SAP Business ByDesign is one of several SAP products offered in the cloud. Another product that is also available in the cloud is presented in the following section.

3.9   The Next Software Generation: SAP S/4HANA

On February 3, 2015, SAP presented the new SAP Business Suite 4 SAP HANA (SAP S/4HANA) at the New York Stock Exchange. SAP S/4HANA is the enterprise's fourth major product generation following SAP R/2, SAP R/3, and SAP ERP (so "4" in the product name is no coincidence). According to SAP, the new platform is characterized by a simple data structure and high user-friendliness. The SAP HANA database forms the technical basis of SAP S/4HANA.

The most essential innovations of SAP S/4HANA are the following:

- **SAP HANA database**
  The SAP HANA in-memory database forms the core of the new database. SAP HANA enables you, for example, to process Big Data and create particularly fast evaluations. SAP HANA Cloud Platform serves as the development environment for SAP HANA.

- **New SAP Fiori UX**
  With SAP S/4HANA, SAP starts to retire from the well-known SAP GUI, which you can see in the system screenshots of this book. SAP Fiori is based on an intuitive usability in the form of apps. Additionally, it's optimized for usage on mobile devices, for example, smartphones and tablets.

Another special feature of SAP S/4HANA is the availability of various types of operations: Besides the installation of the software at the enterprise itself (on-premise)—as you know it from SAP ERP—customers can also use SAP S/4HANA in the cloud. The various cloud versions differ, for example, with regard to functional scope and the option to make individual enhancements (i.e., programming).

With SAP S/4HANA, SAP prepares itself for the increasing digitalization that entails a revolutionary change of all business areas. Today, enterprises must face new challenges, including the use of mobile devices and social media, the rapid development of the Internet of Things (IoT), and the growing amount of data. With SAP S/4HANA, SAP customers have completely new options to respond to these changes.

Additional Information

If you want to learn more about SAP S/4HANA, we recommend the book *SAP S/4HANA: An Introduction* (*www.sap-press.com/4153*).

3.10   The Technical Basis: SAP NetWeaver

SAP NetWeaver forms the technical basis for SAP applications and business processes; it's the operating system, so to speak, that runs all the applications you use. SAP NetWeaver is responsible for the following tasks:

- User integration
- Information integration

- Process integration
- Application basis (application server)

Let's delve into what these tasks mean in the following subsections.

User Integration

The user integration functions allow employees to use functions and information they require for their work. One option is to access the SAP system from different channels—that is, via mobile devices (smartphones) or via a portal (usually an Internet connection). This means that you have access to the system using various frontends. You can use both SAP GUI for Microsoft Windows and an Internet browser to access an SAP system.

Information Integration

In SAP NetWeaver, information integration includes components for master data management, reporting, and analysis (business intelligence), and knowledge management. Master data management ensures that redundant and incorrect data are eliminated. The SAP Business Warehouse component (SAP BW) is a data warehouse, meaning it's where you can collect and format information from different systems and make it available for reports and evaluations. SAP BW is one of the few SAP NetWeaver components that the user may contact directly.

Process Integration

Process integration means, on the one hand, that information from different areas can be connected through interfaces. On the other hand, the term refers to the option to automate business processes beyond system and enterprise boundaries. You can fulfill your tasks without any problems, even if IT systems of different manufacturers (non-SAP systems) are used or if other enterprises are integrated with the processes.

Application Server

The application server is the technical basis for all other SAP products. Besides communication with applications, its tasks include basic functions such as user management, data exchange, monitoring, and transportation. In addition, SAP NetWeaver lets customers expand their systems themselves so they can develop their own software applications using the ABAP and Java (J2EE) programming languages.

Accordingly, SAP NetWeaver primarily forms the technical basis for an SAP system and the required applications so that business processes can be mapped across areas. This way, all participating departments are integrated.

> **NOTE**
>
> **Using Non-SAP Software**
>
> SAP NetWeaver can be used in heterogeneous IT environments (ones in which you can use software products of different manufacturers). Other manufacturers and software companies that provide add-ons for the SAP system can then integrate the software with the system landscapes.

This chapter provided an overview of the SAP products. As you've learned, SAP offers software solutions for all business sizes. Here, a distinction is made between industry-specific and industry-neutral solutions. The components of SAP ERP originate from accounting, human resources, and logistics. Products are offered for which you don't need to provide any system infrastructure because you can access the systems via the Internet. SAP NetWeaver forms the technical basis for all of the described products and solutions, and it provides components so that you can optimally integrate the system with the enterprise structure and expand it as necessary.

The next part of this book focuses on the concrete work in the system and describes the basic operation of SAP.

Part II

Basic Principles of System Operation

4   Organizational Structures and Master Data

Before you can work with the SAP system, you need some background knowledge. Some basic settings in the SAP system remain more or less unchanged over a long period and form the foundation for your business processes. These include organizational structures (created in Customizing) and master data. If you work in a department as a user, you must "tell" the system for which area of the business a specific action is performed. To do this, you must know about the organizational units.

> **In this chapter, you'll learn the following:**
> - How to map enterprise structures in the system
> - Which master data you need for your work with SAP

4.1   Organizational Structures

Every enterprise has its own structure and business processes in purchasing, sales and distribution, and accounting. The structure of the organization reflects these processes and can be presented in an organization chart. Every department maps its structure in this organization chart. Frequently, not all levels and functional areas of the business are presented in the overall organization chart. Instead, each chart is limited to individual areas, such as purchasing, with its corresponding structures (i.e., sales).

Figure 4.1 shows one such part of the organization chart with units from logistics. This example presents the fictional bicycle manufacturer, *Sportbikes International*. The Sportbikes International companies are pooled in a holding. Production occurs at two plants in Germany and one plant in England. The subsidiaries' warehouses are subdivided into two areas: finished products and quality assurance (QA). A purchasing department undertakes the procurement for all production plants across the group through centralized purchasing; an expert team is responsible for procuring finished products, and another group of employees is responsible for purchasing services.

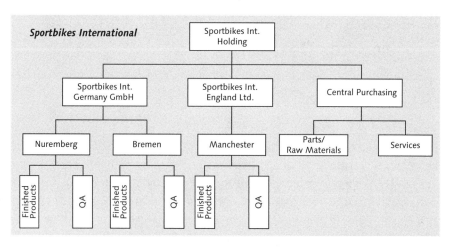

Figure 4.1 *Example of an Enterprise Structure from the Logistics Perspective*

Such organizational structures are mapped and assigned using organizational units in the SAP system. Before you, as the user, can work with the SAP system, you must link your various tasks in the SAP system with the corresponding organizational units. You can create and assign the organizational units through Customizing (see Chapter 2). After this assignment has been made, it's very difficult to implement changes (e.g., problems arise during company takeovers or mergers).

To transfer the business structure to the system, you need several organizational units, which will be discussed in more detail. The organizational units originate from the purchasing area. Other areas in the enterprise—financial accounting, human resources, sales and distribution, and so on—use different organizational units that are customized for their respective needs. Because complete enterprises are mapped in SAP ERP, specific central organizational units must be available to several (user) departments. For example, a plant is the decisive organizational unit for financial accounting, sales and distribution, and materials management (purchasing). Among other things, financial accounting monitors and performs incoming and outgoing payments that result from sales orders (sales and distribution) and purchase orders (purchasing). These are discussed in more detail in the chapters on the respective SAP components (see Part III). This book provides information particularly on the organizational units of Materials Management (MM), Sales and Distribution (SD), SAP ERP Financials (FI), Controlling (CO), and SAP ERP Human Capital Management (SAP ERP HCM).

The following sections detail the most important organizational units of the individual business areas of Sportbikes International that are relevant for the purchasing department. If you transfer the structure of the sample business, Sportbikes International, to the SAP organizational units, you get a result like the one shown in Figure 4.2.

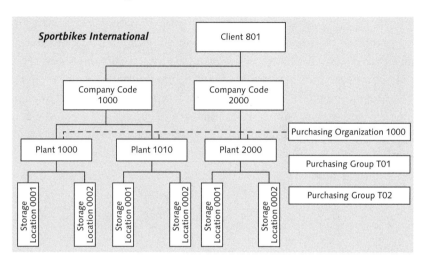

Figure 4.2 *Organizational Units of Sportbikes International in the SAP System (Purchasing Area)*

The client (801) represents the group or the corporate headquarters, and it's the topmost organizational unit. Company codes 1000 and 2000 are located below the client and represent the companies (subsidiaries) in Germany and England. In Germany, there are two production plants, 1000 and 1010, which have corresponding storage locations. In England, plant 2000 has its own storage locations. Purchasing organization 1000 handles all purchasing, and, for this reason, it's not assigned to a company code. Purchasing groups T01 and T02 are intended for purchasing teams with different task areas; purchasing groups aren't assigned to any other organizational element directly.

> **NOTE**
>
> **Keys of the Organizational Units Used**
> In this example, the keys (801, 1000, etc.) were assigned randomly. In real life, however, you should use useful, assignable keys (e.g., existing internal numbers and names such as company number, plant number, warehouse number, or cost centers). Many different approaches and

variants exist here, but some basic rules for keys of specific organizational units are discussed in the next sections.

The following section describes the organizational units from the Sportbikes
International example in detail. The respective organizational units are created for an area (e.g., financial accounting, purchasing, sales and distribution, etc.) and are then available to all relevant application areas. For example, the purchasing department orders materials for a plant, and the internal
valuation of these materials is included in the financial statements created by
financial accounting. (Part III of this book, Chapter 15 through Chapter 20,
provides further organizational units that are required for areas such as
financial accounting or HR.) The sales organization sells the additionally purchased or produced materials to the customers in sales and distribution. Let's
explore those organization units:

- **Client**

  You enter or select the client when you log on to the SAP system. Because
  the client represents the group (and is therefore the highest organizational
  unit in the system), all settings that are made for the client also apply to
  the subordinate units. The key for the client always has three digits and is
  numeric, for instance, 801.

- **Company code**

  Accounting is mapped at the level of the company code, which is representative of an independent balancing unit. A client can contain various
  company codes, but a company code is unique across the client. The key
  for the company code has four digits and is alphanumeric.

- **Plant**

  Because a plant produces goods or sells services, it's a central organizational unit of logistics. A plant can also be used in these roles:

  - Production location (MM, PP)

  - Sales office (SD)

  - Issuing storage location (SD)

  A plant must be assigned to one single company code. It's always unique
  across the client; in other words, a plant number can only be assigned
  once. However, a company code and a plant with the same key can exist
  in one client. The key for the plant has four digits and is alphanumeric.

- **Storage location**
  The storage location lets you differentiate material stocks (stock types) within a plant. For the storage location, only the quantities of materials are relevant and not the values. These are considered at the level of the plant or the company code. A storage location is directly assigned to a plant. The key of the storage location is unique within a plant, so the same key can exist at another plant. The key for the plant has four digits and is alphanumeric.

- **Purchasing organization**
  The purchasing organization maps the business's purchasing department in the system. You can map either a central or a decentralized purchasing department, depending on the requirements. A client can also contain various purchasing organizations, and a purchasing organization can be assigned to a company code. This can also be cross-company code; in other words, it doesn't have to be assigned to a specific company code. Plants for which procurement is to be made must be assigned. When mapping a central purchasing department, the purchasing organization isn't assigned to any company code. The key for the purchasing organization has four digits and is alphanumeric.

- **Purchasing group**
  A team of employees usually forms a purchasing group. The purchasing group itself isn't assigned to any other organizational unit. The key for the purchasing group has three digits and is alphanumeric.

Organizational units aren't just required to map the business in the system, but they are also required if you perform processes in the system. If goods are procured, the system needs to know to which user the documents must be assigned. In other words, the system must know who procures for which company code and for which plant. The example in Figure 4.3 shows the organizational units involved in the transaction to create a purchase order in the SAP system. Transactions in the SAP system are functions that can be called by the user via an alphanumeric code, known as the transaction code; you'll find more information in Chapter 5 and Chapter 6.

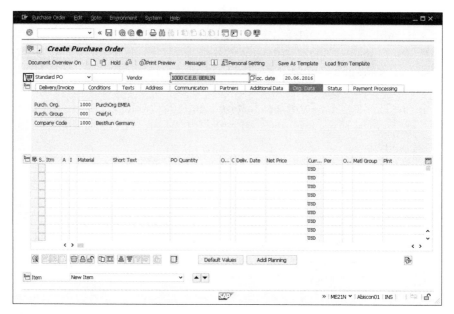

Figure 4.3 *Organizational Units in the Purchase Order (Transaction ME21N)*

Transaction ME21N, the purchase order, shows an example of using organizational units. Here you specify which purchasing organization and purchasing group is responsible for procurement, for which company code the purchase order is to be made, and for which plant procurement is to be made. Organizational structures are defined and assigned (mapped) via Customizing in the SAP system.

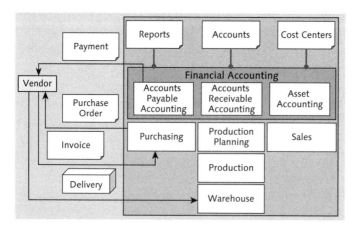

Figure 4.4 *Example of the Joint Use of Organizational Units*

Figure 4.4 and Table 4.1 illustrate which organizational units are relevant for the individual components.

	Com-pany Code	Purchas-ing Orga-nization	Sales Organi-zation	Plant	Storage Location
Purchas-ing (MM)	×	×	–	×	(×)
Accounts Payable Account-ing (FI)	×	–	–	–	–
Sales and Distribu-tion (SD)	×	–	×	×	–

Table 4.1 Interlocking of SAP Components and Organizational Units

EXAMPLE

Organizational Units in Processes

When you enter a purchase order, you must fill in the corresponding fields:

- For which company code do you procure?
- Which purchasing organization and which purchasing group procure?
- For which plant do you procure?
- At which storage location is the material to be stored?

When you enter an order in SD, you must specify the following:

- Which sales organization is responsible?
- Which sales area is responsible? Which plant delivers the goods (delivering plant)?

Now that you've learned the principles of organizational units in the SAP system, let's move to master data in the upcoming section. If you want to learn more about the individual organizational units in the various SAP components, go directly to Chapter 15 through Chapter 18.

4.2 Master Data

Master data information remains unchanged for a long time and is repeatedly required in business processes. After creation, the data are available to various users in different areas. For example, a master record can be the address of a customer or information on a material. Master data information plays a critical role both in SAP implementation and in daily work.

Good maintenance of master data is key to optimizing the SAP system. When you create a purchase order, for example, you only need to enter the supplier number to call the address and additional information automatically.

EXAMPLE

Master Data

- Creditor (supplier): Name, address, and so on
- Debtor (customer): Name, address, customer number, terms of delivery, and so on
- Material (article): Material number, short text, size and weight, valuation, and so on
- Services: Service type, description, service number, and so on
- Employee: Name, address, personnel number, department assignment, and so on

Besides master data, transaction data are also available. Transaction data can be changed; the data are created, edited, and valid for a limited time for a specific transaction only.

EXAMPLE

Transaction Data

- Invoice: Document number, amount, material, quantity, and so on
- Purchase requisition: Material, quantity, preferred supplier, and so on
- Purchase order: Document number, supplier, material, quantity, conditions, and so on
- Standard order: Debtor, conditions, delivery date, material, quantity, and so on
- Material document: Delivered quantity, material, storage location, and so on

Figure 4.5 illustrates the difference between master data and transaction data.

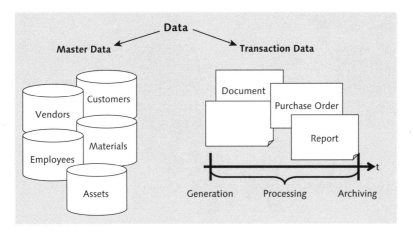

Figure 4.5 *Master Data and Transaction Data*

Because many applications and users can access the same master data if they have the relevant authorizations, redundancies (or multiple data retention) are avoided. However, redundancies can be unavoidable if systems of different manufacturers are deployed in the business.

The most important master data in the SAP system are presented in Part III of this book in the context of specific SAP components.

The following example describes how to create a material master record in the SAP system. A material master record contains information on the material, which is relevant for accounting or logistics processes. In other components, a material is often referred to as an article. If you want to reproduce the example in the system yourself, first read Chapter 5 and Chapter 6, which outline the logon and navigation in the SAP system. To create a material master, follow these steps:

1 In the SAP Easy Access menu, select **SAP Menu ▸ Logistics ▸ Materials Management ▸ Material Master ▸ Material ▸ Create (General)** to call Transaction MM01, and then double-click **MM01 – Immediately**. Alternatively, you can start the transaction directly via the command field.

2 The system displays the initial screen of Transaction MM01 (Figure 4.6). Enter the following test data:

  – **Material:** "ZZTM02"

  – **Industry sector:** "Mechanical Engineering"

  – **Material Type:** "Raw material"

Figure 4.6 *Initial Screen of Transaction MM01*

3 Click the **Select View(s)** button. A material master record is displayed that is subdivided into the various views assigned to the respective user departments (Figure 4.7). Select the **Basic Data 1**, **Purchasing**, and **Accounting 1** views.

Figure 4.7 *Select Views*

4 Click the **Org. Levels** button, and maintain the plant in which the material is to be held by entering "1000" in the **Plant** field (Figure 4.8). Press

Enter or click the **Next** button ✅ to confirm. Alternatively, you can choose **Plant 1000** via the **Help** field button 🗇, which is located to the right of the field.

Figure 4.8 *Organizational Levels*

5️⃣ The system now displays the **Basic Data 1** tab of the new material master record. Enter the following values in the fields listed (Figure 4.9):

- **Material** (short text): "TFT MONITOR 22 INCH WIDESCREEN"
- **Base Unit of Measure**: "PC"
- **Material Group**: "00103"
- **Gross Weight**: "12"
- **Weight unit**: "KG"
- **Net Weight**: "10"

Figure 4.9 *Create Material Basic Data Tab*

These individual pieces of master data represent important properties of the material, which are required for procurement and for internal valuation.

6 When you click ‹ ›, you navigate to the **Purchasing** tab. Here you maintain relevant purchasing information, such as base unit of measure, material group, purchasing value key, goods receipt processing time, underdelivery tolerance, and overdelivery tolerance. You can also open the tab by clicking the title. Then enter the value "000" in the **Purchasing Group** field (Figure 4.10).

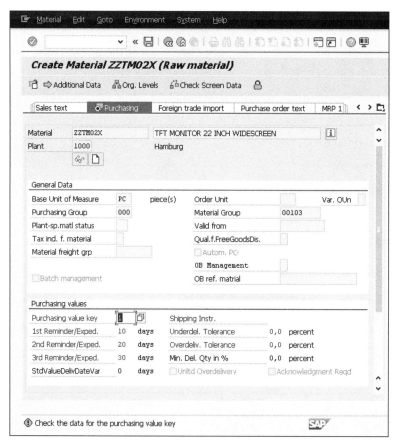

Figure 4.10 *Create Material Purchasing Tab*

7 Click ‹ › to go to the **Accounting 1** tab, or open it by clicking the title. As the name suggests, you maintain data on this tab that is important for accounting, that is, data about how the material is valuated internally.

For this purpose, you must enter the valuation class, valuation price, and the price control (Figure 4.11):

- **Valuation Class**: "3000"

- **Price control**: "V" (moving average price)

- **Moving price**: "150" (EUR)

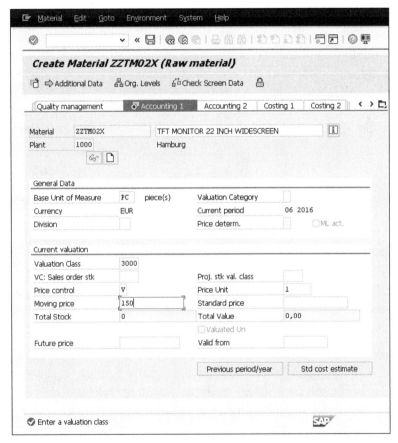

Figure 4.11 *Create Material Accounting Tab*

8 Save the master record by clicking the **Save** button in the upper part of the screen.

You've now successfully created a material master record.

> **NOTE**
>
> **Material Master Quality**
>
> Enter the master data with care. In many cases, insufficient attention is paid to the master data quality. Remember that virtually all business processes in the SAP system access master data. If a field value is missing, the process can't be executed correctly.

This chapter taught you two basic elements in the SAP system: The structure of an enterprise is mapped in the SAP system using organizational units, and all organizational units are defined and assigned in Customizing. The chapter also outlined the difference between master data and transaction data. Master data usually remains in the system for a long time and are available to all applications and all authorized users in the system. Transaction data, on the other hand, are created in the various business cases and change frequently.

Chapter 5 details how to log on to the SAP system.

4.3   Try It!

Exercise 1

In this exercise, you'll create an organizational structure for Engineering Massachusetts Holding Ltd. The focus is on producing and procuring units. The company has three production locations: one in Boston, one in Springfield, and another in Pittsfield.

The production location in Boston is financially independent, but Springfield and Pittsfield belong together. Each location has a warehouse for raw materials and a warehouse for finished products. Within the business, one centralized purchasing department procures materials for all locations.

Outline how you could map this structure in the SAP system using the organizational units in Table 4.2.

Organizational Unit	Key
Client	805
Company code Boston	1000

Table 4.2 *Exercise 1: Organizational Units*

Organizational Unit	Key
Company code Springfield and Pittsfield	2000
Plant Boston	1010
Plant Springfield	2010
Plant Pittsfield	2020
Finished goods warehouse	0001
Raw materials warehouse	0002

Table 4.2 Exercise 1: Organizational Units (Cont.)

Exercise 2

What's the difference between master data and transaction data? Name three examples from different business areas for each.

5 Logging On to the SAP System

The previous chapters provided basic knowledge of the SAP system and described organizational structures and master data. This chapter begins with a description of SAP system operation.

In this chapter, you'll learn the following:
- How to connect with the server using SAP Logon
- How the SAP screen is structured
- How to log on and off from the SAP system
- Which information is provided in the status bar

5.1 SAP Logon

You probably have several links to applications you use frequently on your desktop, such as Microsoft Word or Microsoft Outlook. After your SAP administrator completes the installation of the SAP GUI, you'll find an icon for SAP Logon on your desktop, too (Figure 5.1).

Figure 5.1 *SAP Logon*

Establishing a Connection to the SAP System

Using the SAP Logon, your Windows PC establishes a connection to the SAP system via the network when you carry out the following steps:

1. Double-click the **SAP Logon** icon on your desktop to start SAP Logon, or go to the Windows **Start** menu and choose **Start ▶ Programs ▶ SAP Front End ▶ SAP Logon.**

2 The configured SAP systems are displayed in the **Systems** tab of the opened SAP Logon. To log on to the required system, select the name (in this case, **PROD** for production system), and click the **Log On** button (Figure 5.2).

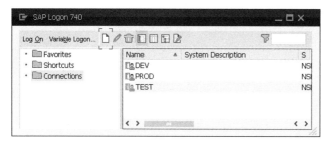

Figure 5.2 *Selecting System for Logon*

A logon screen is displayed if SAP Logon can establish a connection to the SAP system (Figure 5.3).

Figure 5.3 *SAP Logon Screen*

Different SAP Systems in the Enterprise

Most businesses deploy various SAP systems besides the one that you use in your daily work. Figure 5.2 also shows the development system (**DEV**) and the test system (**TEST**).

To log on to the SAP system, you need the following information:

- **Client** number
- **User**
- **Password**

In SAP Logon, you not only have the option to log on to the system, but you can also change the parameters or add a connection to a new SAP system. To define a new system in SAP Logon, you need some SAP system parameters.

NOTE

Settings in SAP Logon

The SAP administrator for your business can provide the parameters for an SAP system. Not every user is authorized to change these parameters or add new systems on his PC. Under Microsoft Windows, you need write authorizations for the *saplogon.ini* file in the Windows system directory.

Configuring Connection Settings for the SAP System

After you've logged on to SAP Logon, you can check, change, or add a connection. For example, you might need to access another system for specific reasons, or the parameters of a test system are changed. To add a connection, follow these steps:

1. You can adjust the settings of a new system via the **Edit** ☐ button. Then click the **Next** ☑ button. You need the respective authorization on your PC.

2. Various parameters for the system connection are available. The following fields are mandatory (Figure 5.4):

   - **Description**: Provide an alphanumeric description for the user.
   - **Application Server**: Provide the IP address or Domain Name System (DNS) name.
   - **Instance Number**: Provide a two-digit number.
   - **System ID**: Provide a three-digit, alphanumeric ID.

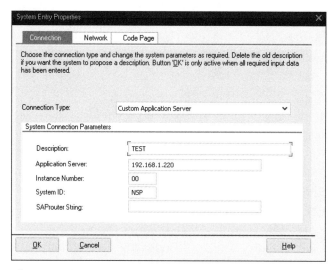

Figure 5.4 *System Connection Parameters*

Whether the **SAProuter String** field must be filled in depends on the network infrastructure. Here you need to enter the IP address or the DNS name.

3 After you've changed the parameters, click **OK**.

The connection information is now stored in your SAP system. The following sections show how to log on to the SAP system.

5.2 Logging On for the First Time

The steps for your initial logon vary from subsequent logons. Initial logon can mean that you want to log on to the system for the first time (e.g., if you have a new employer) or after you receive a new password.

The initial logon requires the following information, which is usually provided by the SAP administration team:

- Client
- User
- Password

The client (three-digit numeric key) is mandatory. Your user account is client-dependent. For example, if you want to log on to the test system, you need a different client than for the logon to the production system. An enterprise may have various clients for different tasks.

NOTE

Password Rules

SAP standard has the following essential rules for passwords:

- The password can be in letters, numbers, and special characters.
- The password must have a length between 3 and 40 characters; the standard system requires a minimum length of 6 characters.
- The first character of the password must not be a question mark or exclamation point.
- The first three characters must differ from those of the user and must not be three identical characters.
- None of the first three characters can be a blank space.
- The password must not be SAP* or PASS because these are reserved for SAP.
- The password must differ from the previous five passwords.

The password is case-sensitive and isn't visible after you enter it. For the initial logon or if you've forgotten your password, the administrator provides you with an initial password. You can use this password only once and must immediately change it after successful logon.

To log on to the system and change your password for the first time, follow these steps:

1 Start SAP Logon by double-clicking the icon on your Windows desktop or via the **Start** menu.

2 SAP Logon is opened. Check that you're on the **Systems** tab.

3 Select the desired **System Entry**, and then click the **Log On** button. When your PC successfully establishes a connection to the SAP system via the network, the logon screen is displayed.

4 Enter the logon data that you received from your system administrator or trainer in the logon screen. Specify **EN** in the **Language** field (Figure 5.5).

Figure 5.5 *Setting the Language Field*

5 Make sure that you enter the logon data exactly as you received it. The system is case-sensitive and doesn't permit any errors, especially if security is concerned. If you're sure that you've entered all data correctly, click the **Next** button ✔ or press Enter.

6 You've logged on to the system successfully! Next, the system prompts you to enter a new password. If the message **Enter a new password** is displayed, click **OK** to confirm the message.

7 Enter the new password twice, once each in the **New Password** and **Repeat Password** fields. The characters aren't visible during entry (Figure 5.6).

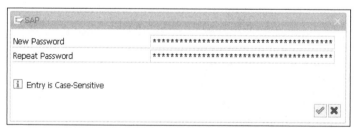

Figure 5.6 *Entering the New Password*

8 Confirm your entry by pressing Enter or clicking the **Next** ✔ button.

The new password is now defined in the system.

> **TIP**
>
> **Defining the Logon Language**
>
> Chapter 7 describes how to define the logon language in the system so that you don't have to specify it each time you log on.

5.3 Logging On to the System

If you want to log on to the SAP system after the initial logon (perhaps when you start your usual workday in the morning), follow these steps:

1. In SAP Logon, select the system to which you want to log on. Then click the **Logon** button.

2. Enter your client's name in the **Client** field.

3. Enter your username in the **User** field.

4. Enter your **Password**.

5. Specify **EN** in the **Language** field.

6. If all entries are correct, click **Next** ✅.

> **NOTE**
>
> **Incorrect Password**
>
> If you've entered the password incorrectly three times in a row, logon is closed. Fortunately, you can restart logon immediately. If you've entered the password incorrectly five times, the user is locked. The lock expires after a maximum of 24 hours. The locked user can be unlocked by the SAP administrator at any time, although a new initial password must be assigned.

The next section discusses the user interface of the SAP system, which you can view after the logon.

5.4 The SAP Graphical User Interface

SAP GUI is the user interface in which you work; it displays the applications that run on the server on your PC. After successful logon to the system, the screen shown in Figure 5.7 is displayed.

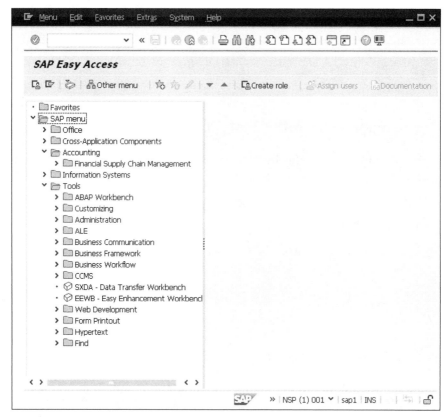

Figure 5.7 *SAP Easy Access (Initial Screen after Logon)*

You can conveniently navigate to the desired application via the user menu, SAP Easy Access menu.

The SAP screen contains many buttons and fields. The following section details the various areas of the SAP GUI that will help you better orient yourself to SAP in your daily work. The elements that you can click in the SAP screen are indicated in **Bold** in this book.

Menu Bar

The menu bar is located at the top of the screen (Figure 5.8). The menus displayed depend on the respective application (transaction) and the level at which you're located within the application. The menu items **System** and **Help** are always available in the menu bar regardless of the transaction you're working on.

Figure 5.8 *Menu Bar*

You can call the menu items by clicking them. They may contain submenus. By clicking ![icon], you can activate a menu that offers the following functions:

- Restore
- Move
- Change size
- Minimize
- Maximize
- Close
- Create session

You can find the buttons for minimizing, maximizing, and closing the window on the right-hand side of the menu bar; these are listed in Table 5.1. They are comparable with the buttons you already know from Microsoft Windows.

Button	Name	Use
![minimize]	Minimize	The application window is minimized and displayed at the bottom of the screen. Its size is restored by clicking it.
![maximize]	Maximize	The application window is displayed in its full size.
![close]	Close	The open application window is closed.

Table 5.1 *Sizing Icons in the Menu Bar*

Standard Toolbar

The standard toolbar is located below the menu bar (Figure 5.9). It contains icons for the most important functions, such as **Save** and **Cancel**. The buttons are displayed in all screens; inactive buttons are grayed out, and you can only use the buttons that are displayed in color. If you move the mouse pointer over the button without clicking it, the system displays brief information about the function, which is also referred to as tooltip.

Figure 5.9 Standard Toolbar

Some functions can also be called via the function keys, which are located at the top of your keyboard ([F1] through [F12]). Remember that some function keys have different settings, depending on the application. Table 5.2 lists the most essential buttons and function keys.

Button	Key/ Key Combination	Name	Use
	[Enter]	Next	Confirm the entered selected data; this is *not* a save function.
	[Ctrl]+[S]	Save	Save changes; this is the same function as **Save** in the **Edit** menu.
	[F3]	Back	Go back to the previous screen.
	[Shift]+[F3]	Exit	Close a transaction without saving the data or changes.
	[F12]	Cancel	Cancel transaction; this is the same function as **Cancel** in the **Edit** menu.
	[Ctrl]+[P]	Print	Print a document or list.
	[Ctrl]+[F]	Search	Find a value in a list.
	–	Create a new session	Open a window with a new session.
	–	Create a link	Create a new link in the SAP GUI.

Table 5.2 Most Essential Buttons of the Standard Toolbar

Button	Key/ Key Combination	Name	Use
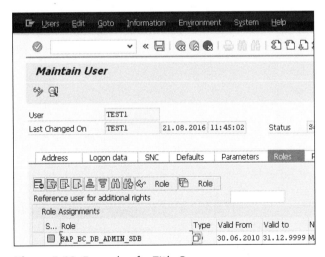	F1	Help	Display descriptions on a field on which the cursor is positioned.
	Alt + F12	Adjust local layout	Enable user-specific settings of the display options.

Table 5.2 *Most Essential Buttons of the Standard Toolbar (Cont.)*

For information on working with sessions, refer to Chapter 6. To learn more about links and adaptations of the local layout, read Chapter 7. The help function is described in Chapter 13.

Title Bar

The structure of the title bar always depends on the transaction you use (Figure 5.10). It can also contain other buttons in addition to the respective transaction name.

Figure 5.10 *Example of a Title Bar*

Command Field

You can navigate in the SAP system without a mouse by using the SAP Easy Access menu via the keyboard. This way, you can start transactions by directly entering the transaction code in the command field, as shown in Figure 5.11 (see also Chapter 6).

Figure 5.11 Command Field

Status Bar

The status bar is located at the bottom of the screen and extends over the entire screen width. On the left side, you can see an area that displays system messages. The right side displays four fields that provide current information on the system's status.

By clicking the **Help** ⌄ button in the first status field, you get various pieces of information on the system and client you're working with. The status bar indicates which program and transaction are currently active. You also find information on the response and interpretation time of the SAP system (Figure 5.12).

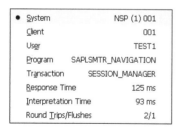

Figure 5.12 Information in the Status Bar

Table 5.3 describes the most essential information available in the status bar.

Description	Explanation
System	System and client to which you're currently logged on
Client	Client
User	Logon name
Program	Program that is currently active
Transaction	Transaction that is currently active
Response Time	Time in milliseconds in which the SAP system responds
Interpretation Time	Time in milliseconds in which commands to the system are executed
Round Trips/Flushes	Connections to one or more SAP systems

Table 5.3 Status Bar Information

In the second status field (Figure 5.13), you can view the name of the server to which you're connected (here, **sap1**).

Figure 5.13 Additional Information in the Status Field

The third status field shows whether you're in overtype mode (**OVR**) or in insert mode (**INS**) (refer to Figure 5.13). If **OVR** is set, you overwrite the existing data on the right side of the cursor when you enter data; if **INS** is set, you add or insert data. You can toggle between the modes by clicking this field.

The next section describes how to exit the SAP system.

5.5   Logging Off the SAP System

You have several options for terminating the SAP GUI. One option is to follow these steps:

1 Click the  button at the top left, and select the **Close** menu item or press [Alt]+[F4], as shown in Figure 5.14.

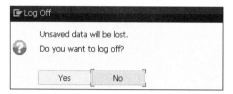

Figure 5.14 *Navigating to the Close Menu Item*

2 Confirm the **Unsaved data will be lost. Do you want to log off?** message by clicking **Yes** (Figure 5.15).

Figure 5.15 *Confirming Log Off*

Alternatively, you can log off as follows:

1 Click the **Close** ✕ button at the top right.

2 Confirm the **Unsaved data will be lost. Do you want to log off?** message by clicking **Yes**.

The message that unsaved data will be lost is displayed at every logoff for security reasons.

This chapter described how to log on to and log off from the SAP system. With SAP Logon, you can configure a connection to an SAP system or start the connection setup. To log on to an SAP system, you require a client, user, and password. Specifying a logon language is optional. SAP GUI is installed on your PC and enables interaction with the system. Chapter 6 presents the options available for navigation and data entry in the SAP system.

5.6 Try It!

Exercise 1

Describe how to establish a connection to the SAP system.

Exercise 2

Which information is mandatory for logging on to the system and which information is optional?

Exercise 3

Which of the following are valid passwords?

- SAP*
- q7
- meier#1
- demo#2010
- swordfish

Exercise 4

What do you enter in the command field to terminate a session without query?

6 Navigating in the SAP System

Chapter 5 taught you how to log on to and log off from the SAP system. After logon, you use the applications that belong to your task area. You fulfill different tasks by editing all screens that belong to the respective action and filling the necessary fields with content.

6

This chapter discusses the following:

- How to navigate in the SAP system
- How to use transaction codes
- How to enter data in the system
- Which options are available to call an application

6.1 Overview of the Navigation Options

Directly after you've logged on to the SAP system, it displays the initial screen shown in Figure 6.1.

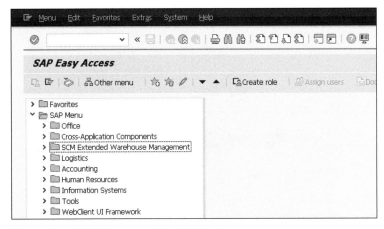

Figure 6.1 *Initial Screen of the SAP System*

The SAP system provides you with three options to navigate to the desired application:

- SAP Easy Access menu
- Transaction codes
- Favorites and links

You can customize the SAP Easy Access menu to your specific needs and set whether transaction codes are shown in the menu tree or in favorites. To make these modifications, select **Extras ▸ Settings** in the menu bar. You can also use the key combination $\boxed{\text{Shift}}+\boxed{\text{F9}}$ to set the following:

- Display transaction codes in the SAP Easy Access menu
- Show or hide the SAP logo
- Display favorites at the end of the menu
- Hide the SAP Easy Access menu and display favorites only

To display the transaction codes in the SAP Easy Access menu, follow these steps:

1 Choose **Settings** under **Extras** (Figure 6.2).

Figure 6.2 *Extras Menu*

2 The **Settings** window is now open. In this window, activate the **Display Technical Names** checkbox to map the transaction codes in the tree structure of the SAP Easy Access menu (Figure 6.3).

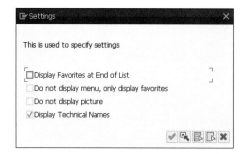

Figure 6.3 *Settings Window*

Here you can also set whether the favorites are displayed in the SAP Easy Access menu (via the **Display Favorites at End of List** checkbox).

The following two sections provide more information on the navigation options via the SAP Easy Access menu and via transaction codes. Favorites and links are discussed in Chapter 7.

6.2 Navigating via the SAP Easy Access Menu

After you've logged on to the SAP system, it displays the SAP Easy Access menu as a tree structure on the left-hand side of the screen.

The SAP Easy Access menu offers a user-specific entry point and navigation options in the SAP system. In this context, "user-specific" means that the tree structure displays only those transactions with which you may work according to your role (see Chapter 14 for details on roles).

Via the SAP Easy Access menu, you can expand the tree structure, which contains the individual folders (nodes), by clicking the ⟩ button. You can close it again with ⌄.

The folders themselves are identified with the **Opened Folder** 📂 or **Closed Folder** 📁 buttons. The executable transactions are marked with a building block 🔷, as shown in Figure 6.4.

Figure 6.4 SAP Easy Access Menu: Nodes and Transactions

To start a transaction via the SAP Easy Access menu, follow these steps:

1 Open the respective subordinate folder by clicking ⟩ . An opened folder is indicated by a triangle pointing downward ⌄ . This folder may contain subordinate folders.

2 Start the desired transaction by double-clicking the ⬡ button, which opens the initial screen of the respective transactions.

NOTE

Presentation of Menu Paths in This Book

Like other SAP books, this book doesn't provide screenshots of the SAP Easy Access menu when describing how to reach a specific transaction, but instead lists the individual steps of the menu path. In this example, the path is **Logistics ▸ Sales and Distribution ▸ Sales ▸ Order ▸ Create**.

TIP

How to Close All Folders in the SAP Easy Access Menu

If you want to close several folders and subfolders in the SAP Easy Access menu, you can close them all in one step by selecting **Menu ▸ Refresh** or pressing Ctrl + F1 .

6.3 Navigating via Transaction Codes

Transaction codes help you quickly access the desired application without navigating via the SAP Easy Access menu. Transaction codes are alphanumeric codes assigned to every application in the SAP system. You must know the transaction code of the desired application to navigate to it. The appendix of this book provides an overview of the most critical transaction codes.

TIP

Overviews for Download

You can download all overviews provided in the appendix free of charge at *https://www.sap-press.com/using-sap_4155/*. At the bottom of the page, click **Supplements list** in the **Product Supplements** box. A window opens where you can view the materials that are available for download.

To use transaction codes in the command field, follow these steps:

1 Click the command field after logon (Figure 6.5). The blinking cursor indicates that this field is active and ready for input.

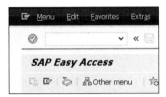

Figure 6.5 *Command Field*

2 Enter a transaction code (Figure 6.6). Confirm your input by clicking the **Next** button or pressing Enter.

Figure 6.6 *Transaction Code*

Transaction codes without preceding parameters can only be entered in the initial screen of the SAP Easy Access menu. If you're already in another transaction, you must enter a parameter in addition to the transaction code.

You can show or hide the command field by clicking the triangle «.

Table 6.1 lists the most important parameters.

Parameter	Explanation
/nend	Logs off from the system, with confirmation.
/nex	Logs off from the system, without confirmation.
MMBE	Example of a transaction code without additional parameters. It starts Transaction MMBE. This is only possible in the SAP Easy Access menu in this form.

Table 6.1 *Parameters Used in the Command Field*

Parameter	Explanation
/nMMBE	Closes the current transaction and starts a new one, such as Transaction MMBE here. Enter "/n" and the desired transaction code without any spaces.
/oMMBE	Starts a transaction in a new session, such as Transaction MMBE here. Enter "/o" and the desired transaction code without any spaces.
/n	Terminates the current transaction.
/i	Deletes the current session.
/o	Shows a list of current sessions.
/*MMBE	Starts a transaction and skips the initial screen, such as Transaction MMBE here. Enter "/*" and the desired transaction code without any spaces.

Table 6.1 *Parameters Used in the Command Field (Cont.)*

To describe the navigation via transaction codes in more detail, let's work through an example in the system. You ultimately want to determine the line items of your customers (debtors) for the current day in company code 1000. Follow these steps:

1 Log on to the SAP system (see Chapter 5, Section 5.3, if you need a reminder).

2 In the SAP Easy Access menu, open the customer line item list via the menu path, **Accounting ▶ Financial Accounting ▶ Accounts Receivable ▶ Account** (Figure 6.7). Alternatively, you can enter Transaction "FBL5N" directly via the command field.

3 Under **Account**, you can find **FBL5N Display/Change Line Items**. A building block icon displayed in front of the transaction means that it can be executed. Double-click the ⊘ button, and the initial screen of Transaction FBL5N opens.

4 Enter the following information:

  – **Company code:** "1000"

  – **Open at key date:** Current date (DD.MM.YYYY)

Click the **Execute** 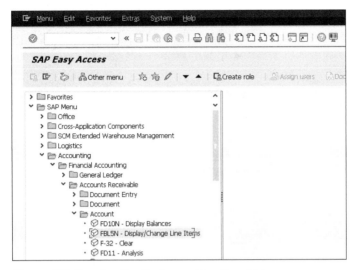 button or press F8.

Figure 6.7 *Opening the Customer Line Item List*

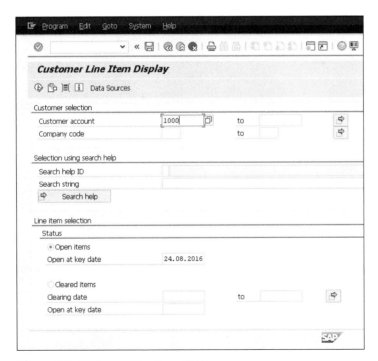

Figure 6.8 *Customer Line Item Screen*

5 Now the system shows the line item list in which you can view which sales were made to the respective customer (Figure 6.9).

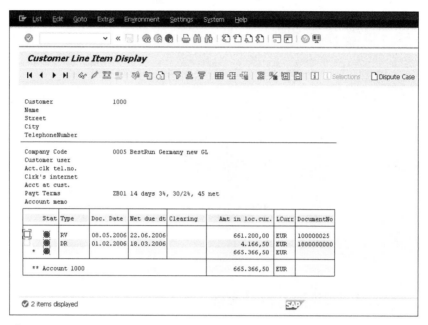

Figure 6.9 *Line Item List*

6 Click the **Close** 🔙 button to close the customer line item list. The system takes you back to the SAP Easy Access menu.

The transaction code is displayed in the SAP Easy Access menu and also in the status bar at the bottom-right of the screen.

6.4   Entering Data in the SAP System

You have various options in the SAP system to enter data and communicate with the system. In Chapter 5, we presented some essential elements of the SAP user interface (UI):

- Menu bar
- Standard toolbar
- Title bar

- Status bar
- Command field

This section now presents an overview of the central UI elements that you'll encounter in a transaction. You can use either mouse navigation or various keys of your keyboard to navigate between these elements.

You can execute specific functions (such as copy and paste) by pressing a specific key combination on your keyboard at the same time (e.g., `Ctrl`+`C` and `Ctrl`+`V`). You usually use the keys, `Ctrl`, `Shift`, or `Alt` in combination with a letter. The appendix provides a comprehensive overview of useful key combinations, and the most important are listed here in Table 6.2.

Action	Key Combination
Cancel actions step by step	`Esc`
Select all	`Ctrl`+`A`
Cut	`Ctrl`+`X`
Insert	`Ctrl`+`V`
Navigate in the list of selectable entries	`←`, `→`, `↓`, `↑`
Copy	`Ctrl`+`C`
Search	`Ctrl`+`F`
Select section	`Ctrl`+`Y`
Go to menu	`Alt`
Navigate to next element	`Tab`
Navigate to previous element	`Shift`+`Tab`
Navigate to next screen area	`Ctrl`+`Tab`
Navigate to previous screen area	`Shift`+`Ctrl`+`Tab`
Undo	`Ctrl`+`Z`

Table 6.2 *Overview of the Most Essential Key Combinations*

After you've entered your data, you must save it so that the system adds the new or changed information to the database.

Tabs

You can conveniently navigate complex contents by switching between the individual tabs. If you click the title of a tab, it's displayed in the foreground (Figure 6.10).

Figure 6.10 *Example of a Tab*

Screen Areas

Screens that include various input options are often subdivided into several area. A screen area, also known as a field group or group box, combines various input options for a specific topic.

Fields

You can enter information in the SAP system via fields (Figure 6.11). The available fields are input fields (white) and display fields (gray).

Figure 6.11 *Example of an Input Field*

In some cases, fields must be filled; required entry fields like these are labeled with a checkmark ☑. The system displays an error message if you miss a required entry field.

You don't have to fill in optional fields, which are frequently information fields.

Moreover, an input help is available for some fields (Figure 6.12). If you're not sure which inputs are expected in the field, use this input help ([F4]). You can also enter the field value manually.

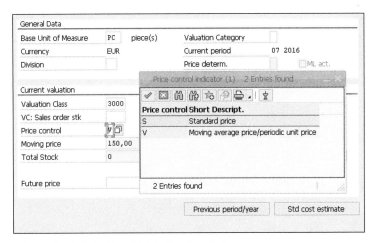

General Data

Base Unit of Measure	PC	piece(s)	Valuation Category	
Currency	EUR		Current period	07 2016
Division			Price determ.	☐ ML act.

Current valuation

Valuation Class	3000
VC: Sales order stk	
Price control	
Moving price	150,00
Total Stock	0

Future price

Price control indicator (1)   2 Entries found

Price control Short Descript.

| S | Standard price |
| V | Moving average price/periodic unit price |

2 Entries found

Previous period/year   Std cost estimate

Figure 6.12 *Selection List in the Input Help*

You can copy the field's content to the clipboard and thus avoid transfer errors by following these steps:

1 Fill in the corresponding field (e.g., the customer name, "John Smith").

2 Select the entry by pressing the left mouse button. Use the key combination Ctrl + C to copy it.

3 Navigate to the field in which you want to insert the content, and press Ctrl + V to insert the information.

Buttons

You can use buttons to execute numerous functions such as create or save. Some buttons are labeled; others bear a symbol or icon. If you position the cursor over a button, its function is shown in a tooltip (Figure 6.13). You can also use the key combination Ctrl + Q to get this tooltip.

Figure 6.13 *Tooltip of a Button*

Function Keys

Your keyboard has a row of keys labeled [F1] to [F12]. Table 6.3 provides an overview of the most important function keys. Remember that some function keys have different settings, depending on the application.

Action	Function Key
Back	[F3]
Cancel transaction	[Shift]+[F3]
Cancel	[F12]
Adjust local layout	[Alt]+[F12]
Help	[F1]

Table 6.3 *Standard Function Keys*

Checkboxes

Using checkboxes, often called indicators or flags, you can select various different options by clicking the box (Figure 6.14). After you click them, a checkmark appears in the box. Unlike radio buttons (discussed next), it's possible to select several checkboxes at a time.

Figure 6.14 *Example of a Checkbox*

Radio Buttons

By selecting a radio button, you can select one single option out of several. After you've clicked on them, they are filled with a black dot (Figure 6.15).

Figure 6.15 *Example of a Radio Button*

Dialog Windows

If you need to make further inputs or if the system wants to display specific information, a dialog window opens. Figure 6.16, for example, shows a warning message dialog window. The original window remains open in the background.

Figure 6.16 *Example of a Dialog Window*

6.5 Input Help

When searching for certain criteria, SAP provides the input help at specific points. You can call the input help with by pressing F4. If no input help can be displayed, a selection list is presented.

Let's use Transaction MMBE as an example to show how the input help can be deployed:

1 Start Transaction MMBE (Material Stock List).

2 Leave the cursor in the **Material** field, and press F4. A search window opens in which you can enter the various criteria that you want to search (Figure 6.17). Press Enter to run the search.

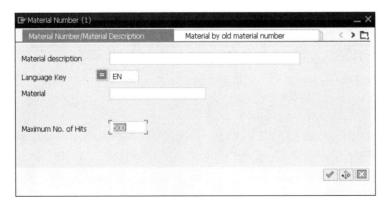

Figure 6.17 *Search Window*

Search Pattern

It isn't necessary to enter the entire search term. If you don't know the entire term, you can use a search pattern. For example, if you search for the **Material** short text "blank", you can use the following search patterns:

- *lank*: Finds all criteria that contain "lank".
- *lank: Finds all criteria that begin with any letter combination and end with "lank".

6.6   Working with Sessions

SAP provides the option to open and work with several sessions at the same time in the system. This allows you to work with up to six transactions in addition to the current one.

Using Various Sessions

You're currently creating a master record for a vendor when a coworker urgently requires the warehouse stock of a material and asks for your help. You don't have to cancel the creation of the master record before you check the warehouse stock in another session.

Follow these steps to generate another session:

1. You're located in any transaction, for instance, Transaction MMBE. Click **System ▸ Create Session** in the menu bar (Figure 6.18).

Figure 6.18 Create Session

2. Alternatively, you can click the 🔲 button in the standard toolbar to create a new session (not displayed in this figure).

To toggle between the sessions, you have the following options:

- Press ⌐Alt⌐+⌐Tab⌐ to toggle between the sessions. The inactive sessions are indicated in gray.

- Click the desired session in the Windows taskbar (Figure 6.19).

Figure 6.19 *Sessions in the Windows Taskbar*

- Enter the parameter "/o" in the command field to obtain an overview of the active sessions (Figure 6.20). Here you can also delete sessions that are no longer required.

Figure 6.20 *Session List*

6

> **NOTE**
> **How Many Sessions Are Permitted?**
> The SAP system administrator can set the number of permitted sessions between 2 and 16 sessions. By default, 6 sessions are permitted.

There are three different options to close a session:

- Choose **System ▶ Delete Session**.
- Click the **Close** ✖ button in the menu bar.
- Enter the parameter "/i" in the command field.

> **NOTE**
> **Performance**
> Open sessions have a negative effect on the system performance (or the speed of the user's PC). Always make sure to close sessions that you're not using.

In this chapter, you learned how to navigate in the SAP system and work with transactions, or applications, of an SAP system. These can be started via the SAP Easy Access menu or by entering a transaction code in the command field. You can use parameters in combination with the transaction code. You also learned about the various data input options and how to work with sessions.

6.7   Try It!

Exercise 1

What is a session?

Exercise 2

What do you enter in the command field to start Transaction ME21 in a new session?

Exercise 3

Name three options to toggle between sessions.

Exercise 4

What happens if you enter the parameter "/o" in the command field?

Exercise 5

Which settings can you make in the SAP system in the menu under **Extras ▸ Settings**?

7 Maintaining the System Layout and User Data

Just as you can organize your workplace, you can also make custom settings in the SAP system to make work more convenient for you. These personal settings affect only the user with which you're logged on to the system. Other user accounts remain unaffected by these settings.

In this chapter, you'll learn the following:

- How to create links
- How to adapt the SAP system interface to your requirements
- How to work with favorites
- How to prepopulate fields to reduce input work

7.1 Creating Links on the Desktop

If you primarily work with one or only a few transactions and don't want to navigate via the SAP Easy Access menu each time, you can create a link to a transaction on your Windows desktop. To do so, follow these steps:

1 In the SAP Easy Access menu, select the transaction that you want to link on your Windows desktop (here, Transaction MMBE, Stock Overview).

2 Go to **Edit ▸ Create shortcut on the Desktop** in the menu bar (Figure 7.1), or press Ctrl+F3.

3 The system displays a message informing you that the shortcut was created successfully.

4 The shortcut was created on the Windows desktop. The next time you log on, you can directly use the transaction by double-clicking the shortcut (Figure 7.2).

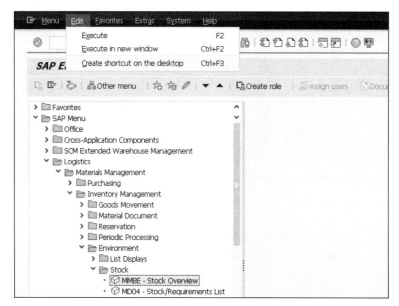

Figure 7.1 *Create a Shortcut on the Desktop*

Figure 7.2 *Shortcut*

7.2   Maintaining Your Own User Data

You can define user-specific settings such as logon language, printer settings, and parameters in user settings. Follow these steps to maintain your own user data:

1 Start Transaction SU3 via the command field, or select **System ▶ User Profiles ▶ Own Data** from the menu bar (Figure 7.3).

2 After you've called the transaction for maintaining your own user data, the system shows the **Address** tab. Here, you can maintain a variety of information:

– In the **Person** area, you can maintain your personal data such as **Title**, **First name**, and **Last name** in the respective fields. Use the 🖫 button to save each field change in this transaction.

- In the **Language** area, you can change the language that is used in the system after logon. Use **EN English**. In addition, you can also maintain further information in this area, such as telephone numbers and email addresses. Remember to save each field change via the 🖫 button.

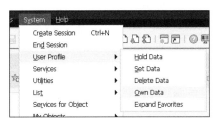

Figure 7.3 *Define User-Specific Settings*

3 You can also change your password using the **Password** button at the top-left of the screen (Figure 7.4).

Figure 7.4 *Address Tab*

4 Now click the **Defaults** tab (Figure 7.5), where you can determine the presentation of figures and dates. You can specify the following information:

- **Start menu**: Here you can assign an enterprise-specific area menu to your user. In this area, you can combine transactions for your task area. The SAP administration team usually sets these parameters.
- **Logon Language**: If no language is selected in the logon screen, the language specified here is used. If you define a language here (e.g., **EN** for English), you don't need to specify a language during logon.
- **Decimal Notation**: With this selection field, you define how the SAP system displays decimal numbers. For example, you can choose between 1.234.567,89 (a period for thousand separators and a comma for decimal digits, which is standard in Germany); 1 234567,89 (with a blank for thousand separators and a comma for decimal digits); or 1,234,567.89 (with a comma for thousand separators and a point for decimal digits, which is standard in the United States).
- **Date Format**: In this selection field, you define the date format, for instance, DD.MM.YYYY or MM/DD/YYYY.
- **Time Format (12/24h)**: In this selection field, you specify which time format is used. For example, choose between 11:10:15 (hours, minutes, seconds) or 11:10:15 PM. The time zone must be set if an international business has employees in Germany and in the United States, for example.
- **OutputDevice**: 1oc1 is the name of the default Windows printer that is installed in this SAP system (see Chapter 9). The default Windows printer refers to the printer installed on the workplace computer.

5 In the **Parameters** tab (Figure 7.6), you can set the default values for fields in transactions. These fields are populated with default values in the respective transactions to save the user the trouble of unnecessary inputs. Section 7.4 describes how this works. If you primarily work in company code 1000, then you can prepopulate fields in transactions with this key.

The following section shows how you can create favorites to facilitate navigation within the SAP system.

Figure 7.5 *Defaults Tab*

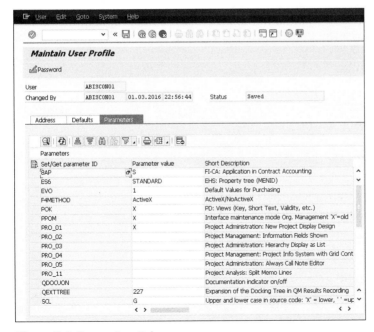

Figure 7.6 *Parameters Tab*

7.3   Creating Favorites

You already know about favorites from using Internet browsers, where you identify pages you frequently open as "Favorites." SAP offers the same concept for SAP GUI. You can identify the following objects you frequently use as favorites in the SAP Easy Access menu:

■ Transactions

■ Internet pages

■ Files or programs located on your computer or the network drive

The latter is useful if you require a document, such as a PDF regularly. You can access this file via your favorites as necessary using Microsoft Windows Explorer. The following section presents these options.

Adding Transactions to the Favorites

You can add transactions to your favorites in the following three ways:

■ Via drag and drop

■ Via the menu bar

■ Via the right mouse button

We describe these alternatives in the following.

You can add a transaction via drag and drop to your favorites by following these steps:

1 Open the SAP Easy Access menu, and search for the transaction you want to add to your favorites.

2 Position the mouse pointer on the transaction, and keep the left mouse button pressed.

3 Keeping the left mouse button pressed, set the mouse pointer on the **Favorites** folder, and release the left mouse button again. The transaction is added to your favorites.

Alternatively, you can add transactions to your favorites via the menu bar. Follow these steps:

1 In the SAP Easy Access menu, select the transaction you want to add to your favorites.

2 Click **Favorites** ▸ **Add** (Figure 7.7). The transaction selected is added to your favorites.

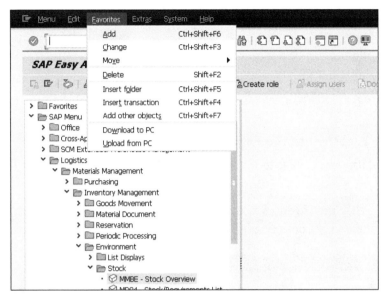

Figure 7.7 *Adding Favorites*

The third option is to add transactions via the right mouse button to the **Favorites** folder. Follow these steps:

1 Right-click the **Favorites** folder, and the context menu opens (Figure 7.8).

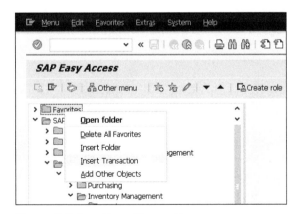

Figure 7.8 *Inserting a Transaction*

2 In the context menu, select **Insert Transaction**. Then enter the transaction code to add it to your favorites (Figure 7.9).

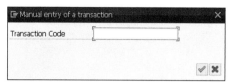

Figure 7.9 *Entering a Transaction Code*

Adding Websites to the Favorites

You can also save a link to a website in your favorites by following these steps:

1 Right-click the **Favorites** folder. Select **Add Other Objects** from the context menu that opens (Figure 7.10).

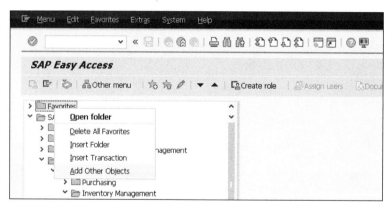

Figure 7.10 *Adding Other Objects*

2 Double-click **Web address or file** in the dialog window that opens (Figure 7.11).

3 Input a description of the favorite in the **Text** field, and enter the URL (e.g., *https://www.sap-press.com*) in the **Web Address or File** field. Confirm your entries by clicking the **Next** icon. The desired website is added to your favorites (Figure 7.12).

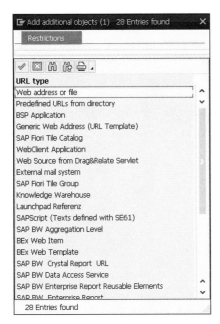

Figure 7.11 *Selecting Object to Add*

Figure 7.12 *Favorite URLs*

Adding Files or Programs to the Favorites

To add files or programs from your local drive or a network drive to your favorites, proceed as described in the previous section. Enter or select the file name or the path in the **Web Address or File** field instead of the web address (Figure 7.13).

Figure 7.13 *Adding a File to the Favorites*

Deleting Favorites

You can also delete your favorites if you don't need them anymore by right-clicking the unwanted favorite and choosing **Delete Favorite** from the context menu, as shown in Figure 7.14.

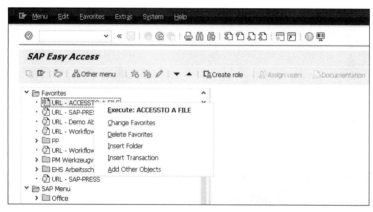

Figure 7.14 *Deleting Favorites*

Importing and Exporting Favorites

You've already seen how favorites are created. In this section, you'll now learn how to export and import favorites. Because favorites are saved locally, importing and exporting favorites can be useful if you want to transfer them to a different PC (e.g., when a PC is replaced). Another scenario could be that you want to help a new colleague getting started with the system by importing your favorites into his GUI.

Follow these steps:

1 To save the favorites, select **Favorites ▸ Download to PC** from the menu bar (Figure 7.15).

2 The **Save as** menu opens. Enter a file name in the **File name** field. We used * for our example. Select a file format, in this case, **All files (*.*)**, from the **File type** dropdown menu.

3 You can then choose a location on your PC or network drive by entering a path in the **Save in**. Alternatively, you can use the buttons in the left window pane to specify a location (e.g., **Desktop** to save the file locally on the desktop).

4 Save your changes by clicking the **Save** button.

Figure 7.15 *Download to PC*

To import favorites, you need a file (an original export) containing the favorites. This file is then saved on your desktop PC. Select **Favorites ▶ Upload from PC** to import the favorites. Navigate to the location of the file containing the favorites, select the file, and click the **Open** button.

> **NOTE**
>
> **List of Favorites for Download**
>
> In the download area for this book (*https://www.sap-press.com/using-sap_4155/*), you'll find a list of favorites containing all important transactions for the individual chapters that you can import. At the bottom of the page, click **Supplements list** in the **Product Supplements** box. A window opens where you can view the materials that are available for download.

7.4   Prepopulating Parameters for Fields

In specific cases, you must enter the same data repeatedly. To spare having to do repeated entries, you can save specific parameters as default values. These default values are permanently available to you within your username and will be prepopulated in the corresponding fields the next time you log on to the system.

Transaction VD03 (Customer Master Data) should be used to show how you can prepopulate fields with parameters. The key of this organizational unit (1000) should be used as a default value in the **Sales Organization** field.

First, you must determine the parameter ID for the desired field. Then, specify the default value for the field under **System ▶ User Profile ▶ Own Data**. The individual steps are as follows:

1 Navigate to the field in which you want to insert a default value by either using the corresponding transaction or following the respective menu path.

To reproduce this concrete example, open Transaction VD03 by entering the transaction code in the command field or navigating via the SAP Easy Access menu path: **Logistics ▸ Sales and Distribution ▸ Master Data ▸ Business Partner ▸ Customer ▸ Display ▸ VD03 – Sales and Distribution** (Figure 7.16).

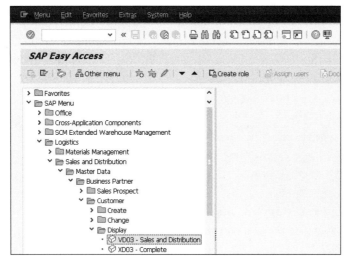

Figure 7.16 *Navigating to the Field*

2 The system displays the initial screen of Transaction VD03. Click the **Sales Organization** field (Figure 7.17), and then press F1 (field help).

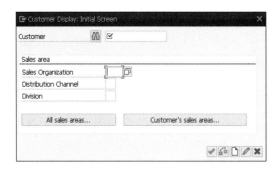

Figure 7.17 *Initial Screen*

3 Click the **Technical Information** 🖼 icon to determine the parameter ID. Every field has its own parameter ID.

4 Memorize the parameter ID: For the **Sales Organization** field, in which you're currently located, the **Parameter ID** is VKO (Figure 7.18).

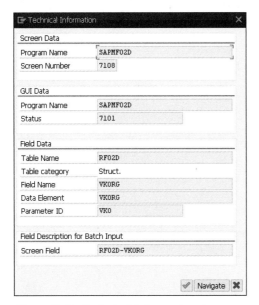

Figure 7.18 *Technical Information Screen*

5 Exit the transaction by clicking **Cancel** ☒.

6 Change your profiles. To do so, open your own user data by starting Transaction SU3 (Maintain Users Own Data) via the command field; or select **System ▸ User Profile ▸ Own Data** in the menu.

7 Click the **Parameters** tab, and enter "VKO" in the **Set/Get- Parameter ID** field and "1000" in the **Parameter Value** column (Figure 7.19). If you've entered a correct parameter ID (i.e., one known to the system) and confirmed it by pressing ⌨Enter⌨, the system displays the short description. This way, you can also check whether the parameter ID is correct.

8 Save your settings by clicking the **Save** button 💾. You've prepopulated the field for the sales organization with the parameter value **1000**.

9 Test your settings by starting Transaction VD03 again. If it worked, the **Sales Organization** field is now prepopulated with the value **1000** in the initial screen of the transaction (Figure 7.20).

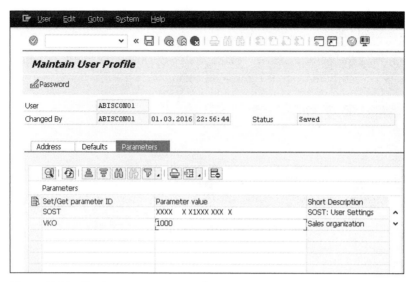

Figure 7.19 *Checking Parameter ID for Correctness*

Figure 7.20 *Testing Sales Organization Field*

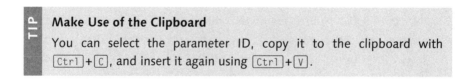

TIP

Make Use of the Clipboard

You can select the parameter ID, copy it to the clipboard with [Ctrl]+[C], and insert it again using [Ctrl]+[V].

7.5   Holding, Setting, and Deleting Data

The functions **Hold Data**, **Set Data**, and **Delete Data** save time by lowering the number of inputs in the SAP system (Figure 7.21). The settings are retained during one session only, which is different from prepopulation with parameters.

Figure 7.21 *Hold Data, Set Data, And Delete Data*

You have the following options:

- **Hold Data**
  Data can be held (i.e., default values can be defined) in various transactions. The fields filled this way are prepopulated with the default values from the previous processing when the transaction is called again. These default values can still be overwritten.

- **Set Data**
  The **Set Data** function also automatically fills the fields with default values. In contrast to **Hold Data**, the prepopulated fields can no longer be changed after **Set Data**.

- **Delete Data**
  With this function, you reset both the **Hold Data** and the **Set Data** functions so that the fields are no longer automatically populated with default values. You can see how the **Hold Data** fields are filled by taking the following steps:

  1. Start Transaction VA01 (Create Standard Order).

  2. In the initial screen, select **ST** (Standard Order) in the **Order Type** field. Choose **1000** in the **Sales Organization** field.

  3. Enter the article numbers for the items. Then choose **System ▸ User Profile ▸ Hold Data** from the menu.

  4. Exit the transaction, and restart it. Your field entries should be prepopulated again.

This chapter so far described various options that make your work with the SAP system easier. For example, if you require only a few transactions for your work, you can create links to them on the Windows desktop. This way, after you've logged on to the system, you can directly navigate to the desired transaction with a simple double-click. Furthermore, SAP GUI allows you to manage your favorites, so you can store frequently required transactions or websites in your favorites menu. It's also very useful to prepopulate a parameter ID of a field with a default value. The parameter ID can be defined in your personal settings and is valid for the current user only.

7.6 Adapting the User Interface

The look and feel of the SAP GUI can be changed according to your requirements. In this section, we'll describe some of the settings that can be adapted.

In the standard toolbar, click the **Adapt Local Layout** button. Select **Options**. Alternatively, you can press [Alt]+[F12] and then click the **Options** menu item.

> **NOTE**
>
> **New Logon Required**
>
> Some settings are only applied after logging off the system and restarting the SAP Logon Pad.

The screen shown in Figure 7.22 opens.

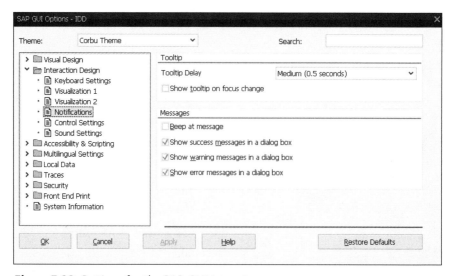

Figure 7.22 Settings for the SAP GUI Layout

You can configure the following settings:

- **Visual Design**
  In this area, you can adapt the design, font, and font size. You can set a complete theme (appearance and colors) or individual colors.

- **Interaction Design**
  In this area, you can configure settings for a personalized keyboard and audiovisual settings.

> **Display Keys in Dropdown Lists**
>
> In the **Adapt Local Layout** menu, under **Options**, select the **Display Keys in Dropdown Lists** checkbox under **Interaction Design ▶ Visualization & Interaction** to display descriptions and keys in dropdown lists.
>
> Under **Interaction Design ▶ Notifications**, you can configure if a pop-up with the corresponding information is displayed for every success, warning, or error message.

- **Accessibility & Scripting**
  In this area, users with visual impairments can adjust SAP GUI to improve readability and appearance.

- **Multilingual Settings**
  Use this folder to configure explicit settings for other languages.

- **Local Data**
  This folder can be used to adapt local options such as the size of the input history and the location for local data.

- **Traces**
  Use this folder to activate log files for diagnosis purposes. System administrators can then use these logs to identify problems within a program if malfunctions need to be corrected.

- **Security**
  This folder can be used to adjust security rules. For example, if data are exported to a file on your local PC, this process must be confirmed.

- **Front End Print**
  Here you can configure the options for the printer frontend and display printer logs.

- **System Information**
  This area provides detailed information on the installed SAP GUI version.

7.7 Try It!

Exercise 1

Describe how to create a link to Transaction VA01 (Create Standard Order) on your Windows desktop.

Exercise 2

Name the four objects for which you can create favorites.

Exercise 3

Describe three methods of creating favorites.

Exercise 4

Describe how you can determine the parameter ID for a field. For this purpose, start Transaction XK01 (Create Vendor) in the system, and determine the parameter ID of the sales organization.

8   Creating Evaluations and Reports

If your daily work frequently requires you to create reports and lists, you can print, send, and use these lists for the decision-making process via the SAP reporting options.

Besides the tools contained in SAP ERP, there are further powerful tools (e.g., within SAP NetWeaver) that aren't discussed in this book. This chapter is limited to the information system in SAP ERP.

In this chapter, you'll learn the following:
- How to call standard reports in the SAP system
- How to use the SAP List Viewer for presentation
- How to export reports to Microsoft Excel
- How to use variants
- How to access further reporting tools provided in SAP ERP

8.1   Using Standard Reports in the SAP System

Reporting and analysis play a central role in the success of a business. The wealth of information stored in the SAP system can be evaluated and presented in reports (e.g., in lists) for analysis.

The different areas and departments of your business have diverse information requirements. In the HR area, the employees and managers require personal data that ranges from simple lists of employees to more complex reports. In logistics, reports can involve stock lists or lists of orders from a specific time period. In accounting, you can display all items of a debtor (customer), the costs and revenues of a specific area, and much more.

Part III of this book provides a selection of the most important reports in the Purchasing, Sales and Distribution (SD), Human Resources (HR), SAP ERP Financials (FI), and Controlling (CO) components.

> **INFO**
>
> **SAP List Viewer (ALV)**
>
> The SAP system provides various options to display queried data. One of the most important display tools is the SAP List Viewer (ALV). ALV stands for ABAP List Viewer, which is the name of the tool in older releases. Different list operations such as search, filter, and sort are available within the ALV. With the ALV grid control, SAP gives you a standardized tool for displaying lists in the system. Grid control lets you define which information is displayed in the list and choose the criteria used to filter it.

Let's use an example to illustrate how to call standard reports. You must determine in the SAP system which sales were generated by a specific sales organization (in this example, 1000) within a specific time period (three months). Follow these steps:

1. Open the **Logistics ‣ Logistics Controlling ‣ Logistics Information System ‣ Standard Analyses ‣ Sales and Distribution ‣ MCTA – Customer** path in the SAP Easy Access menu (Figure 8.1). Alternatively, start Transaction MCTA by entering the transaction code in the command field.

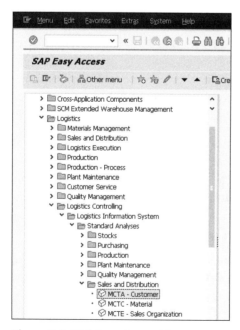

Figure 8.1 SAP Easy Access Menu

2 In the initial screen of the customer analysis, enter the sales organization in the corresponding field for which you want to create the evaluation. Enter "1000" in this example. Limit the period to analyze to four years (01.2012 to 01.2016) using the fields, **Month** and To (Figure 8.2). To run the evaluation, click the **Next** button or press F8.

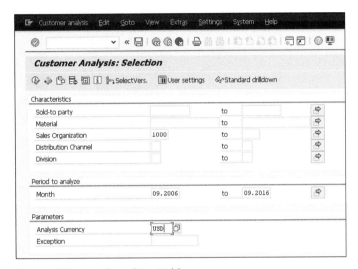

Figure 8.2 *Month and To Fields*

3 After the selection is executed, the basic list is displayed (Figure 8.3). You can now modify the report using the buttons that are detailed in the upcoming Table 8.1.

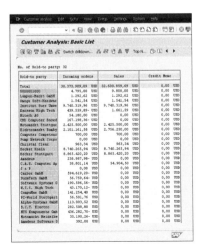

Figure 8.3 *Customer Analysis: Basic List*

123

You've now successfully created a sales report. The list, which was output in ALV format, offers various navigation options. The ALV grid control has a special toolbar for this that offers the important buttons shown in Table 8.1.

Button	Name	Key Combination	Explanation
	First Page	Ctrl + Page ↑	Navigates to the beginning of the list
	Previous Page	Page ↑	Navigates to the previous page in the list
	Next Page	Page ↓	Navigates to the next page in the list
	Last Page	Ctrl + Page ↓	Navigates to the end of the list
	Select (Details)	F2	Shows detailed information on the selection
	Save in PC File	Shift + F8	Exports the list to a PC file
	Send	Ctrl + F1	Sends a link of this list to another user
	Graphic	F5	Creates a graphic
	Sort in Ascending Order	Ctrl + F5	Sorts a selected column by contents in ascending order
	Sort in Descending Order	Shift + F4	Sorts a selected column by contents in descending order
	Other Info Structure	Ctrl + F4	Changes the list structure

Table 8.1 Buttons in the ALV Grid Control

Button	Name	Key Combination	Explanation
Switch drilldown...	Change Drill-down	F7	Changes the first column
¥	Analysis Currency	Ctrl + F7	Changes the currency to the selected currency
	Drilldown by	F8	Provides further drilldown of a selected criterion
Top N...	Top N Values	Shift + F6	Shows the highest values of a selected column

Table 8.1 *Buttons in the ALV Grid Control (Cont.)*

The next section describes how to find the report that meets your evaluation purposes best.

8.2   Finding Standard Reports

If you receive a specific report request, you can check in the SAP system for a standard report that meets your requirements. The following section presents three options to find the reports in the SAP standard version.

Searching for Reports

If you know the name of the report required, you can call it quickly and easily. To call reports and search them via the search help, you can activate the reporting function via the menu bar (**System ▸ Services ▸ Reporting**). Follow these steps:

1 Open the **System ▸ Services ▸ Reporting** menu item in the menu bar (Figure 8.4).

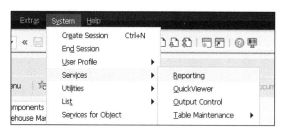

Figure 8.4 *Opening Up Reporting*

2. Open the **ABAP: Execute Program** window; enter the name of the report in the **Program** field, and execute it directly (Figure 8.5). Additionally, you can select the associated variants via the **Overview of variants** button.

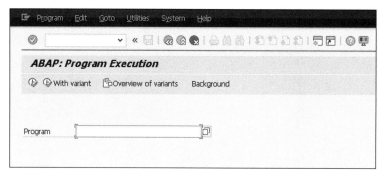

Figure 8.5 *ABAP Program Execution*

3. If you don't know the program name, you can use a search window (also known as a program directory) to determine the program name according to different selection criteria. For this purpose, open the value help via the [⊡] button in the **Program** field.

Effective Search

The less precise your selection criteria are, the more time the system requires for the search. If you only enter "*" in the **Program** field, it can take several minutes to obtain a result.

4 Specify your search term in the program directory, and enter any part of the report name in the **Program** field. You can use the following placeholders for unknown characters:

- Asterisk (*): Character string
- Plus sign (+): One character exactly

5 Choose **Execute** 🔄 (Figure 8.6).

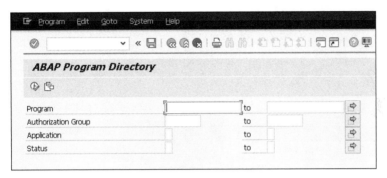

Figure 8.6 *ABAP Program Directory*

6 The system displays a list with reports. Double-click the desired report to select it. Alternatively, position the cursor on the report name and choose **Execute** 🔄.

7 The system displays the selection screen of the report if no variant is required. If you need a variant, you must return to the initial screen via the **Back** 🔙 button or [F3] to enter the program and variant name there. Before you do so, write down the name of the report.

8 Enter your selection values in the selection screen. Choose **Program ▶ Execute**. The report is displayed in a list.

Calling Reports in the SAP Easy Access Menu

You can find the reports on the individual components in the corresponding information systems. You can also directly navigate to the reports of the information system from the top level of the SAP Easy Access menu (Figure 8.7).

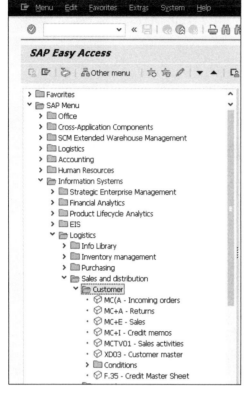

Figure 8.7 *Information Systems in the SAP Easy Access Menu*

8.3   Exporting Lists to Microsoft Excel

You can also process data outside the SAP system by exporting it to other programs. For example, you can export a list as a Microsoft Excel file to view and change it there.

Let's continue the example of the previous section, in which you ran a customer analysis. Now export the list created there as a Microsoft Excel file by following these steps:

1 In the SAP Easy Access menu, select **Customer Analysis ▸ Export ▸ Save to PC File** (or press Shift + F8).

2 In the dialog window that appears, select the **Spreadsheet** radio button (Figure 8.8), and then click the **Next** ✅ button (or press Enter).

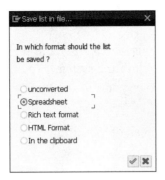

Figure 8.8 *Saving the List into a Spreadsheet*

3 Another dialog window opens in which you can specify the directory (folder) where the file is to be saved on your computer and name the file.

Note that you may not have write authorizations in all directories of your business. Click the **Generate** button after you've specified the directory and file name.

4 Next, a dialog window opens that details the number of bytes that were transferred to the file. You can now further process the generated file in Microsoft Excel by starting Microsoft Excel and opening the file in the directory in which you've saved it (Figure 8.9).

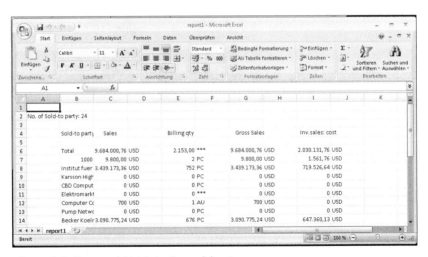

Figure 8.9 *Exported List into Spreadsheet*

You now have the option to format the selected data graphically in Microsoft Excel charts.

8.4   Using Variants

A variant includes saved selection criteria (various search criteria in the corresponding fields that you use to restrict a search in the system). You don't need to reenter these selection criteria whenever you call the transaction, but you can save them.

If you want to save your entries in the initial screen of the customer analysis as a variant, follow these steps:

1 In the initial screen of Transaction MCTA, choose **Goto ▸ Variants ▸ Save as Variant** (Figure 8.10).

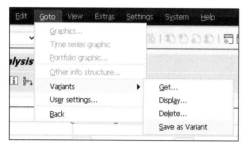

Figure 8.10 *Saving as a Variant*

2 Enter the variant name (**Variant Name**) and a descriptive text (**Description**) in the relevant fields of the **Variant Attributes** screen (Figure 8.11). Then click **Save** 🖫.

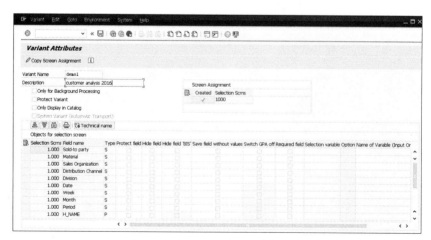

Figure 8.11 *Defining Variant Attributes*

3 After you've saved your entries, the SAP system displays the message **Variant ... was saved.**

To load a saved variant, follow these steps:

1 Choose **Goto ▸ Variants ▸ Get** in the initial screen of Transaction MCTA (Figure 8.12).

Figure 8.12 *Loading a Saved Variant*

2 A variant catalog is displayed from which you can select the saved variant (Figure 8.13). The fields are then filled accordingly.

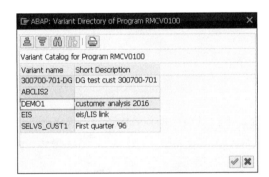

Figure 8.13 *Saved Variants*

8.5 Other Reporting Options in SAP ERP

The SAP system provides numerous reports with which you can access the saved data. In the SAP standard system, many predefined reports can be executed in the ABAP programs directly.

For advanced reporting requirements, SAP ERP offers its own reporting tools you can use to define custom evaluations according to your requirements.

(This also involves ABAP report generators.) The following are the most critical reporting tools in SAP ERP, with which you can create custom evaluations:

- SAP Query (including components of SAP Query, InfoSet Query, and QuickViewer)
- Report Painter/Report Writer
- Drilldown Reporting
- Logistics Information System (LIS)

The use of the appropriate tool depends on the specific report requirement. Influencing factors include data format, options for further processing, and (graphical) presentation options. Table 8.2 lists the reporting tools and their main usage areas. The scope of this book doesn't cover the versatile characteristics of each tool.

Reporting Tool		Main Usage Area
SAP Query	SAP Query	All SAP components (In SAP ERP HCM, InfoSet Query is referred to as Ad-Hoc Query)
	InfoSet Query	
	QuickViewer	
Drilldown Reporting		Accounting (FI, CO, TR, IM, PS)
Report Painter/Report Writer		Accounting (CO, FI)
Logistics Information System (LIS)		Logistics (SD, MM, QM, PM, PP)

Table 8.2 *Overview of the Most Critical Reporting Tools in SAP ERP*

Beyond that, SAP Business Warehouse (SAP BW) includes various reporting tools (see Chapter 3) that aren't discussed in this book either. One example is SAP Business Explorer (SAP BEx). A few years ago, further tools, such as SAP Crystal Reports, were added with the acquisition of Business Objects.

8.6   Try It!

Exercise 1

Create an evaluation that shows the 20 customers that generated the highest sales figures in sales organization 1000 over the past 12 months. Then export this data to Microsoft Excel.

9 Printing

Because the paperless office hasn't become reality yet, it's still often necessary to print documents. You can print everything that you can view on the
SAP screen. Although you usually need to print lists, purchase orders, or
invoices, sometimes you might want to print the entire screen—that is, to
make a screenshot. In this chapter, you'll learn about the most important
printing functions and settings.

This chapter discusses the following:
- Setting up a default printer
- Understanding pool requests and output requests
- Printing lists from the SAP system
- Creating screenshots

9.1 Overview of the Print Functions

The SAP system provides two options for outputting documents: working
with immediate outputs and using the spool system. To print the document
immediately, follow these steps:

1 Open the document (e.g., the list that you want to print), and click **Print**
🖨. Alternatively, you can press `Ctrl`+`P` or use the **List ▸ Print** menu
path.

2 The system now displays a window with the print options. Maintain the
other print options, and select the printer (Figure 9.1).

3 The list will be output.

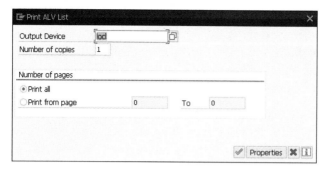

Figure 9.1 *Printing the ALV List*

If you use the spool system, the print requests aren't output immediately (Figure 9.2). Instead, the print request is stored in a spool file. This file can then be sent to a printer or another output device, such as a fax machine. An output request finally initiates the print process.

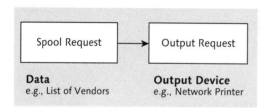

Figure 9.2 *Spool Request and Output Request*

Let's explore spool requests and output requests further:

- **Spool request**
  Your document isn't directly output on a printer or another device after you select a print function for it. Instead, the system stores the output files of the print document in a data store until they are sent to a specific output device (via an output request). With the spool request, the print data are temporarily stored, and you can access and display this data.

- **Output request**
  For output requests, the print data of a spool request are output on a specific output device. There can be numerous output requests with different printers or print settings for one spool request.

It might seem easier to output a Microsoft Word document on a printer than go through these steps. However, output control has to cover several additional requirements: the flexibility to output documents or lists again or on a different device, or the ability to send documents to a telefax gateway controlled via the SAP system in the business network. Output control also supports further processing via the Electronic Data Interchange (EDI). The spool system makes this possible by storing print data temporarily and differentiating between spool requests and output requests.

> **INFO**
>
> **Electronic Data Interchange**
>
> EDI is the electronic data interchange between computer systems; for example, a customer electronically transfers a purchase order to your business's SAP system, where the purchase order is further processed. Data are exchanged in the form of Intermediate Documents (IDocs) between SAP systems. For further information on this, please read Chapter 12.

The following section describes the usage of spool requests in detail.

9.2   Using Spool Requests

The print process in the system has two phases: First, a spool request is created at which time the system formats the data required for the output. Then you can generate an output request where you define when and on which device the data will be output.

Let's take a look at the print function using the list of vendors as an example:

1   Call Transaction MKVZ via the SAP Easy Access menu by following the menu path, **Logistics ▸ Materials Management ▸ Purchasing ▸ Master Data ▸ Vendor ▸ List Displays ▸ MKVZ Purchasing List**. Alternatively, call Transaction MKVZ via the command field.

2   In the initial screen of the list of vendors, enter "1000" in the **Purchasing Organization** field (Figure 9.3). This means that the output should list all vendors that are assigned to the purchasing organization 1000.

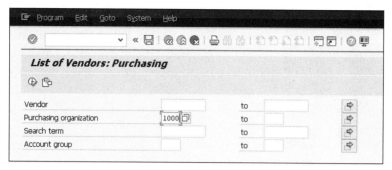

Figure 9.3 *Initial Screen for the List of Vendors*

3 Clicking **Next**. The screen displays the list of vendors (Figure 9.4).

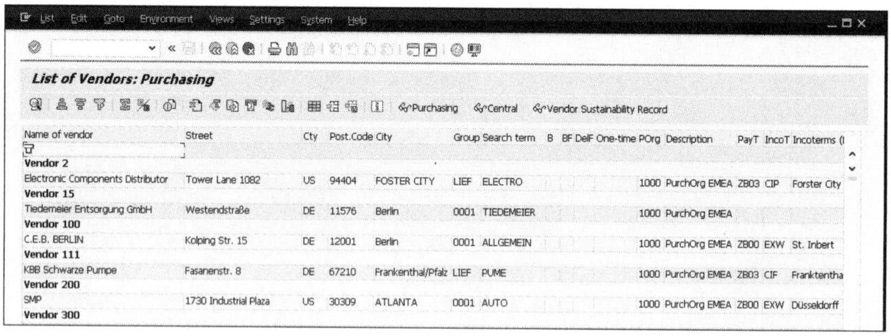

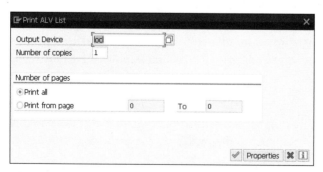

Figure 9.4 *List of Vendors*

4 To print this list, click the **Print** button in the menu bar, or press
[Ctrl]+[P]. The system displays the **Print ALV List** dialog box (Figure 9.5).
The print window may look different, depending on the application you
use.

Figure 9.5 *Printing the List of Vendors*

5 In this print window, you can make the settings that are necessary for your output.

- **Output Device**: Enter which printer you want to use. The **Input Help** button beside the field lets you view the available printers and select one by double-clicking it. You can create a PDF if a PDF printer driver is installed on your PC.

- **Number of copies**: Define how many copies you want to print.

- **Number of pages**: The **Print all** or **Print from page** radio buttons let you choose whether you want to print the entire document or individual pages.

Press ⌈Enter⌋, or click **Next** ✓. The system displays a status message that confirms the creation of the spool request (Figure 9.6). Every spool request has a unique identification number.

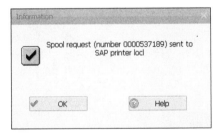

Figure 9.6 *Creation of a Spool Request*

6 Follow the **System ▸ Services ▸ Output Control** path in the menu bar to open the output control (Figure 9.7).

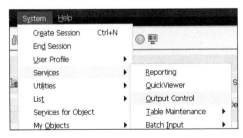

Figure 9.7 *Navigating to Output Control*

7 Click the **Further Selection Criteria** button at the top in the output control to restrict your search result (Figure 9.8).

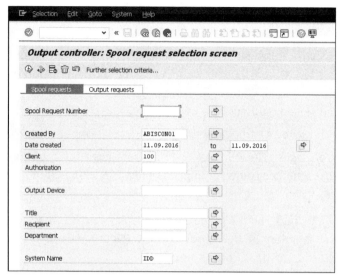

Figure 9.8 *Output Controller*

8 When you click the **Further Selection Criteria** button, a window opens that provides the selection criteria as required (Figure 9.9). In this case, the fields of the **Standard** selection criterion are displayed.

Figure 9.9 *Selecting Spool Requests*

9 Press ⟨Enter⟩ to return to the output control. Click **Execute** 🔲 to display the output control. The system may display several requests, depending on the restriction for your selection criteria. Select the spool request that you want to output by activating the checkbox next to the spool number (Figure 9.10). Click **Print** 🖨, or press ⟨Ctrl⟩+⟨P⟩.

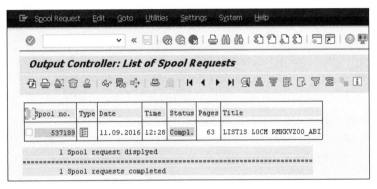

Figure 9.10 *List of Spool Requests*

10 The system generates the output request and outputs it on the printer. When you receive the message **Spool request created without immediate output**, confirm with **OK** (Figure 9.11). The system then outputs your document on the selected printer.

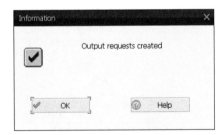

Figure 9.11 *Outputting Spool Request to Printer*

The following section describes how you configure the default printer in the SAP system.

9.3   Changing the Default Printer

In the SAP system, the printers are defined centrally and assigned to individual users.

> **NOTE**
>
> **Printer Setup**
>
> In a live SAP system, the administrator of your SAP system is responsible for the printer configuration, not you. However, for testing purposes, it may be necessary to use an installed Microsoft Windows or network printer, which you may need to manage.

It's also possible to use the default Windows printer—the one the Windows operating system proposes when you use the print function in an Office application to output a document. To set up the default printer in the SAP system, follow these steps:

1 Open **System ▸ User Profile ▸ Own Data** in the menu bar. Then click the **Defaults** tab (Figure 9.12).

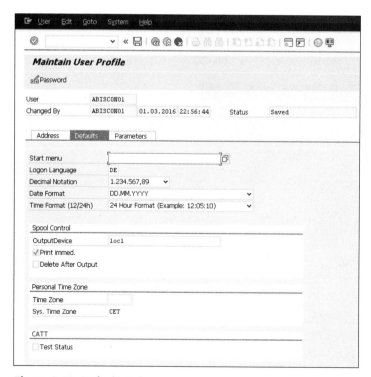

Figure 9.12 *Defaults Tab*

2 Select **1oc1** in the **OutputDevice** field to use the default Windows printer. You can also select the output device in the input help for the ▢ field, and copy it by double-clicking it.

Make sure that the **Print immed.** checkbox is activated. This way, the system will generate an output request immediately after the spool request, and the output will be carried out directly after the print command. The **Delete After Output** setting ensures that print formatting (spool) doesn't remain in the SAP system. This means that the spool doesn't need to be regenerated for a new output.

The next section illustrates how you can create screenshots of the SAP system.

9.4 Creating Screenshots

9

If you have to create documentation, it's useful to illustrate your text with images from the SAP system, known as screenshots or hardcopy in the SAP system. There are two methods for creating screenshots:

- Using Microsoft Office
- Using the **Hard Copy** function in the SAP system

To create screenshots using standard Microsoft functions, follow these steps:

1 Open the required screen, and select a section (if applicable).

2 Copy the screenshot to the clipboard with `Ctrl`+`Print`.

3 You can then insert the screenshot from the clipboard in various applications using `Ctrl`+`V`:

- Open Microsoft Paint via the Windows **Start** menu, insert the screenshot with `Ctrl`+`V`, and store it as a *.tif file.

- Open Microsoft PowerPoint, insert the screenshot with `Ctrl`+`V`, and save the presentation.

- Open Microsoft Word, insert the screenshot with `Ctrl`+`V`, and save the Word document.

4 Then you can further process the created screenshots in the programs mentioned in various ways.

You can also directly output a screenshot in the SAP system on a default Windows printer by following these steps:

1 In the standard toolbar, click the **Adapt Local Layout** 🖳 button (Figure 9.13). Then click the **Hard Copy** button. You can also use the key combination Shift + H in the displayed menu.

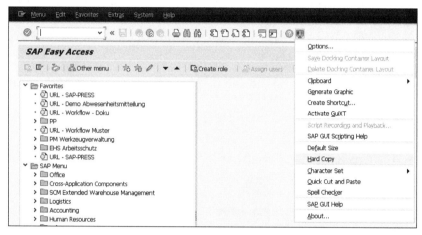

Figure 9.13 *The Hard Copy Button*

2 The screenshot is output on the printer.

This chapter introduced you to print functions in the SAP system. Printing in SAP usually requires a spool request and an output request. You can output documents, lists, and reports.

9.5 Try It!

Exercise 1
Describe how to define a default printer in the SAP system for your user.

Exercise 2
What's the difference between a spool request and an output request?

Exercise 3
Print a list of all sales orders (Transaction VA04).

10 Automating Tasks

This chapter shows you how to automate specific work steps so you can simplify your work. The SAP system runs specific routine tasks automatically in the background or in batch processing (also known as batch input) to save you time.

In this chapter, you'll learn about the following:

- Online and background processing
- Simplifying work by using jobs
- Using batch processing with batch input sessions

10.1 Background Jobs

Background processing in the SAP system is used to automate routine tasks. Background processing occurs if the SAP system performs tasks (jobs) without user intervention. Of course, you must first tell the SAP system what programs to trigger and when. This way, jobs are processed in the background without needing further help or attention from the user.

> **INFO**
>
> **Reports**
>
> In the SAP context, a report is an executable ABAP program that reads database tables and uses them to output results according to specific criteria. For example, the sales department requires an evaluation that lists all customers from a specific state who purchased goods worth $10,000 in the previous fiscal year. If such a report is executed, the task list can be displayed, printed, or saved.

Online processing is the opposite of background processing. Unlike the traditional definition in IT, the term *online* doesn't refer to the Internet connection here. In this context, online is used when a user starts transactions directly in the SAP system.

Background jobs are particularly suitable for recurring tasks that must be performed in the SAP system but that require no interaction between the user and the SAP system. The benefit that background jobs offer is that you can schedule the tasks to be performed at times when SAP system use is as low as possible (e.g., at night). You should coordinate this time window with the SAP administration team.

The following tasks are run as background jobs:

- Printing dunnings
- Creating reports
- Transferring data via Electronic Data Interchange (EDI)

To work with background jobs successfully, you must first learn how to create a job. Determine the name of the report that you want to run in the background job, and then define the job using the Job Wizard in the SAP system. The Job Wizard guides you through job creation, including helping you to specify the job name, job class, task, start time, and output.

In this example, the system is supposed to create an up-to-date list of vendors in a background job. Follow these steps:

1 With Transaction MKVZ, you can output a list of vendors in the SAP system. Call this transaction via the SAP Easy Access menu path: **Logistics ▶ Materials Management ▶ Purchasing ▶ Master Data ▶ Vendor ▶ List Displays** (Figure 10.1). Another option is to enter Transaction MKVZ in the command field.

2 The initial screen of the list of vendors opens. Before continuing this transaction, however, determine the name of the report. You'll need this report name to automate the step later. Select **System ▶ Status...** in the menu bar (Figure 10.2).

Figure 10.1 *Navigating to Purchasing List*

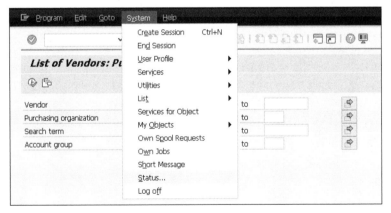

Figure 10.2 *Navigating to the Report Details*

3 Determine the name of the report in the **System: Status** window (Figure 10.3). In this example, the name of the report is RMKKVZ00. Either write down this report name or copy it to the clipboard by selecting it with the mouse and pressing Ctrl+C.

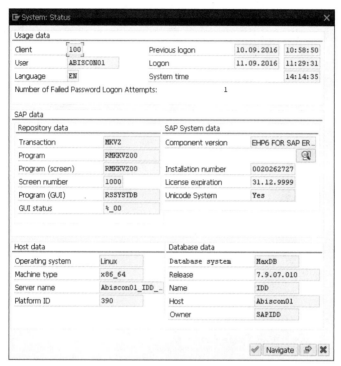

Figure 10.3 Naming the Report

4 You'll specify specific parameters when you define the job in the SAP system later. For this purpose, create a variant for the list of vendors by selecting **Goto ▶ Variants ▶ Save as Variant** in the menu bar (Figure 10.4).

Figure 10.4 Saving as Variant

5 The **Variant Attributes** screen opens (Figure 10.5). Here you must enter the **Variant Name** (here, "zz_vendor1") and **Description** ("List of vendors") so that you can assign and uniquely identify the variant later.

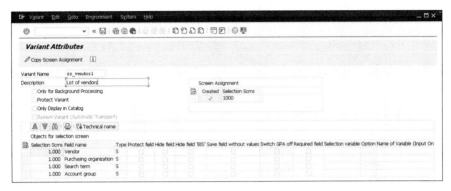

Figure 10.5 *The Variant Attributes Screen*

6 Click the **Save** 🖫 button in the standard toolbar to save the variant. The system displays the message **Variant ZZ_VENDOR1 saved** after saving (Figure 10.6).

Figure 10.6 *ZZ_VENDOR1 Saved*

7 Next, you need to schedule the background job in the SAP system. Select **System ▸ Services ▸ Jobs ▸ Define Job** in the menu bar (Figure 10.7). Alternatively, you can enter Transaction SM36 in the command field.

8 Call the Job Wizard in Transaction SM36 (Define Background Job). Similar to a Microsoft Office application wizard, the Job Wizard guides you through the background job creation. To begin, click the **Job wizard** button (Figure 10.8).

Figure 10.7 *Defining Jobs in the Easy Access Menu*

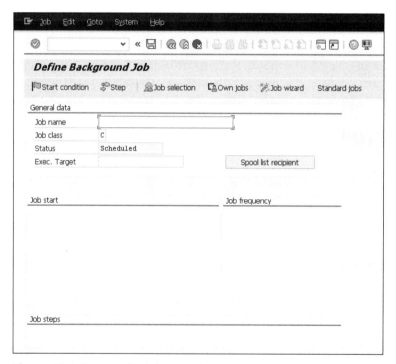

Figure 10.8 *Starting the Job Wizard*

9 The initial **Create a job** screen of the Job Wizard opens in the subsequent step (Figure 10.9). Click **Continue**.

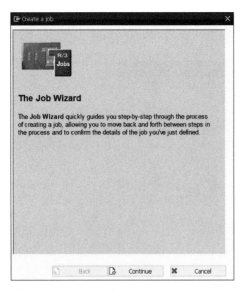

Figure 10.9 *The Job Wizard*

10

In the next screen, enter the **Job Name** and select the **Job Class** (Figure 10.10). The **Job Class** determines the priority with which the job is processed. If available, choose **C – Prio low** here. Leave the **TargetServer** field blank. Choose **Scheduled** in the **Job Status** field. Then click **Continue**.

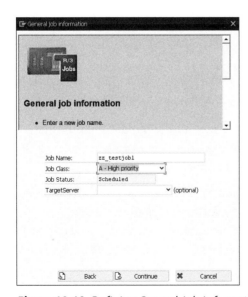

Figure 10.10 *Defining General Job Information*

11 In the next dialog window, make sure that the **ABAP program step** radio button is selected (Figure 10.11). Click **Continue** again.

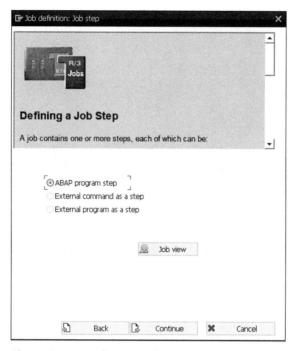

Figure 10.11 *Defining a Job Step*

12 You now need to specify which ABAP program to process with which variant. In the **ABAP program name** field, enter the report name ("RMK-KVZ00"). If you've saved the report name in the clipboard, place the cursor on the **ABAP program name** field and press Ctrl + V .

13 Click the **Value Help** button next to the **Variant** field. In the pop-up that appears, find and double-click your saved variant to select it (Figure 10.12). Continue by clicking **Continue**.

14 In the next screen, you can add further steps (another ABAP program). Because you don't require any further steps in this example, leave the **Add additional steps (optional)** checkbox deactivated, and click **Continue** (Figure 10.13).

Figure 10.12 *Saved Variants*

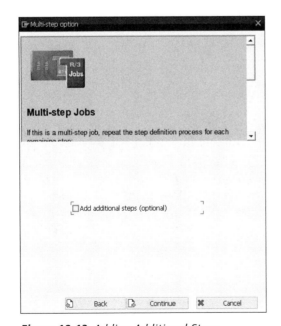

Figure 10.13 *Adding Additional Steps*

15 Next you must specify when and how to start the job. For this example, choose the **Immediately** button to reproduce the result in the SAP system as fast as possible (Figure 10.14). In real life, however, you'll select a more suitable point in time. Click **Continue**.

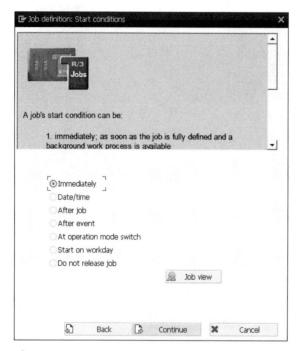

Figure 10.14 *Setting Job Start Time*

16 A message appears stating that the job can be executed immediately (Figure 10.15). The system load permits this, and the job starts immediately. In this screen, you can also view how many processes run in the background. Click **Continue**.

17 The system provides a summary of the scheduled job in the next dialog window. You can revise the job definition via the **Back** button or terminate the entire process via the **Cancel** button. Click **Complete** to create a job with the current definition in the SAP system (Figure 10.16). The Job Wizard is closed.

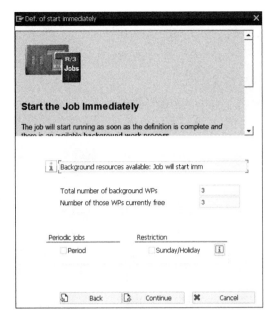

Figure 10.15 *Job Starting Immediately*

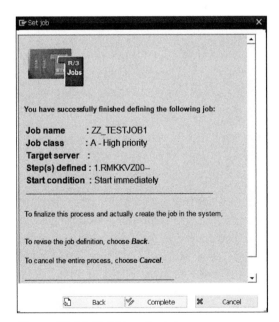

Figure 10.16 *Finishing the Job*

18   You then receive a status message confirming that the job was saved (in this example, **Job ZZ_TESTJOB1 saved with status: Released**). Click **OK** to confirm this message (Figure 10.17).

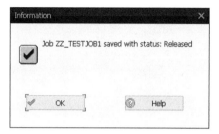

Figure 10.17 Job Save Confirmation

19   Now view the result by going to **System ▸ Services ▸ Output Control** in the menu bar (Figure 10.18).

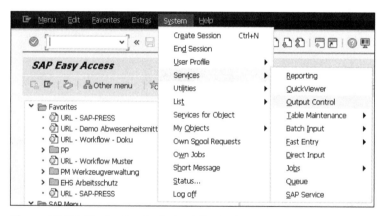

Figure 10.18 Navigating to Output Control

20   Call your job again. In the output control, you can filter the search by the jobs available in the SAP system (e.g., by accepting your username in the **Created By** field and setting the **Date created** field to the correct date; both values are proposed by the SAP system). Check the fields for accuracy (Figure 10.19), and click **Execute** or press F8.

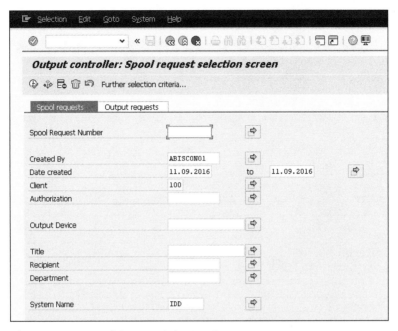

Figure 10.19 *Spool Request Selection Screen*

21 You get an overview of all spool requests (Figure 10.20). Here you should view the list generated by the job; you can identify the job you've created based on the title. Select the checkbox next to the spool request; if you click the **Display Content** 🔍 button, the system displays a preview of the list of vendors. You can also press F6.

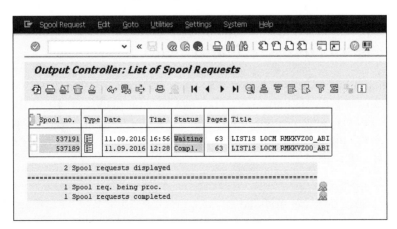

Figure 10.20 *List of Spool Requests*

22 The system displays the list of vendors (Figure 10.21).

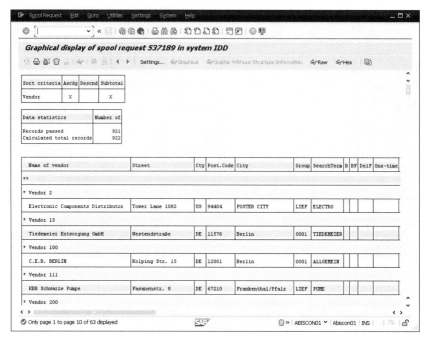

Figure 10.21 *List of Vendors*

In the SAP system, you can control which jobs you've created and whether these jobs are released, active, or already completed. To do this, choose **System ▶ Own Jobs** in the menu bar.

10.2   Batch Processing (Batch Input)

The batch input technique is useful if you must process larger quantities of data (e.g., for mass data transfers). You can transfer data from one SAP system (or a third-party system) to another SAP system. A batch input is often used for the nonrecurring import of data from a legacy system to a newly installed SAP system.

Transactions run automatically in such a batch processing. The data required for this transaction are provided in batch input sessions, which are then processed together with the transaction. You can use batch input sessions to automatically import data into the SAP system without requiring your attention or involvement during import.

A batch input session consists of the process of one or more transactions and the associated data. In a batch input session, the transactions and data are recorded in such a way that they can be processed by the SAP system. If a batch input session is implemented, the SAP system processes the inputs of transaction codes and data (as if you were executing the transaction yourself).

The batch input consists of two key steps:

1 The batch input session is created.

2 The batch input session is processed; the contained data are then imported into the SAP system.

The main menu of the batch input session is available by choosing **System ▶ Services ▶ Batch Input ▶ Sessions** on the menu bar or by using Transaction SM35. The next two sections discuss how to create and process a batch input session.

10

Creating Batch Input Sessions

This section uses an example to walk you through creating a batch input session. You learn how to create a "mini-record" of a transaction using the transaction recorder. The transaction recorder is similar to a macro recorder in an Office application. It records every step you take. From this record, you can create any number of batch input sessions for testing.

Though this example shows a transaction with only a few user interactions, you can also transfer this process to more complex applications (e.g., to create materials or customer master records). For the sake of simplicity, this example uses a transaction you already know: Transaction MMBE (Stock Overview).

Follow these steps:

1 To start the transaction recorder, select **System ▶ Services ▶ Batch Input ▶ Recorder**, or enter Transaction code SHDB in the command field.

2 Click the **New Recording** button.

3 Enter a name in the **Recording** field; either memorize this name or write it down. Enter the transaction name in the **Transaction code** field (here, "mmbe"). Leave all other settings unchanged. Then click the **Start recording** button (Figure 10.22).

Figure 10.22 *Creating a Recording*

4   The transaction is now being recorded. If you have an Internet Demonstration and Evaluation System (IDES) system available, you can use
Material "t-t100" and **Plant** "1000", as shown in Figure 10.23. Finish the
transaction completely. Initially, click **Next** to run the transaction.

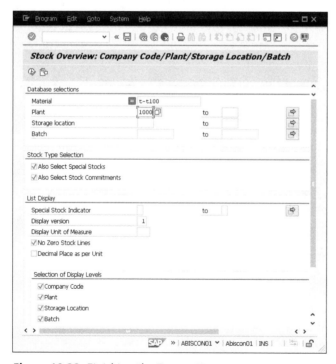

Figure 10.23 *Finishing the Transaction*

5 Exit the stock overview transaction by clicking the **Exit** button (Figure 10.24).

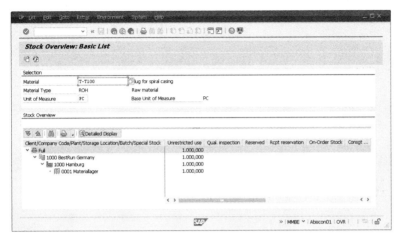

Figure 10.24 *Exiting the Stock Overview Transaction*

6 The system displays a message informing you that the recording is complete (Figure 10.25). Confirm the message by clicking the **OK** button.

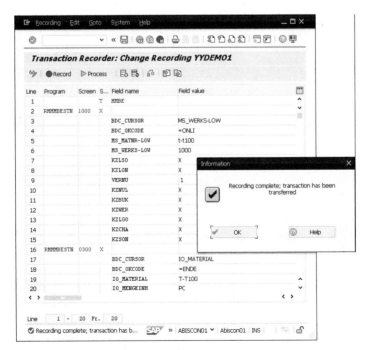

Figure 10.25 *Recording Complete*

7 Click the **Save** 🖫 button to save the recording, and the **Process** button to test it. When you click the **Exit** 🖈 button, the system returns you to the recording overview (Figure 10.26). Your recording is now included in this list.

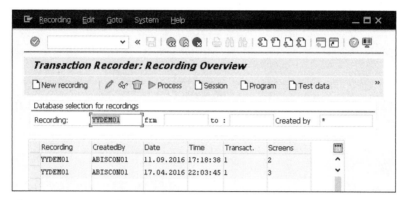

Figure 10.26 *Recording Overview*

8 Select the recording, and then choose **Edit ▸ Create Session** (Figure 10.27).

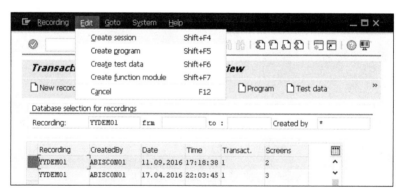

Figure 10.27 *Creating a New Session*

9 Enter a name for your new batch input session (here, "YYDEMO1"), and click the **Create** button (Figure 10.28).

10 The batch input session was created successfully and can be started now (Figure 10.29). Select **System ▸ Services ▸ Batch Input ▸ Sessions** in the menu.

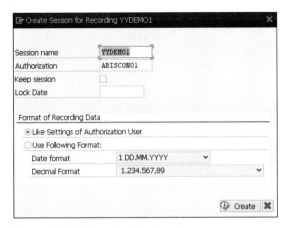

Figure 10.28 *Naming the Session*

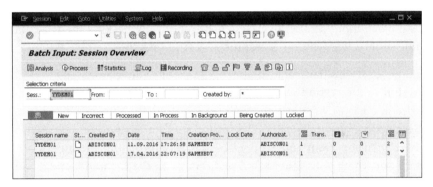

Figure 10.29 *Session Overview*

You can always test the session or create a new one at any time by starting the transaction recorder again.

Processing Batch Input Sessions

In this section, you learn how to process a batch input session. To go to the sessions defined in the SAP system and located in the session overview, follow these steps:

1. Select **System ▸ Services ▸ Batch Input ▸ Sessions** in the menu (Figure 10.30).

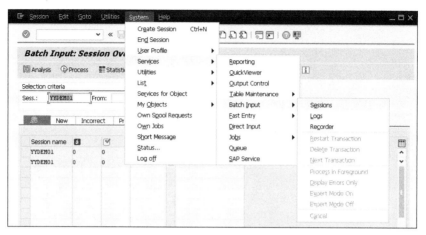

Figure 10.30 Navigating to Batch Input Sessions

2 The batch input session overview is displayed. By clicking the left-hand side of the table, you can select the row (and thus the desired session).

3 If the overview contains too many sessions, you can use the search option in the session overview to find the one you want. The **Selection criteria** area provides various selection options for this purpose: In the **Sess.** field, enter the name of the session that you want to process (Figure 10.31). In the **From** and **To** fields, enter a point in time or a period of time for which you want to find sessions. With the **Created by** field, you can select the session of a specific person.

Check whether the selected session is marked as locked. If it is, you can unlock it by clicking the **Unlock Session** 🔓 button or selecting the **Session ▸ Unlock** menu option.

Figure 10.31 Processing Batch Input Sessions

You have the option to edit the batch input session in the session overview.

4 Click the **Process** button to select a processing mode. The following processing modes for batch input sessions are available.

- **Process Foreground**: This mode displays interactions with the user and requires confirmation for individual screens. The user can intervene if an error occurs.
- **Background**: The system processes the batch input session in the background.
- **Display Errors Only**: If the batch input doesn't have any errors, then no user interaction is required.

5 Enter a target host in the **Target Host** field. Press F4 to use the value help.

6 You can process the selected session by clicking the **Process** button.

Table 10.1 gives an overview of the processing options available in the session overview.

Button	Function
Analysis	Analyze
Process	Process session
	Unlock session
	Release session
	Delete session
	Lock session
Log	Log

Table 10.1 *Processing Options of Batch Input Sessions*

In this chapter, you learned how to work with background jobs, which can be used for recurring system tasks. You also learned how to control transactions in the process using batch input.

10.3   Try It!

Exercise 1
Give an example for when to use variants.

Exercise 2
How do you determine a report name?

Exercise 3
What's the difference between online processing and background processing?

Exercise 4
State three options for processing batch input sessions.

Exercise 5
Create a batch input session for displaying an evaluation on customer returns using Transaction MC+A (menu path: **Information systems ▸ Logistics ▸ Sales and Distribution ▸ Customer**).

11 Working with Messages and Business Workplace

The Business Workplace in the SAP system offers functions for efficient office communication to support your work. You can edit and manage documents, maintain calendars, and send short messages.

This chapter describes the following:

- How to send short messages in the SAP system
- How to use folders
- How to set up automatic replies
- How to use the calendar

11.1 Overview of the Business Workplace

The Business Workplace gives you a work environment within the SAP system that supports you with functions for managing messages, documents, and appointments. It's available to every SAP user, regardless of department.

The Business Workplace provides support for the following tasks:

- Creating workflows and editing work items
- Sending short messages
- Submitting documents
- Distributing and replying to received documents
- Creating, editing, and deleting documents
- Creating and editing folders
- Managing notes
- Using resubmission functions for documents
- Maintaining calendars
- Using out-of-office functions

This chapter introduces you to some of these functions. You can call the Business Workplace via the SAP Easy Access menu by following the **Office ▸ Workplace** path or by entering Transaction SBWP in the command field. The Business Workplace screen is divided into three areas:

- **Folder**

  The folders of your Business Workplace are displayed in a menu tree (left side of Figure 11.1). You can call the contents by clicking a folder.

- **Content list**

  The contents of the folders (contained work items, documents, etc.) that are selected in the menu tree are displayed on the right-hand side of the figure.

- **Preview**

  The preview (bottom-right area) displays the list entry that is selected in the contents list. The example shows a test message.

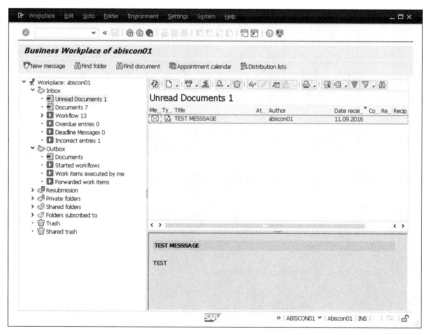

Figure 11.1 *The Business Workplace*

In the initial screen of the Business Workplace, you can directly use the functions listed in Table 11.1.

Button	Function
New message	Create and send a new message (Shift + F4)
Find folder	Search for a folder (Shift + F5)
Find document	Search for a document with specific criteria (F5)
Appointment calendar	Your calendar (Shift + F7)
Distribution lists	Distribution lists (Shift + F8)

Table 11.1 *Buttons in the Business Workplace*

In the next section, you'll learn how you can send short messages in the SAP system.

11.2 Sending Short Messages

The SAP system lets you create and submit short messages. In fact, it's similar to an email system with extended functions. You can send messages to and receive messages from colleagues. These short messages can be used within the SAP system but also on the Internet (although the latter requires appropriate server configuration). In addition, the SAP system can also send short messages to you (e.g., to notify you that a specific action was performed in the background). You also can direct the system to send this system information to another user. Via this message, the user can then directly navigate to the respective object in the SAP system.

> **EXAMPLE**
>
> **Sending Short Messages**
>
> Let's say you want to make an evaluation available to a colleague. Instead of exporting the evaluation and sending it as an attachment in an email, you can use a short message to send a link to the object. This way, you can make sure that the central data basis is accessed by your colleague and that you're not each using different statuses of data.

The message functions are part of the Business Workplace, but you don't have to call the Business Workplace to send a message. Instead, follow these steps:

11

1️⃣ Select **System ▸ Short Message** in the menu bar (Figure 11.2).

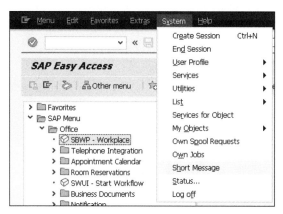

Figure 11.2 *Creating a Short Message*

2️⃣ This opens a screen in which you can enter your short message. You have the following options:

- **Title**: Enter a subject line for your message as you would in any other email program. In this example, enter "Test".

- **Document contents**: Enter your message text. The upcoming table explains the functions of the individual buttons.

- **Attachments**: If you want to add an attachment to your message, click the **Add Attachment** button 📷 or press ⌜Ctrl⌝+⌜Shift⌝+⌜F3⌝.

- **Recipient**: Enter the recipient of the short message by his username. You can have the system search for the recipient by clicking the **Selection** button 🔲 in the **Recipient** field, which gives you various search options. If you send the message to the username, you don't have to specify a recipient type. The **Recipient** tab provides additional send options: Select the **Express Mail** 📋 checkbox to have the system send the recipient a notification on his screen if he is logged on to the SAP system. Select the **Send as Copy** 📋 checkbox to send the message to other colleagues. If you activate the **Send as Blind Copy** 🔒 checkbox, each recipient is hidden from all other recipients of the message.

- **Attributes**: Choose whether the document can be changed retroactively and forwarded to an external Internet address. You can also set the priority of the message (medium, high, or low).

– **Trans options:** Specify the date on which the document is supposed to be sent and whether the recipient can forward to others.

After entering values in all fields, you can submit the message by clicking **Send** ⊞ (Figure 11.3).

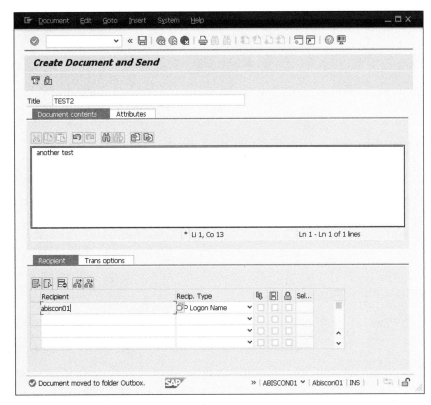

Figure 11.3 *Document Contents Tab*

Table 11.2 lists the functions of the buttons on the **Document Contents** tab.

Button	Function
✂	Cut ([Ctrl]+[X]) selected text
🗐	Copy ([Ctrl]+[C]) selected text
🗐	Insert ([Ctrl]+[V]) objects from the clipboard
↩	Undo ([Ctrl]+[Z]) the last action

Table 11.2 *Buttons on the Document Contents Tab*

Button	Function
🔁	Restore (Ctrl + Y) deleted text
🔍	Find/replace (Ctrl + F) in the text
🔎	Find next (Ctrl + G)
📥	Load local file from PC
📤	Save as local file on PC

Table 11.2 *Buttons on the Document Contents Tab (Cont.)*

11.3   SAP Business Workflow

SAP Business Workflow facilitates business processes. A workflow controls the flow of documents that are usually processed by several people and must be handled in a specific sequence. A workflow can include release or approval procedures but also complex processes, such as the creation of a master record that involves multiple departments. Workflows can also be started automatically when predefined events occur (e.g., when an error is detected in a process).

EXAMPLE

Usage Options of SAP Business Workflow

A team lead assigns a task (creating a master record) to an employee. When the employee accepts the task with a workflow object, the team lead can track the processing status via the Business Workplace.

The Business Workplace provides an overview of all the activities that you have to carry out for the workflow. You can perform your tasks from the Business Workplace. Figure 11.4 shows three screen areas that are used when workflows are processed.

At the top right in the Business Workplace, you can see the worklist. At the bottom right, the preview displays a work item (an object that represents a task or an action of the workflow) that is selected in the worklist.

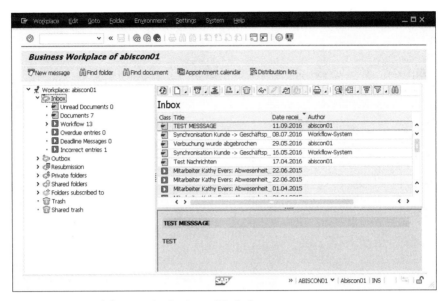

Figure 11.4 *Workflow in the Business Workplace*

11.4 Folders

Folders help you manage your documents and messages and organize group-specific objects. You can even link archiving systems and integrate third-party software if the provider offers software that can be licensed for SAP systems.

The Business Workplace provides several work environments to process documents and messages. To view the contents of a work environment, click the required work environment in the folder tree; the system will display the corresponding folder content list (Figure 11.5).

Figure 11.5 *Folders in the Business Workplace*

The work environments are mapped through the buttons described in Table 11.3.

Button	Work Environment	Function
	Inbox	Contains all documents and resubmissions you've received
	Outbox	Contains all documents sent by you
	Resubmission	Contains documents that are resubmitted to your inbox on a defined date
	Private folders	Manages documents and messages in a folder structure that you've created for your own use
	Shared folders	Stores group-specific or cross-enterprise documents and messages in these folders
	Subscribed folders	Contains all folders you subscribe to
	Trash	Temporarily contains all deleted folders, documents, and messages

Table 11.3 Work Environments and Thier Corresponding Buttons in the Business Workplace

By right-clicking the **Private Folders** object, you can create subfolders for your personal document administration so you can manage your documents and messages individually.

11.5 Office Organization

Office organization functions include automatic message forwarding to a substitute, resubmissions, automatic replies to the sender of a message, and a calendar. The following sections describe how you set up automatic replies and use the calendar functions.

Setting Up Auto Reply

You can use the Business Workplace to instruct the SAP system to reply automatically to incoming messages (auto reply). This function is useful if you want to automatically inform people who send you messages that you're absent from the office. Follow these steps:

1 In the Business Workplace, select **Settings ▸ Office Settings** in the menu bar. The **Automatic reply** tab lets you define the activation period (start date and end date). With the **To** and **From** fields, you specify how long to enable the setting for automatic activation.

In the **Title** field in the **Document** area, enter the text for your subject line of the automatic reply.

In the text box field, enter the message text (Figure 11.6).

2 After making these settings, press ⌜Enter⌝ or click **Next** ✅ to save the settings.

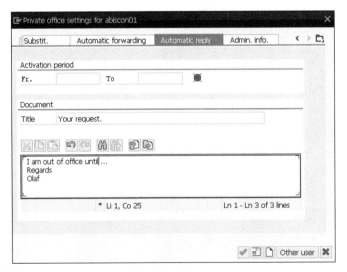

Figure 11.6 *Automatic Reply Tab*

Managing Appointments

The Business Workplace also provides a calendar for your private and business appointments.

To create an entry in the calendar, follow these steps:

1 Start the appointment calendar by clicking the **Appointment Calendar** in the Business Workplace or via the **Environment ▸ Private Calendar** menu. Alternatively, you can also use the key combination [Shift]+[F7]. There (as illustrated in Figure 11.7), you have the following options:

- To create a new calendar item, click **Create Appointment** 🗋.
- To adjust personal settings—for example, the presentation of the days of the week or time intervals on your calendar—click **Settings** 🖾.
- To change the view of the current day (daily view), click 🖾 Today.
- To change the view of the current week (weekly view), click 🖾 Current week.

Figure 11.7 *Managing Appointments*

2 Choose **Create Appointment** 🗋 to create a new calendar entry.

3 A dialog window opens for the title, time frame, and notes about the appointment. When you're done, click **Next** ✅, or press [Enter].

This chapter described how you can use the Business Workplace in the SAP system to send messages as well as manage documents and appointments. Chapter 12 deals with Electronic Data Exchange (EDI).

11.6 Try It!

Exercise 1

If you want to send a message to yourself or a colleague via the SAP system, how do you proceed?

Exercise 2

Name one real-life example of a workflow that is implemented in your business.

11

12 Electronic Data Interchange

To accelerate data exchange with other SAP systems and make sure the data are transferred correctly, many companies use Electronic Data Interchange (EDI). This chapter introduces EDI.

> **This chapter discusses the following:**
> - How EDI is used in practice
> - How data are exchanged between SAP systems

12.1 Overview of the Electronic Data Interchange Process

EDI refers to the communication between different IT systems. When using EDI, data are sent in such a way to be further processed immediately by the recipient's IT systems.

> **NOTE**
>
> **Data Exchange between Different Systems**
>
> EDI is not only used to exchange data between SAP systems. Because EDI uses system-independent standards (e.g., United Nations Electronic Data Interchange for Administration, Commerce and Transport [EDIFACT]), it can also be used for communication with other vendor's enterprise resource planning systems (Oracle, Navision, Baan, etc.).

To be able to exchange data between IT systems, the data must be available in a certain structure. These information packages are combined in the SAP system in Intermediate Documents (IDocs). In the SAP system, IDocs are used to transfer information within a company or between different companies. For example, a separate IDoc is generated for every document (purchase order, invoice, confirmation, etc.). This IDoc is then transferred to the target system. At this point, you can only check if the IDoc was transferred. You can't access the target systems to which the data were transferred.

Table 12.1 lists important transactions that can be used in the SAP system to check if IDocs were transferred.

Transaction	Application
Transaction SM59	Display and maintain RFC destinations
Transaction WE05	IDoc list
Transaction WE19	Test tool for IDoc processing
Transaction WE20	Partner agreements
Transaction WE21	Ports used for IDoc processing
Transaction WE60	Documentation

Table 12.1 *Important IDoc Transactions*

An IDoc comprises several components (as seen in Figure 12.1): a control record (identical for all IDocs), different data records that include an administration and a data part, and status records containing information on the current processing status.

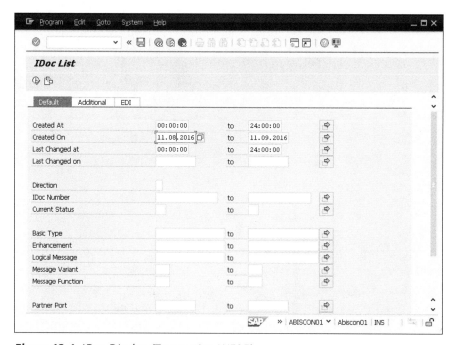

Figure 12.1 *IDoc Display (Transaction WE05)*

12.2 Electronic Data Interchange in Practice

By using EDI, you can automate several process steps. The example in this section shows how EDI is used in the procurement process.

Let's quickly explore procurement without EDI, to highlight the advantages of using EDI. A purchase order is entered in the customer's SAP system (Step ❶ in Figure 12.2) and transferred to the vendor via email, mail, or fax. The purchase order is then entered in the vendor's SAP system (Step ❷). The vendor creates the delivery in the SAP system and posts the goods issue (Step ❸). At the same time, a delivery note is sent to the customer. Upon receipt of the goods, the customer checks the delivery note and posts the goods receipt (Step ❹). The vendor enters the invoice and sends it to the customer (Step ❺). The customer checks and pays the invoice (Step ❻).

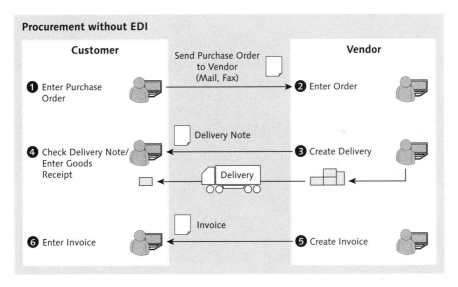

Figure 12.2 *Procurement without EDI*

When using EDI, the documents are transferred electronically. Because the data do not need to be entered several times, this saves both the customer and the vendor a lot of time. Instead of manually entering information, the SAP system automatically transfers the data. This reduces the risk of transfer errors. To what extent this process is automated depends on each environment's requirements.

12.3   Try It!

Exercise 1

Check if there are IDocs in your system that weren't transferred and for which an error status is displayed. To do so, familiarize yourself with Transaction WE05.

13 Using Help Functions

If you come to a dead end as you work in the SAP system, you can find information in several places to help you. This chapter presents the various help functions of the SAP system, focusing on those you can call via the F1 and F4 function keys and by using the **Help** menu in the menu bar.

This chapter discusses the following:
- Getting field help via the F1 function key
- Getting input help via the F4 function key
- Information found in the **Help** menu
- SAP Library and glossary data
- The information content of the release notes
- Using the SAP Service Marketplace
- Customizing the help functions

13.1 Field Helps and Search Windows

Help is available in the SAP system. If you get stuck, you can call a field help or an input help (an overview of the entries that are expected or accepted by the system). You can also use search windows. The following sections introduce you to these options.

Help via Function Keys

If you need information on a certain field in the SAP system, you can use field help and input help (value help):

- **Field help**
  If you press F1, the system provides a general description of the field on which the cursor is currently placed.
- **Input help**
  If you press F4, the system opens a list of the possible input values for

the field on which the cursor is currently placed. You can enter the value by double-clicking the field. Alternatively, you can enter the value using the keyboard.

Cursor Placement

The field and input help always refer to the field on which the cursor is currently placed.

The [F1] and [F4] helps are cross-system standard functions, so you can't assign other function codes to them.

In the example shown in Figure 13.1, you're running the **Maintain Users** profile (Transaction SU3). The cursor is positioned in the **First name** field. If you press [F1] now, the system displays general information on the **First name** field. Because the information in the help can be very detailed, you can scroll down in the help window to see more.

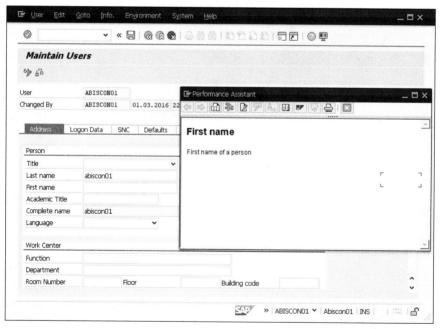

Figure 13.1 Field Help Using the F1 Key

In the example shown in Figure 13.2, you're on the **Defaults** tab as in the previous example of the F1 help. Position the cursor in the **Logon Language** field, but display the possible input values by pressing F4. You can copy the required value from the list displayed by double-clicking it.

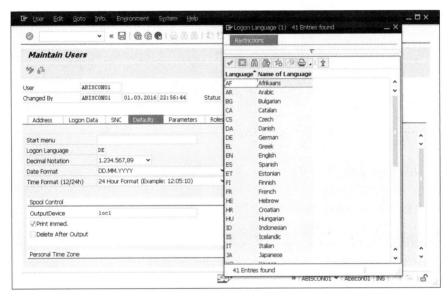

Figure 13.2 *Input Help Using the F4 Key*

13

Not every field has an input help. The next section describes how you can still determine the required value in these cases.

Search Windows

The field type determines whether a list of possible input values is available. If no input help is available, you can determine a value using search windows. Press F4 to open the search window.

In Figure 13.3, the system displays the initial screen of Transaction MM02 (Change Material). The cursor is in the **Material** field. Press F4 to open the search window. The search window now lets you search for the material based on several criteria.

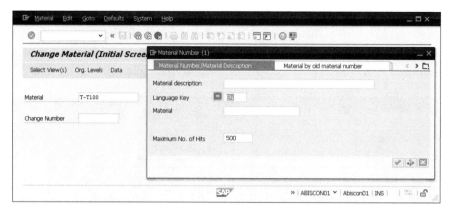

Figure 13.3 *Search Window for a Field*

In this example, we want to find a specific slug but don't know the exact material description. You can use search patterns even if you know only a part of the search term. When working with search patterns, you define a pattern—that is, a character string—with which the required value can be identified in the SAP system. The pattern can contain both characters and digits and can be of any length. It can also contain various meta characters (e.g., + and *). Table 13.1 lists some examples of search patterns.

Search Pattern	Result
Slug 4711	Searches for the exact phrase "Slug 4711"
Slug*	Outputs all hits that start with "slug"
ug	Outputs all hits that contain the "ug" character string, irrespective of the character strings before or after it
+lug 4711	Outputs all hits that start with any character but then contain "lug 4711"

Table 13.1 *Examples of Search Patterns*

13.2   The Help Menu

The **Help** menu in the menu bar (Figure 13.4) provides additional support options and includes a wide range of information sources:

- Application help
- SAP Library
- Glossary
- Release notes
- SAP Service Marketplace
- An option for creating support messages
- An option to customize the help (**Settings**)

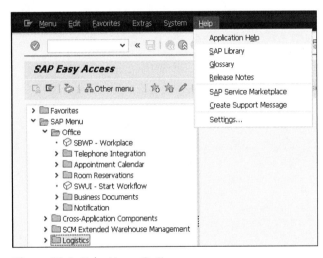

Figure 13.4 *Help Menu Options*

The following sections describe the options provided in the **Help** menu.

Application Help

Application help offers the user context-sensitive help, that is, help executed based on the transaction the user is running. "Context-sensitive" means that the system doesn't display a general help but instead offers help topics that refer to the specific transaction or business process that is currently used.

SAP Library

The SAP Library provides the entire documentation of the SAP system (Figure 13.5). Directly after logging on to the SAP system, you can use the menu bar to navigate to this documentation via the **Help ▶ SAP Library** path.

Here you'll find instructions for operating the SAP system and for using individual components' functions. In the SAP Library, you can navigate through a tree structure that is similar to the SAP Easy Access menu.

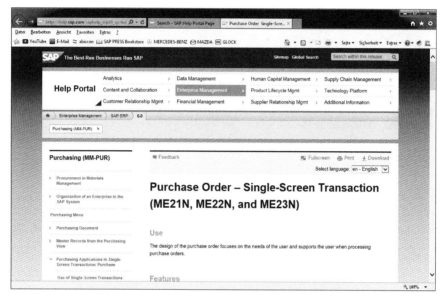

Figure 13.5 *SAP Library*

> **SAP Documentation: The SAP Help Portal**
>
> The SAP documentation is available on CD-ROM. Users with a web browser also have free online access to the documentation via *http:// help.sap.com*.

Glossary

The glossary lists and explains alphabetized technical concepts of the SAP world (Figure 13.6). You can access, search, and navigate the glossary via the **Help ▸ Glossary** path. Because the meaning and use of some concepts differs in various business departments, some keywords have multiple entries. The abbreviation of the respective SAP component is indicated in parentheses. You can navigate using the index and a full-text search.

Figure 13.6 *Glossary of the SAP Library*

Release Notes

Release notes contain the release version of the SAP system in use. Through release notes, you can learn which updates have been installed and which functions have changed since the previous release.

To call the release notes, select **Help ▶ Release Notes** in the menu bar. The information is sorted by components (Figure 13.7).

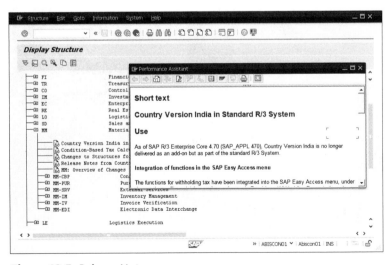

Figure 13.7 *Release Notes*

SAP Service Marketplace

The SAP Service Marketplace provides SAP customers, developers, partners, and interested parties with additional information and tools via an Internet portal (Figure 13.8). The following are included in the SAP Service Marketplace:

- **SAP Support Portal**

  This portal supports all SAP Business Suite solutions (e.g., customer messages and SAP notes, which require an account—that is, a username and password).

- **SAP Help Portal**

  The SAP Help Portal provides web-based documentation on all SAP solutions in the SAP Library. This offer is available to all Internet users free of charge at *http://help.sap.com/*.

- **SAP Community Network**

  The SAP Community and SAP Developer Network (*http://scn.sap.com/ welcome*) is a social network for SAP experts and developers. The information tends to be rather technical.

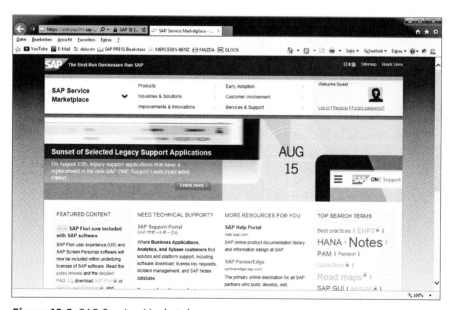

Figure 13.8 *SAP Service Marketplace*

You can access the SAP Service Marketplace at *https://websmp201.sap-ag.de/*. Though some areas can be accessed by anyone with an Internet connection, many areas require a username and password to enter. You can also navigate to the marketplace portal via the **Help ▸ SAP Service Marketplace** menu item.

Creating Support Messages

If an error occurs while you're using a transaction, you can create an error message using the **Help ▸ Create Support Message** path in the menu bar. The message is then forwarded directly to your business's support team (SAP Competence Center). The team will either solve the problem or forward it to someone else, and then provide feedback. The support message can only be created if this was set up accordingly in the system environment. In many cases, other tools for error detection and monitoring are also used. If you have any questions regarding this topic, please contact your SAP support.

13.3   Customizing the Help

You can customize the help that you have access to. The **Help ▸ Settings** path in the menu bar lets you choose how help windows are displayed.

You can view the predefined settings on the **F4 Help** tab in the **System defaults** area, and adjust them in the **User-specific settings** and **Display** areas (Figure 13.9). You can command the system not to display the personal value list when you call the input help (**Do not display pers. value list automatic.** checkbox) and, if the search results in only one hit, whether this hit is directly displayed in the corresponding field and not in a hit list (**Only return value directly if only one hit** checkbox). You can also specify how many hits a list of the input help is supposed to display. In the **Display** area, you can determine the display type of the hit list: If you select the **Control (amodal)** (the more recent display format) or **Dialog (modal)** radio button, the hit list is displayed in the Performance Assistant or as a dialog box.

13

Figure 13.9 *Help Settings: F4 Help Tab*

On the **F1 Help** tab, you can choose whether the help is displayed as a search help control in the Performance Assistant or in a dialog box (modal window). For this purpose, select either the **Control** radio button (result shown in Figure 13.10) or the **Dialog** radio button (result shown in Figure 13.11) in the smaller **Display** area to the right of the screen.

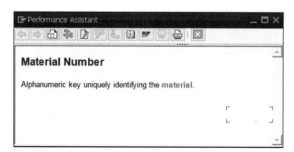

Figure 13.10 *Help in the Performance Assistant (Control Radio Button)*

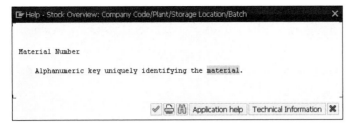

Figure 13.11 Help in a Dialog Box (Dialog Radio Button)

The **Application help** tab lets you define whether you want to access the Internet help or the CD-ROM in the business network (Figure 13.12).

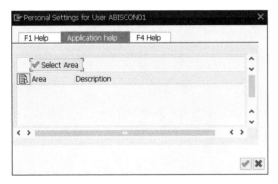

Figure 13.12 Application Help Tab

13.4 Try It!

Exercise 1

Start Transaction MM03 (Display Material) in the SAP Easy Access menu via the following menu path: **Logistics ▶ Sales and Distribution ▶ Master Data ▶ Products ▶ Material ▶ Trading Goods.**

- If you want the system to display general information on the **Material** field, how do you proceed?

- Make use of the search window. Search for the "slug*" material description, and have the system display the material (select the **Basic Data 1** tab, and click the **Next** button). How many hits do you get?

- Position the cursor in the **Base Unit of Measure** field, and tell the system to display the list of possible base units of measure. How many base units of measure does the system display?

- What do you do to have the system display the help for the transaction you're currently working with?

Exercise 2

How can you effectively create a support message in a live environment?

Exercise 3

Which menu items do all SAP screens display?

Exercise 4

What is the SAP Service Marketplace?

Exercise 5

You're an SAP user and want to work with the SAP system over the weekend. Unfortunately, you can't access the business network. What options do you have for getting information on the system?

14 The Role and Authorization Concept

This chapter provides an overview of the roles and authorizations in SAP systems. An authorization concept in the SAP system protects functions and data against unauthorized access.

This chapter explains the following:

- Authorizations
- Tasks of an authorization concept
- Role concepts

14.1 Authorizations

In general, *authorization* gives you permission to do something. With regard to IT systems, authorization means that a specific user (or the corresponding username in the system) is allowed to view (read) and change (write) specific data and use specific functions and transactions. Therefore, SAP authorizations control access to certain functions and data in the SAP system.

Every employee in a business has specific tasks assigned to his position. As the employee of a business in the SAP system, you receive the authorizations that are necessary for your tasks. If the authorizations are insufficient, then the tasks can't be completed, but if the authorizations are unrestricted, then the user can access data that are outside his level of expertise. Consequently, authorizations should be as restrictive as possible; the users and the business are better protected when there are occasionally too few authorizations than if there are too many. In addition to user identities that correspond to specific employees, sometimes the implementation of certain programs requires authorization for technical users.

Authorizations in the SAP system restrict access to the following objects:

- Organizational units
- Transactions/programs
- Database tables

14

The assignment of authorizations is based on a business's authorization concept, which has both business and technical dimensions. The authorization concept defines how authorizations are assigned and checked in the SAP system. On the business side, it specifies a company's business processes and the necessary tasks associated with them.

The authorization concept must cover requirements that arise from various legal principles (e.g., Generally Accepted Accounting Principles [GAAP] and data protection law).

> **INFO**
>
> **Separation of Duties**
>
> Certain tasks or functions should always be carried out by different people to avoid the temptation to commit or the actual commission of criminal activities. For example, if the same employee can both maintain vendors in the SAP system and also trigger payments, then he could embezzle funds by creating fictitious vendors and paying fictitious invoices from which he benefits.

On the technical side, the authorization concept defines how authorizations are set up and checked.

These authorizations are controlled by authorization objects, which are defined in Customizing. An authorization object (e.g., a transaction or a resource) consists of the individual authorization fields that define the authorizations in the SAP system. You then assign the authorizations to users using roles, which are discussed in the next section.

14.2   Roles

SAP uses a role-based authorization concept, which means that roles are assigned to employees. A *role* combines the authorizations that are assigned to users or groups of users to affect certain parts of a business process.

> **EXAMPLE**
>
> **Authorization Concept**
>
> User "Lisa S." logs on to the SAP system using her username and password. She works in accounts payable accounting and is responsible for posting outgoing payments. After a successful logon, Lisa is assigned a

> user role and is authorized for the transactions and objects (organizational structures) for which she is responsible. The SAP Easy Access menu in which Lisa navigates is tailored to her user role and contains all transactions that she needs for her task area. These authorizations are combined in an authorization profile that is assigned to her role.

From a technical view, authorizations release access to objects in the SAP system. From the business view, roles define the process-oriented assignment of tasks.

A role is a package of executable transactions, reports, and other functions that are usually combined in a menu. When you assign a role in combination with an object (e.g., an organizational unit) to a user, you determine that this person is authorized to perform the role-specific tasks for the respective object. It's important that SAP administration has first created and enabled the roles and that the business's organizational structure is maintained. SAP administration (with the corresponding roles and authorizations) assigns and maintains roles and authorizations for others.

Table 14.1 lists some examples of roles.

User	Role	Transaction	Authorizations
Karl B.	REPRUE	Transaction MIRO	Invoice verification
Lisa S.	BH_ACCOUNTSPAYABLE	Transaction FB60	Posting invoices

Table 14.1 Examples of Roles

14

If you want to know which roles a user has, you can have the system display his role assignment via Transaction SU01. Follow these steps:

1 Start the user maintenance by entering Transaction SU01 in the command field. The system displays the **User Maintenance: Initial Screen** (Figure 14.1).

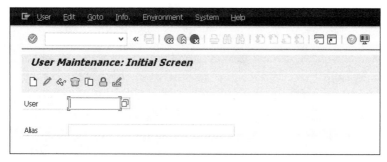

Figure 14.1 *User Maintenance Screen*

2 Enter his username in the **User** field, and click **Display** [icon].

3 The **Groups** tab displays the user group that is assigned to the user (in this case, his logon name).

In this chapter, you learned about the basic characteristics of the authorization concept. As a user, you have limited influence on the control of authorizations because they are maintained and monitored by the administration. However, knowing that roles and authorizations exist and how they function is critical to understanding why you can't change or view certain transactions and data in the SAP system.

14.3   Try It!

Exercise 1

Describe the SAP role concept.

Exercise 2

Your colleague wants to change a customer master record. How would you explain to him why he can view but not change the master record?

Most Important Processes in the SAP System

15 Materials Management

Materials management is at the beginning of the supply chain. It ensures that the materials and services needed by the business are available at the right time and place, as well as procured from the best vendor at a reasonable price. However, the price isn't the only crucial factor; delivery reliability and quality are important criteria, too. This chapter provides an overview of the Materials Management (MM) component in SAP ERP.

> **This chapter describes the following:**
> - The tasks of materials management
> - Organizational units used in purchasing
> - Creating material vendor master records and purchasing info records
> - Creating a purchase order
> - Performing inventory management and invoice verification
> - Evaluations used in the standard version

15.1 Materials Management Tasks

The goal of the purchasing department is to provide the business with the goods and services that its business processes require but that can't be produced in-house. Additional strategic tasks fall into this area; purchasing in particular is increasingly significant because it's an area in which high costs arise, which means there is major savings potential in this area.

> **INFO**
>
> **Purchasing or Procurement?**
> The terms "purchasing" and "procurement" are often used synonymously. However, *procurement* refers to strategic purchasing that determines the procurement strategies, is responsible for vendor selection and evaluation, conducts market research, and negotiates long-term agreements. Operative *purchasing*, on the other hand, is responsible for the actual purchase orders. However, purchasing and procurement can't be

> separated entirely because materials can also be procured or produced internally. In this book, we'll use the term *purchasing* for the sake of simplicity.

The next section gives an overview of the basic purchasing process (i.e., the purchase order, goods receipt, and invoice verification) before discussing purchasing in the SAP system in more detail. Frequently, a purchase requisition (PReq) triggers a corresponding purchase order.

> **INFO**
>
> **Purchase Order Requisition**
>
> A user department issues a purchase requisition (PReq) to notify purchasing of a material or service requirement. The requisition doesn't constitute a purchase order yet because it only triggers the purchase order. Usually, the members of a user department deploy an online form, which is forwarded to purchasing. The PReq must be released by the cost center manager, depending on the costs and the relevant business guidelines. For this purpose, a release procedure can be set up in the SAP system.

As shown in Figure 15.1, at least three different departments are involved in this process: the purchasing department, the goods receiving department, and invoice verification, which, in some enterprises, isn't performed by purchasing but by accounts payable accounting.

Figure 15.1 *Basic Purchasing Process*

You can further subdivide the purchasing process into the following phases:

1 Demand determination

Demand determination is the starting point (Figure 15.2). A user department can inform purchasing about demand for a material or enter a PReq (Transaction ME51N) in the system. This document is then transferred to the purchasing department. The demand determination can even be done by the SAP system in a process called automatic material requirements planning (MRP). Moreover, forecasting and replenishment (F&R)

systems and SAP Advanced Planning and Optimization (SAP APO) systems are used depending on the sector. These systems go beyond automatic MRP because future customer requirements are also considered in their order calculations.

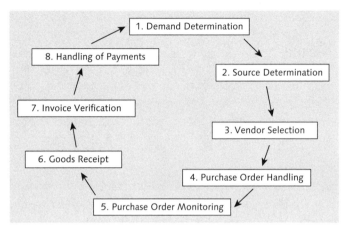

Figure 15.2 *Advanced Purchasing Cycle*

2 Source determination
It can make sense to take previous purchase orders into account when selecting a vendor (i.e., a source). Before you decide on a new source, make sure that there are no suitable sources already available for the requirement. The source can be determined automatically in the SAP system.

3 Vendor selection
The vendor selection requires the user to obtain and compare different quotations from vendors, and choose the most favorable one.

4 Purchase order handling
The actual purchase order is handled in the next step, in which you determine the quantities, dates, and locations of the delivery, and then transfer these to the vendor in a purchase order. A written purchase order gives legal weight to the framework conditions.

5 Purchase order monitoring
The purchase order can also be used for documentation within the business. Because several departments (requesting department, purchasing department, and goods receiving department) are involved in the process, the entire purchase order history can be reproduced.

15

6 **Goods receipt**
In this step, the person responsible refers to the purchase order as the preceding document. The quantity and quality of the goods are checked. Then the delivered goods are posted in specific stock types (i.e., unrestricted-use stock or quality control). In accounting, the warehouse stock is increased.

7 **Invoice verification**
The last step of the purchasing cycle from the MM perspective involves invoice verification. The invoice verification usually requires preceding documents such as the purchase order and material document from goods receipt. Again, the content, price, and figures are checked against the vendor invoice for accuracy.

8 **Handling of payments**
The handling of payments is responsible for clearing vendor invoices. However, this step is assigned to accounting and is no longer within the responsibility of MM.

In SAP ERP, purchasing is implemented in the MM component. MM, in turn, consists of the following subcomponents:

- **Purchasing**
  The Purchasing component of MM undertakes the tasks of stock determination, source determination, pricing, vendor selection, purchase order, and monitoring goods delivery (phases 1 to 5 in the process). Purchasing implements the requirements of the user departments and is the interface between the enterprise and the vendors.

- **Inventory Management**
  This MM component deals with the quantity-based and value-based management of material stocks, the management of goods movements, and the implementation of inventory. These tasks are included in phase 6 of the process presented.

- **Invoice verification**
  The MM component (phase 7) supports the completion of the purchasing process by checking the vendor invoice.

The three areas of the basic purchasing process are discussed in more detail in this chapter. Let's first take a look at the organizational structures that are relevant for MM in the SAP system.

15.2   Organizational Structures

You can use organizational units to map an enterprise in the system. These units are defined in Customizing and are assigned to the corresponding tables; both client and company code are relevant for all SAP components. The organizational units are described in the following list:

- **Client**
  The client forms a unit that is closed in terms of commercial law and organization or represents a corporate group or head office. Master data and tables are assigned to the client in the system. You must enter the three-digit numeric key of the client when you log on to the SAP system.

- **Company code**
  The company code is an organizational unit of external accounting (see Chapter 17) and maps self-contained accounting in the SAP system. All commercial law-related events, including the business's profit and loss, are implemented at the company code level. The company code key is unique to a client.

- **Plant**
  The plant is a central sorganizational unit of logistics. Using a plant, you can map a business's production location, headquarters, central warehouse, or sales office. In the system, the plant is assigned to exactly one company code. The value-based inventory management of materials is done at the plant level.

- **Storage location**
  The quantity-based inventory management of different stock types is done at the storage location level. A storage location is assigned to a plant.

- **Purchasing organization**
  The purchasing organization is an organizational unit of purchasing. It's assigned to at most one company code and always to the plant it procures for. For this reason, central purchasing isn't assigned to a company code.

- **Purchasing group**
  A purchasing group combines a group of purchasers and can, for example, be assigned for the procurement of certain areas (raw materials, finished products, or services). It's not assigned to any other organizational units in the SAP system.

Figure 15.3 shows an example of a purchasing organizational structure.

15

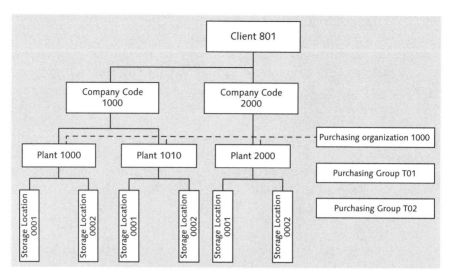

Figure 15.3 *Example of an Organizational Structure in Central Purchasing (Purchasing Organization 1000)*

15.3   Master Data

Master data are stored in the system for a long time and are available to all authorized users and applications. The most important master data in MM include the following:

- Material master
- Vendor master
- Purchasing info records

The following section describes how to create this master data so that you can comprehend its relevance in the SAP system.

Material Master

A material master record contains various pieces of information arranged in different tabs (views). These are assigned to the user departments that work with the material master (e.g., purchasing or accounting). In production systems, authorization roles (see Chapter 14) control which users receive read or write access to which view or whether this view is displayed to the users at all. The material master record is relevant not only for MM but also to the sales and quality management business processes. Table 15.1 lists examples of the role that the material master record plays for the areas indicated.

SAP Component	Usage
Any component	Material number, short description, weights, dimensions, and plant
MM	Material group, purchasing group, automatic purchase order, and goods receipt processing time
SAP ERP Financials (FI)	Internal material evaluation (effect on financial statements), price control, and moving average price (MAP) or standard price
Sales and Distribution (SD)	Procurement times
Quality Management (QM)	Inspection settings and posting in inspection stock

Table 15.1 *Usage of Material Master Records in SAP ERP*

> **INFO**
>
> **Material and Article**
>
> Instead of using the term *article*, SAP ERP uses *material*. In the industry business solution SAP for Retail, however, the common term *article* is used.

15

To create a material, follow these steps:

1 Call Transaction MM01 via the command field or in the SAP Easy Access menu via **Logistics ▸ Materials Management ▸ Material Master ▸ Create (General)**.

2 In the initial screen of the transaction, enter the **Material** (here, "XMDEMO_1000"), **Industry sector** (select **Mechanical Engineering**), and **Material Type** (select **Raw material**) in the corresponding fields (Figure 15.4). Press [Enter].

Figure 15.4 *Creating a Material*

3 Select the tabs that are relevant for you in the view selection pane that opens. Choose the views **Basic Data 1**, **Purchasing**, and **Accounting 1**.

4 You may have to scroll down to view the other required views (as seen in Figure 15.5). To predefine this selection for the next time, click the **Default Setting** button. Press Enter.

The other views, such as **MRP**, are relevant if the system is supposed to plan the material automatically or procure it with quality assurance. In this example, you create the material so that external procurement (purchasing) is possible.

Figure 15.5 *Selecting Views*

5 In the next step, specify the plant in which the new material is to be kept. For this example, enter "1000" for the **Plant** (Figure 15.6), and then press ⌐Enter⌐.

Figure 15.6 *Setting the Organizational Levels*

6 In the next step, define the material name, base unit of measure, gross weight, and weight unit in the **Basic data 1** tab (Figure 15.7). If you want to reproduce this example in the SAP system, enter the following data:

- **Material**: "Cooling Element"
- **Base Unit of Measure**: "PC"
- **Material Group**: "00103"
- **Gross Weight**: "0,5"
- **Net Weight**: "0,3"
- **Weight unit**: "KG"

15

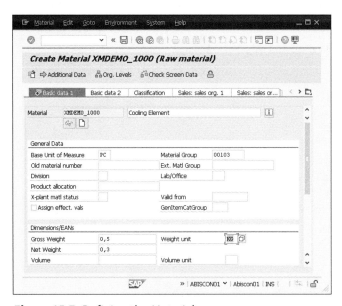

Figure 15.7 *Defining the Material*

209

7 Click the **Purchasing** tab. Enter the purchasing group, purchasing value key, and goods receipt processing time (known as the **GR Processing Time**). The following data are used for this example (Figure 15.8):

- **Purchasing Group**: "000"
- **Purchasing value key**: "1"
- **GR Processing Time**: "1" (day)

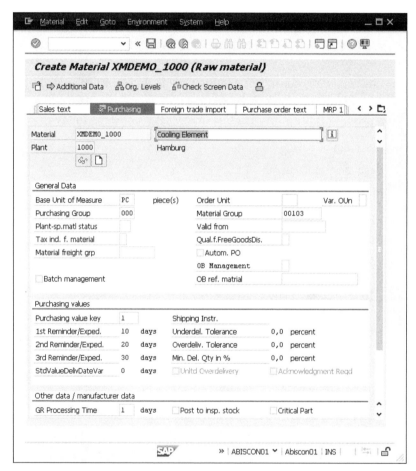

Figure 15.8 *Setting Purchasing Information*

8 Click the **Accounting 1** tab. Enter the valuation class, price control, and MAP. Use the following data for this example (Figure 15.9):

– **Valuation Class**: "3000" (relevant for controlling SAP General Ledger [G/L] accounts, which are updated in cases of goods movement)

– **Price control**: "V" (MAP for internal material valuation)

– **Moving price**: "10" (EUR)

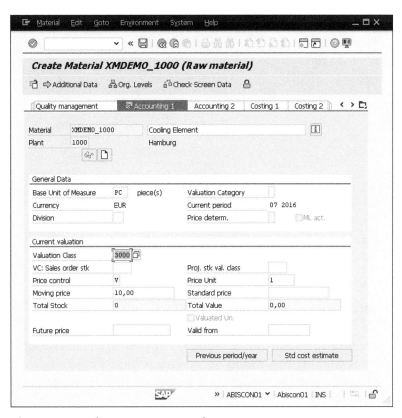

Figure 15.9 *Defining Accounting Information*

9 You've filled in all fields relevant for the material and can now save the new master record by clicking the **Save** button 🖫. The system displays a message informing you that the new material was created in the system: **Material XMDEMO_1000 is created.**

> **INFO**
>
> **Moving Average Price**
>
> MAP is used for inventory valuation for materials that were purchased at different prices. An average price is calculated from the moving average (Table 15.2). Inventory management that uses the historic prices at which the materials were actually purchased would be unnecessarily complex.

Action	Moving Average Price
Creation of a master record	–
Purchase: 10 pieces, $10 each	$\dfrac{10 \text{ pieces} \times \$10}{10 \text{ pieces total stock}} = \$10$
Purchase: 10 pieces, $20 each	$\dfrac{10 \text{ pieces} \times \$10 + 10 \text{ pieces} \times \$20}{20 \text{ pieces total stock}} = \$15$

Table 15.2 *Example of Calculating the Moving Average Price*

After discussing the material master, let's move on to the vendor master.

Vendor Master

The vendor master record in the SAP system contains information on the business's vendors. Besides the name and address of the vendor, the vendor master record also includes information on currencies, payment terms, and contact persons. The information on vendors is used not only in MM but also in FI. Follow these steps to create a vendor master record in the SAP system:

1 Start Transaction XK01 via the command field or in the SAP Easy Access menu path: **Logistics ▶ Materials Management ▶ Purchasing ▶ Master Data ▶ Vendor ▶ Central ▶ Create.**

2 In the initial screen, enter the vendor number, company code, purchasing organization, and the account group. Use the following data in this example (Figure 15.10):

- Vendor: "Z9999"

- Company Code: "1000"

- PurchasingOrganization: "1000"

- Account group: "0006"

Press ⌈Enter⌋.

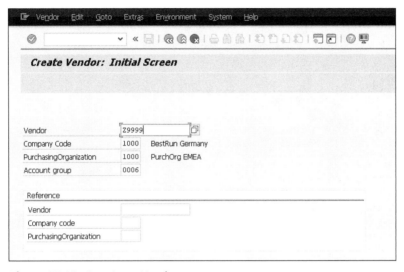

Figure 15.10 *Creating a Vendor*

3 In the next screen, enter the title, name, address, and language. Use the following data for this example (Figure 15.11):

- **Name:** "Mechanical Eng. and Cons"

- **Search term 1/2:** "DEMO"

- **Street/House number:** "West Park" "357"

- **Postal Code/City:** "90449" "Nuremberg"

- **Country:** "DE"

- **Region:** "09" **Bavaria**

- **Language:** English

15

213

Figure 15.11 *Creating a Vendor Address*

4 Select the button to navigate to the **Create Vendor: Accounting informa-tion Accounting** screen. Enter the reconciliation account (here "160000") in the **Recon. account** field (Figure 15.12).

5 Navigate to the **Create Vendor: Payment Transactions Accounting** screen via the button. Enter the terms of payment (here "0002").

6 Navigate to the **Purchasing data** tab. Select **EUR** in the **Order currency** field (Figure 15.13).

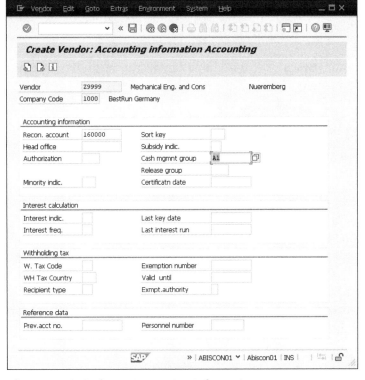

Figure 15.12 *Defining Accounting Information*

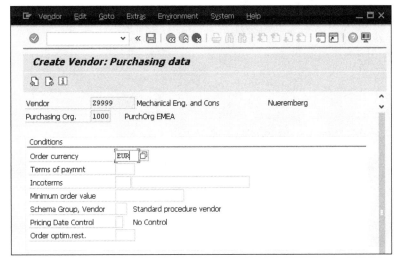

Figure 15.13 *Purchasing Data Tab*

7 Save the vendor master record by clicking the **Save** 🖫 button. The system displays a success message (**Vendor Z9999 was created for company code 1000 and purchasing organization 1000**).

The next section presents the third important master record in MM: the purchasing information record.

Purchasing Information Record

The purchasing information record (or simply information record) connects a vendor master record and a material master record so you can procure a specific material from different vendors with different conditions (Figure 15.14).

You can create an information record either manually or automatically in the SAP system. If you define a price in the information record, it will be proposed in the next purchase order. If the purchaser agrees on a new price with the vendor and changes it in the existing purchase order, the new price will be proposed in the next purchase order. The information record is an important source of information for purchasing.

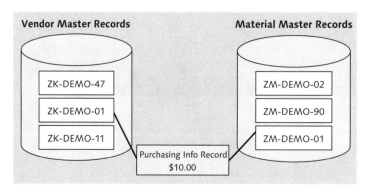

Figure 15.14 *Purchasing Information Record*

So far, you've already defined a material and a vendor in the system. Now create an information record for this combination by following these steps:

1 An information record can be created via Transaction ME11. Start Transaction ME11 via the command field or in the SAP Easy Access menu path: **Logistics ▸ Materials Management ▸ Purchasing ▸ Master Data ▸ Info Record ▸ Create**.

2 In the initial transaction screen, enter the vendor, material, and purchasing organization (Figure 15.15). In addition, enter the path here because different conditions may apply in another plant. Use the following data in this example:

- **Vendor**: "Z9999"
- **Material**: "XMDEMO_1000"
- **Purchasing Org.**: "1000"
- **Plant**: "1000"

Press [Enter].

Figure 15.15 Initial Transaction Screen

3 The system takes you to the general data from the initial screen. In this example, you don't have to enter any information in the general data. Click **Purch. Org. Data 1** (Figure 15.16).

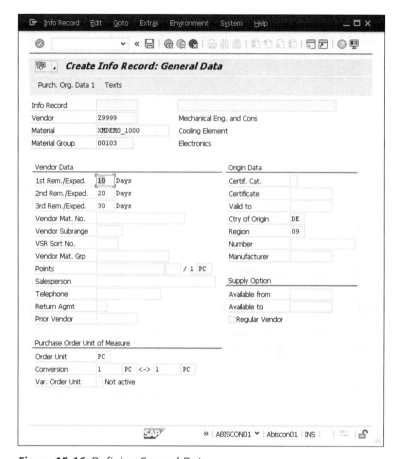

Figure 15.16 *Defining General Data*

4️⃣ Specify the planned delivery time, purchasing group, standard quantity, and net price in the **Create Info Record: Purch. Organization Data 1** screen (Figure 15.17). Enter the following data for this purpose:

- **Pl. Deliv. Time** (planned delivery time): "1" day
- **Purch. Group:** "000"
- **Standard Qty:** "1" PC
- **Net Price:** "10" EUR

Click the **Save** button 🖫 to save your entries.

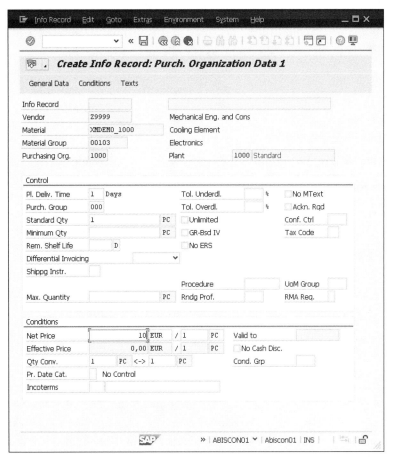

Figure 15.17 *Creating an Info Record*

5 The system saves the information record and displays the following message: **Purchasing information record 5300006151 1000 1000 has been added.**

With the master data, you've now formed the basis for the purchasing process, which you can reproduce in the next step using your own data.

15.4   Purchase Order

With a purchase order, you request a vendor to deliver a material or service based on the agreed conditions. The purchasing process may differ depending on whether you want to purchase stock material or consumable material.

Stock material is used to restock the business's inventory stock, whereas consumable material is used directly. Stock and consumable material are handled differently in the SAP system, as is indicated in Table 15.3.

	Stock Material	Consumable Material
Input of material number	Mandatory	Optional
Account assignment group	–	Mandatory
Goods receipt	Mandatory	Optional
Posting	Material stock account	Consumption account
Update	Quantity and value in the material master, adjustment of the MAP	No value update, update of quantity and consumption possible

Table 15.3 *Differences Between Stock and Consumable Material*

This section uses an example to show how to order a stock material.

In the SAP system, you can find the transaction for the purchase order in the SAP Easy Access menu under **Logistics ▸ Materials Management ▸ Purchasing ▸ Purchase Order ▸ Create ▸ Vendor/Delivering Plant Unknown**. The transactions are Transaction ME21N (Create Purchase Order), Transaction ME22N (Change Purchase Order), and Transaction ME23N (Display Purchase Order). The transaction for creating a purchase order is subdivided into various areas (see Figure 15.18).

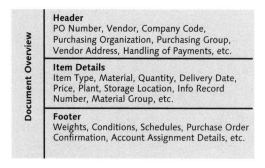

Figure 15.18 *Purchase Order Structure*

You can create a purchase order with a reference to the PReq (Transaction ME51N) or without a reference, as in this example.

The following step-by-step example shows how you can order a stock material without creating a PReq in advance. In this example, you use the master records you created at the beginning of this chapter. Follow these steps:

1 Start Transaction ME21N in the command field or in the SAP Easy Access menu path: **Logistics ▸ Materials Management ▸ Purchasing ▸ Purchase Order ▸ Create ▸ Vendor/Delivering Plant Known**.

2 You can show or hide the screen areas of the purchase order using the 🗔 and 🗔 buttons, respectively. Alternatively, you can use the key combinations shown in Table 15.4.

Function	Key Combination
Display header	Ctrl + F2
Hide header	Ctrl + F5
Show item overview	Ctrl + F3
Hide item overview	Ctrl + F6
Show item details	Ctrl + F4
Hide item details	Ctrl + F7

Table 15.4 *Key Combinations for Showing and Hiding Screen Areas*

15

3 Enter the vendor, material number, order quantity, plant, and storage location. To reproduce this example in the system, use the following data (Figure 15.19):

- **Vendor:** "Z9999"
- **Purch. Org.:** "1000"
- **Purch. Group:** "000"
- **Company Code:** "1000"
- **Material:** "ZZ-DEMO-01"
- **Order Quantity:** "100"
- **Plant:** "1000" (Hamburg)
- **Storage location:** "0001" (materials store)

4 After you've pressed ⌈Enter⌋, the system determines the net price for the material from the information record.

Figure 15.19 Defining Purchase Order Information

5 With the **Check** button 📋, you can check the purchase orders for completeness and plausibility. If the information is complete and conclusive, then the system displays a success message stating **No messages issued during check**. Confirm by clicking **OK**.

6 Click the **Save** 💾 button to save your purchase order. A dialog window opens that contains a confirmation and a document number. In this example, it's **Standard PO 4500017149 has been created**. Write down the document number for the upcoming steps. In the real business environment, you won't write down any document numbers, but in these exercises, it's useful because you can easily refer to the unique document number in the next steps.

The vendor sends the goods (or services) based on the purchase order. The following section describes what happens next.

15.5   Inventory Management

After you've sent a purchase order, the ordered goods are delivered to the business and recorded in goods receipt in the SAP system. All tasks associated with goods movement are performed with the Inventory Management component (MM-IM). MM-IM includes the following tasks:

- Manage material stocks (with regard to quantities and values)
- Plan and record goods movements
- Run inventories

The following are the different types of goods movements:

- **Goods receipt**
  In goods receipt, you post the delivery of goods that you've ordered. Goods receipt increases the warehouse stock, which is also relevant for accounting purposes because the value of materials in the stock (i.e., the stock value) increases.

- **Goods issue**
  Goods issue occurs if goods are delivered to a customer or another department (e.g., to production). Goods issue reduces the warehouse stock.

- **Stock transfer**
  In case of stock transfer, goods are moved to another storage location within the business, either within a plant or between two different plants.

- **Transfer posting**
  A transfer posting is the system recording of a goods movement; its effects on internal accounts are similar to physical goods movement.

15

With the movement type, you control which of these goods movements is used. The stock type indicates the material's usability; you need this piece of information to determine the available stock in MRP, for the withdrawal of goods, and to implement the inventory. The following three stock types can be found at one storage location:

- Unrestricted use stock
- Quality inspection stock (for when the quality of goods is being checked)
- Blocked stock

In addition, special stocks at the vendor or at the customer can be unre-stricted-use stock or quality inspection stock. The individual stock types can be reposted via a goods movement.

This chapter focuses on both goods receipt and stock transfer.

When you post a goods receipt, you usually refer to a preceding purchase order (the preceding document). Because the entire process was mapped uniformly in the SAP system, you can copy data from the preceding document and thus reduce the entry effort and avoid possible input errors. Follow these steps:

1. Start Transaction MIGO by entering the transaction code in the command field or selecting the SAP Easy Access menu path: **Logistics ▶ Materials Management ▶ Inventory Management ▶ Goods Movement ▶ MIGO – Goods Movement**.

2. Check that the selections **Goods Receipt, Purchase Order, Plant, and GR goods receipt** are set (as seen in Figure 15.20). Enter the preceding purchase order number (here, "R01 Purchase Order"), and then press Enter. The SAP system will propose the material and the quantity from the purchase order.

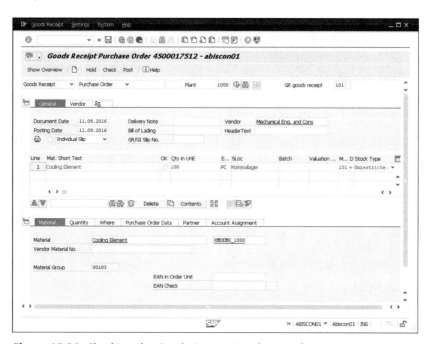

Figure 15.20 *Checking the Goods Receipt Purchase Order*

3 If the quantity and material that was delivered corresponds to the figures stated in the purchase order, then every item must be marked as **OK**. Then you can post the goods receipt by clicking the **Post** or **Save** 🖫 button. The system displays the material document number (here, the message is **Material document 5000011937 has been posted**).

After the goods receipt has been confirmed and completed in the system, the system creates a material document and an accounting document.

Stock or material transfer postings can be made within a plant or across plants within the corporate group. The material is physically moved (transferred) to another location. The goods movement is posted in the SAP system, which increases or decreases the stock value.

In the example in Figure 15.21, 30 of the 100 cooling elements in stock are transferred and posted to another storage location.

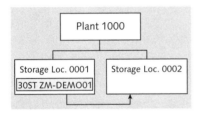

Figure 15.21 *Stock Transfer of Material ZM-DEMO01 in the Same Plant*

Follow these steps:

1 Call Transaction MIGO. Set the transaction to **Transfer Posting – Other**, and enter the appropriate field values in the **Transfer Posting** tab (Figure 15.22). Then post the material document by clicking the **Save** 🖫 button.

2 You can check the transfer posting's result using Transaction MMBE. When you enter the material and the plant in the initial screen of the transaction, the stock overview (basic list) is displayed

After you've created the purchase order and posted the goods receipt, you can run the invoice verification in the next step.

15

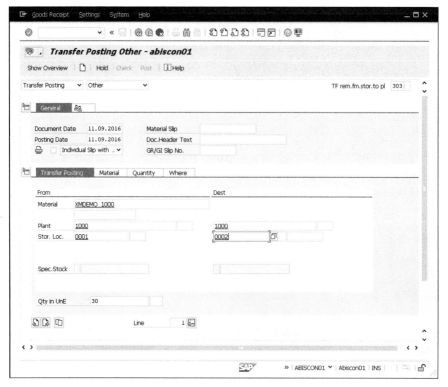

Figure 15.22 *Transfer Posting Tab*

15.6   Invoice Verification

In the Invoice Verification component (MM-IV), you compare the conditions of the purchase order with the invoice you received from the vendor with an eye for content, price, and figures. The SAP system determines possible deviations, which must then be coordinated with the vendor. The material document of the goods receipt tells you which quantities were actually delivered. The following conditions must be met to perform ideal invoice verification:

- A purchase order is created in the SAP system.
- Goods receipt is posted in the SAP system.
- The vendor's invoice is available.

The SAP system has three types of invoice verification: ▪

- **PO-based invoice verification**
  In this case, all items of the preceding purchase order are settled. A goods receipt isn't necessary.

- **GR-based invoice verification**
  Here, every goods receipt is settled separately.

- **Invoice verification without purchase order reference**
  No preceding document exists in this process, so after invoice verification, a post is made directly to a material account, fixed asset account, or G/L account. Consider, for example, a purchase order by telephone, which doesn't directly enter a purchase order into the SAP system without additional steps.

Let's use a short example to understand invoice verification. The data from the previous purchase order example is used here.

Follow these steps:

1 Start Transaction MIRO by entering it in the command field or selecting **Logistics ▸ Materials Management ▸ Logistics Invoice Verification ▸ Document Entry ▸ Enter Invoice**.

2 Enter the following information in the invoice verification:

- **Invoice date**: invoice document (current date; here "11.09.2016")
- **Amount**: gross amount of invoice (here "1.000,00" EUR)
- **Tax amount**: 0I (Input tax 0%)

3 Enter the document number of the entered purchase order in the **Purchase Order/Scheduling Agreement** field on the **PO Reference** tab.

4 Press ⎣Enter⎦, and make sure that the indicator **0I (input tax 0%)** is set for the item (Figure 15.23).

15

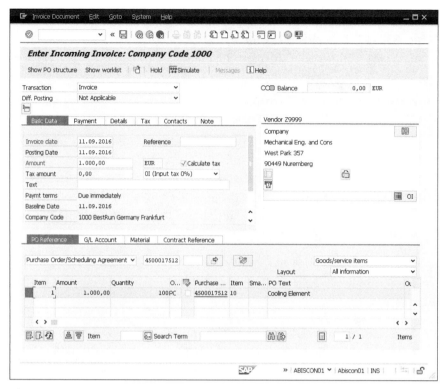

Figure 15.23 *Invoice Verification*

[5] If you get a balance of 0.00 EUR, no deviations were found, and you can post the invoice by clicking the **Save** 🖫 button. The message **Document No. 5105608681 has been added** is displayed in this example.

Invoice verification results in two documents: logistics invoice document (see Figure 15.24) and accounting document (Figure 15.25).

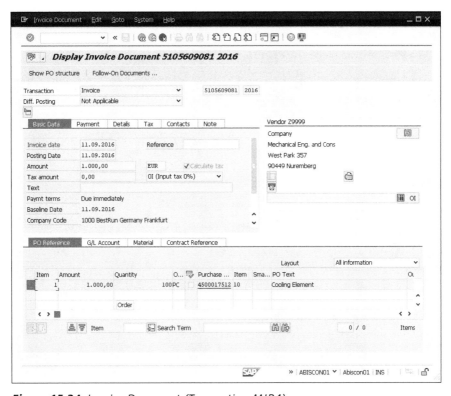

Figure 15.24 *Invoice Document (Transaction MIR4)*

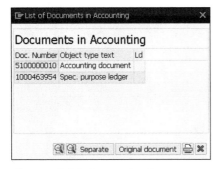

Figure 15.25 *Accounting Document*

15

> **NOTE**
>
> **Display Invoice Document Again**
>
> Using Transaction MIR4, you can display the invoice document again.
> From there, you can also navigate to the accounting document.

IV-MM is closely integrated with the adjacent components, FI and CO. It forwards the information required to settle the invoice amount and to post to FI and CO.

Sometimes goods are delivered for which no invoice exists yet, and sometimes the goods haven't been delivered yet when the invoices are received. In this case, a goods receipt/invoice receipt clearing account (GR/IR account) is used. After the missing goods or invoices are received, the GR/IR account is credited. The corresponding items aren't cleared.

Let's discuss an example to clarify this (Figure 15.26):

1 A. Initial Situation
The opening balance of the material stock account ❶ is $1,000.

2 B. Goods receipt for purchase order
Goods are ordered for another $1,000, and goods receipt occurs. The material stock account ❷ and the GR/IR account ❷ are posted to.

3 C. Invoice receipt (invoice verification)
After the invoice has been entered, the GR/IR account is cleared, and the vendor account receives the posts until it, too, is cleared after the outgoing payments of accounts payable accounting are made.

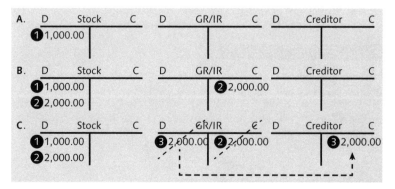

Figure 15.26 Account Movements for Goods Receipt and Invoice Receipt

The invoice of the vendor is entered into the SAP system. It doesn't have any deviations from the purchase order, and the correct materials were delivered in the correct quantity. The GR/IR account ❸ is cleared, and the vendor account ❸ is posted to. The vendor account is cleared when the invoice is paid.

15.7   Automatic Material Requirements Planning

Automatic MRP (automatic procurement) is responsible for punctual and accurate goods procurement. In this process, procurement processes are triggered systematically. Automatic MRP focuses on an optimal supply, primarily of the production and stores, with materials and supplies used for manufacturing. Its goal is to ensure availability of the materials, while keeping the storage costs to a minimum. The benefit is less capital commitment, shorter lead times, higher on-time delivery performance, and more flexibility in production. To conclude the chapter on MM, we'll introduce automatic MRP.

Automatic MRP is used to monitor stocks at the plant level and at the MRP area. MRP at the plant level refers to the plant and all its assigned storage locations. An MRP area, on the other hand, is an independently planning organizational unit.

Automatic planning runs determine shortages (i.e., the stock is about to fall below a defined threshold) and can create the following procurement elements, if necessary:

- PReq
- Planned order
- Delivery schedules

A delivery schedule is an outline agreement with a vendor defining which materials are delivered at certain dates.

Procurement elements can only be created if certain system settings are configured both in the material and vendor master and in the purchasing info record.

MRP can be consumption-based or plan-based. With consumption-based MRP, the current stock level of a material is considered; with plan-based MRP, the current and the future sales are considered. As an example, we'll now contemplate the simple consumption-based MRP, which only considers stock levels, while reservations and sales orders aren't taken into consideration.

15

Figure 15.27 shows the stock levels of a material at a plant. If the stock level reaches the reorder point, procurement processes are triggered (e.g., a PReq is created). The material is then replenished to the maximum stock level, and the process is started all over again. A previously defined safety stock can only be withdrawn after an explicit approval. When using this procedure, the delivery time and the GR processing time must be considered for the respective material.

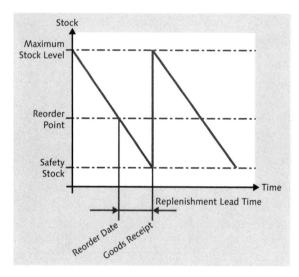

Figure 15.27 *Consumption-Based MRP*

15.8   Standard Reporting

The standard version of the system analyzes the logistics area in several ways to evaluate the data basis and use this information to derive future decision-making bases. Evaluation options are available in the SAP Easy Access menu under **Information Systems ▸ Logistics ▸ Purchasing**.

Figure 15.28 shows an overview of purchase orders for a vendor (Transaction ME2L).

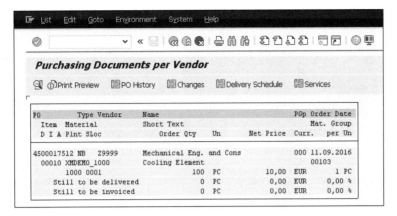

Figure 15.28 *Purchase Orders by Vendor*

Table 15.5 shows some more examples for standard reports in MM.

Transaction	Evaluation
Transaction ME2L	Purchase orders by vendor
Transaction ME80	General evaluations
Transaction MC$0	Purchasing group purchase values
Transaction MC$G	Purchase values

Table 15.5 *Examples of Standard Reports in Materials Management*

15

TIP

Additional Information

Detailed information on MM is available in *Materials Management with SAP ERP: Functionality and Technical Configuration* (*www.sap-press.com/4062*).

16 Sales and Distribution

Sales and distribution is the link between a business and its customers. It's responsible for creating quotations, entering sales orders, and invoicing the delivered goods or services. In the SAP system, the sales tasks are supported by the Sales and Distribution component (SD).

This chapter discusses the following:
- Critical tasks of sales
- Entering and processing sales orders
- Specific invoicing concerns
- Availability checks
- Complaints processing
- Sales and distribution evaluation options

16.1 Sales and Distribution Tasks

This chapter describes all sales and distribution processes, from customer inquiry or quotation, to entry of sales order, to invoicing. In the business world, many companies distribute these tasks among various user departments and thus SAP users. For example, customer accounting monitors the handling of payments.

16

As shown in Figure 16.1, several steps must happen before the customers receive the desired goods (or a service is rendered):

1 Customer inquiry and quotation
In the presales phase (which is optional), customer inquiries and quotations are entered. For example, a customer inquires whether specific goods are in stock or how much they cost. The quotation presents a legally binding readiness to deliver goods or render a service to the customer on the established conditions. The data stored in the inquiry and quotation form the basis for subsequent documents in the SAP system.

2 **Sales order**

The sales order forms the starting point of the sales process. For example, a customer calls and orders goods or a service, and the sales representative enters the sales order into the SAP system. This can be either a one-time purchase order or a long-term agreement. In this case, special conditions can be stipulated and defined in the SAP system condition master records.

3 **Availability check**

During order entry, the sales representative checks whether the inquired materials are available for the requested delivery date. After the sales order has been saved in the SAP system—and if the material is indeed available in the required quantity at the desired point in time—then a delivery can be created. If the material isn't available at that time, the system suggests a new delivery date. The delivery can be made in partial deliveries or as a full delivery at a later point in time.

INFO

Standard Orders

An order type is made up of control parameters that guide further processing in the system, such as which fields must be completed by the order taker. The default order type in the SAP system is the standard sales order.

4 **Delivery**

Next, the delivery to the customer is triggered.

5 **Transport order**

The transport order that is now created in the SAP system involves the transport of goods to picking, not the transport of goods to the customer.

6 **Picking**

Here the goods are packaged, and the shipping documents are added.

7 **Goods issue**

After the goods issue has been posted in the SAP system, the goods are sent to the customer.

8 **Invoicing**

Next, the delivery is invoiced, and the customer account is debited.

⑨ Payment

The incoming payments are monitored in SAP ERP Financials (FI). The debited customer account is cleared.

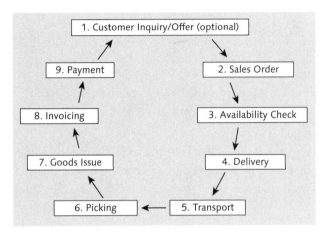

Figure 16.1 *The Sales Cycle*

If customers receive incorrect or defective goods, or if the invoice is incorrect, they send a complaint. Complaint processing in the SAP system offers a solution for these complaints: the customer can return the goods and receive a replacement or a credit memo.

In addition, the output or subsequent processing of documents in the SAP system is mapped via message control and documents (orders, invoices, etc.). Transactions use specific interfaces to make this easier.

Prices are calculated through the pricing and condition technique, which takes specific conditions into consideration.

SD consists of functions that support the employees in sales processes. This chapter focuses on sales order processing, availability check, and complaints processing. The following sections show how sales are mapped in the SAP system with organizational units.

16.2   Organizational Structures

In the SAP system, the sales department of a business is mapped with organizational units. In addition to units used only in sales, the company code and plant organizational units are also relevant in this department. The plant

16

organizational unit is the delivering plant in sales with SAP—that is, from where the customers are provided with products. Beyond these, the following are some organizational units that are maintained and used in sales:

- **Sales area**
  The sales area is responsible for selling materials to the customers. It's assigned to a company code.

- **Sales organization**
  All sales documents are assigned to the sales organization. One or more sales organizations can be assigned to a sales area.

- **Distribution channel**
  The distribution channel is the way materials and services reach the customers. Typical distribution channels are wholesale trade (business-to-business [B2B]), retail trade (business-to-consumer [B2C]), and mail order or direct sales.

- **Division**
  Similar products are combined in a division—that is, a grouping of materials and services that are distributed by the business—which organizes the responsibilities for these products within the business. Examples of cross-division sales include the sales of the product groups "pumps" and "motorcycles."

- **Storage location**
  Materials are managed on a quantity basis (not on a value basis) at the storage location level. One or more storage locations are assigned to a plant.

- **Shipping point**
  The shipping point handles shipping. They may be physically detached from the business (e.g., loading ramps or airports). The shipping point can be determined automatically during order entry.

The next section discusses the master data in sales.

16.3 Master Data

Up-to-date and accurate information about the customers, goods (materials), and sales conditions are crucial for effective execution of sales processes. The following important master data are included in SD:

- Customer master data
- Material master data
- Condition master records

You need to know the master data to understand the activities in the sales process. The following section describes how to create customer, material, and condition master records using the required fields.

Creating Customer Master Records

A company's customers are managed in a customer master, where all information relevant for sales are maintained. Customer master records are created in sales and then made available to the entire SAP system to avoid redundancies and data inconsistencies. Consequently, the users in accounting also work with the customer master data. However, different departments work with different views (or tabs). The relevant data are defined on various levels in the customer master record. There is a general level that applies to the entire client, as well as views for accounting and sales, which are each subdivided into the following data areas:

- General data at the client level, such as addresses and communications links
- Accounting data at the company code level, such as bank details
- Sales data at the sales area level, such as delivery locations

Let's walk through an example to practice creating a customer master record:

1 To call the transaction that creates a customer master record (Transaction XD01), enter the transaction code in the command field or select **Logistics ▸ Sales and Distribution ▸ Master Data ▸ Business Partner ▸ Customer ▸ Create ▸ Complete** in the SAP Easy Access menu.

2 In the initial screen, enter the account group, customer (customer number), company code, sales organization, distribution channel, and division:

- **Account Group:** "ZK01"
- **Customer:** "ZXCUST01"
- **Company Code:** "1000 IDES AG"
- **Sales organization:** "1000 Germany Frankfurt"

16

- **Distribution channel**: "12 reseller"
- **Division**: "00 cross-division"

3 To exit the initial screen, press ⌈Enter⌉. The system takes you to the **Create Customer: General Data** view.

4 You can now enter the remaining data in the respective tabs. By clicking the **Company Code Data** and **Sales Area Data** buttons, you navigate to the corresponding tabs.

5 You maintain the customer's address and other details in the **Address** tab for the general data. Use the following data for this example (Figure 16.2):

- **Title**: "Company"
- **Name**: "Special Machinery Inc."
- **Search term 1/2**: "ZZCUST"
- **Street/House number**: "Mainstreet" "1"
- **Postal Code/City**: "91056" "Erlangen"
- **Country**: "DE"
- **Region**: "09" (Bavaria)
- **Transportation zone**: "D000090000" (Region Nuremberg)

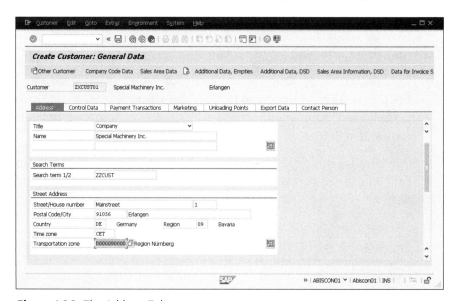

Figure 16.2 *The Address Tab*

6 For this example, enter **Tax ID** "DE47110815" in the **Control Data** tab.

7 For the company code data (available via the **Company Code Data** button), enter **Reconciliation Account** "140000" in the **Account Management** tab (see Chapter 17 for a description of the reconciliation account's function).

8 For the sales area data (available via the **Sales Area Data** button), enter the **Customer Group** "02" in the **Sales** tab.

9 Enter the following sample data in the **Shipment** tab:

- **Shipping Condition**: "10" (immediately)
- **Delivering Plant**: "1000" (Hamburg)

10 You maintain the data required for issuing an invoice in the **Invoice** tab. Use the following data in this example:

- **Incoterms**: "CFR"
- **Terms of Payment**: "ZB01" (payable immediately without deduction)
- **Tax Classification**: "1" (subject to tax)

11 Finally, save the customer master record by clicking the **Save** 🖫 button or pressing ⌨Ctrl+⌨S.

Creating a Material Master Record

When you require a material that the purchasing department procures (see Chapter 15) that will be resold to the customer, you need to create the material in the system. To do so, start Transaction MMH1 via the command field or select **Logistics ▶ Sales and Distribution ▶ Master Data ▶ Products ▶ Material ▶ Trading Goods ▶ Create** in the SAP Easy Access menu (Figure 16.3).

16

> **NOTE**
>
> **Creating Material Master Records**
> Chapter 15 provides a detailed description of material master record creation.

Table 16.1 contains the data that you need to reproduce this example, separated by the screen views they appear in.

Material Number	ZXMAT01
Industry	Mechanical Engineering
Material Type	Finished good
Required Views	Basic Data 1, Sales: Sales Organization Data 1, Sales: Plant Data, Purchasing, Purchase Order Text, Accounting 1
Plant	1000
Sales Organization	1000
Distribution Channel	12
Basic Data 1 view	
Material	Control panel block of 10
Base Unit of Measure	Piece (PC)
Material Group	00103 Electronics/hardware
Gross Weight	1 kg
Net Weight	0.5 kg
Sales Organization 1 View	
Base Unit of Measure	Piece (PC)
Delivering Plant	1000
Material Group	002
Tax Data	1 Full tax
Sales General Plant View	
Transport Group	0001 Pallets
Loading Group	0003 Manual
Sales Text View	
Purchase order text	Control panel block of 10; splashproof

Table 16.1 *Sample Data for the Material Master Record*

Purchasing View	
Purchasing Group	000
Base Unit of Measure	Piece (PC)
Material Group	002
Purchasing Value Key	1
Accounting 1 View	
Valuation Class	3000
Price Control	MAP
Moving average price	100.00 EUR

Table 16.1 *Sample Data for the Material Master Record (Cont.)*

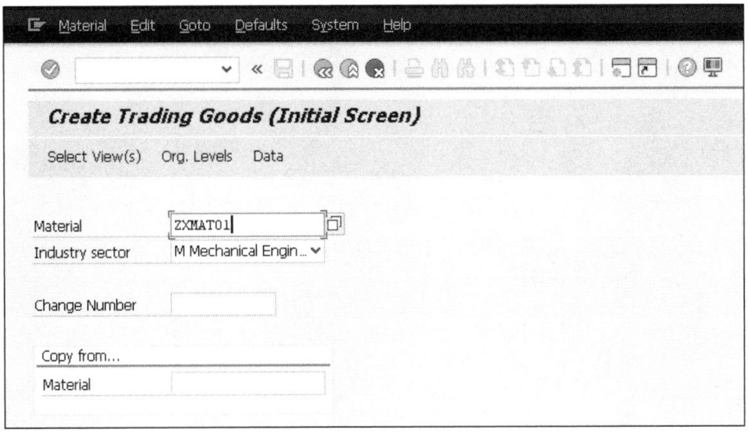

Figure 16.3 *Material Master Record*

Because the master record has been recently created and no material has been procured yet, the stock is 0. The basic procurement process has already been described in Chapter 15.

Now use Transaction ME21N to order 1,000 pieces of the material (ZXMAT01) from vendor 1000, and implement the goods receipt (Transaction MIGO).

Creating Condition Master Records

A condition master record is created in the SAP system if a business relationship has existed with a customer for a long time. After you define the agreed conditions in the condition master record, they will be proposed when you enter a purchase order in the future. This section uses an example to describe how to create a condition master record for a customer and the material.

In this example, you define a price of €200 per piece in the system. This means that if customer ZXCUST01 orders material ZXMAT01, the purchase order will automatically propose a price of €200 during the order entry. Follow these steps:

1. To create the condition master record, start Transaction VK11 via the command field or the SAP Easy Access menu path: **Logistics ▸ Sales and Distribution ▸ Master Data ▸ Conditions ▸ Select Using Condition Type ▸ Create**.

2. Select **PR00 Price** from the CTyp (condition type) column in the initial screen (Figure 16.4).

   A condition type maps a specific criterion for pricing in the system. Surcharges, discounts, and prices that arise during the business process are assigned to the condition types.

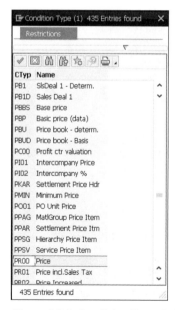

Figure 16.4 *Condition Type Column*

3 Confirm the key combination **Customer/Material with Release Status**, and then define condition **PR00**. A key combination determines the type of combination with which the condition master record is created.

4 You then maintain the conditions in the next screen: If customer ZXCUST01 orders material ZXMAT01, a price of €200 is proposed during the order entry (Figure 16.5).

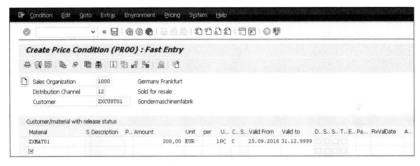

Figure 16.5 *Maintaining Conditions*

5 Save the defined condition via the **Save** 🖫 button (Ctrl+S).

Now that you know the most important organizational structures and master data, the following sections focus on central sales processes.

16.4   Sales Order Processing

Master data forms the basis for sales work. Now bring your attention to the processes that occur in daily sales work that include the creation of a sales order, delivery, and invoice (Figure 16.6).

Figure 16.6 *Basic Sales Process*

The following section discusses the actual sales process and the most important steps of sales order, delivery, and invoice. The presales process often includes the customer inquiry and the quotation (Transactions VA11 and

VA21, respectively). After a customer agrees to a quotation, you'll reference this document when you create the standard order.

Entering Sales Orders

This section gives you an example to show how you can enter a sales (standard) order in the SAP system. A customer calls and wants to order 10 pieces of material ZXMAT01. For this, the condition master record will propose the condition €200 per piece. Follow these steps:

1 To enter the standard order, start Transaction VA01 via the command field or via the **Logistics ▶ Sales and Distribution ▶ Sales ▶ Order ▶ Create** path in the SAP Easy Access menu.

2 In the initial screen, specify **Order Type** "DL" (standard order), **Sales Organization** "1000", **Distribution Channel** "12", and **Division** "00" (Figure 16.7). Press ⌷Enter⌷ or choose the **Continue** ⊘ button to open the screen that creates the purchase order.

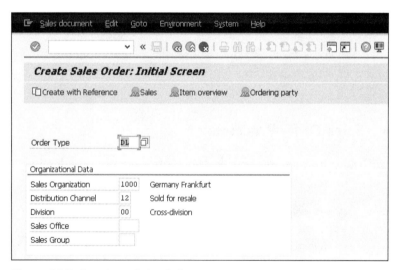

Figure 16.7 *Creating a Sales Order*

3 Subsequently, in the standard order screen, enter the **Sold-To Party** and any **PO Number** in the header, for instance, "DEMO[current date]". For the requested delivery date (**Req. deliv. date**), enter the current date plus

10 days. Specify the **Material** number and the **Order Quantity** (10 pieces) of the items (Figure 16.8). Press ⌊Enter⌋ to transfer the €200 per piece condition from the condition record to the standard order.

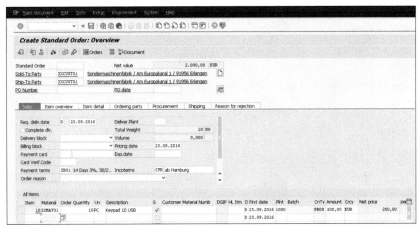

Figure 16.8 *Maintaining Standard Order Information*

■ After you've entered the order, save it by clicking the **Save** 🔲 button or by pressing ⌊Ctrl⌋+⌊S⌋.

The order entry is now complete. The SAP system provides internal documents for the next steps in the process.

Creating Deliveries

In the next step, you create a delivery in the SAP system by following these steps:

■ Call Transaction VL01N via the command field or via the SAP Easy Access menu path: **Logistics ▸ Sales and Distribution ▸ Shipping and Transportation ▸ Outbound Delivery ▸ Create ▸ Single Document ▸ With Reference to Sales Order**. For this example, enter "1000" in the **Shipping point** field as the date that is 10 days in the future in the **Selection date** field (in this case, "25.09.2016"), and enter the document number of the sales order in the **Order** field (Figure 16.9).

16

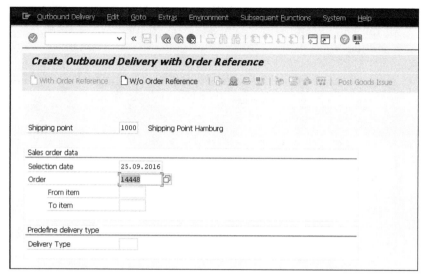

Figure 16.9 *Creating Deilveries*

2 Save your delivery in the subsequent **Delivery Create: Overview** screen (Figure 16.10). Don't post a goods issue yet because the delivery hasn't been created in the SAP system yet.

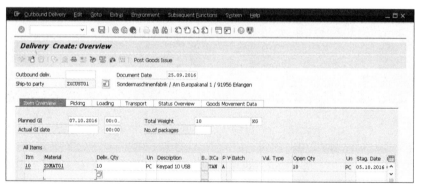

Figure 16.10 *Delivery Overview Screen*

3 Write down the document number of the delivery. To post the goods issue, start Transaction VL02N via the command field or use the SAP Easy Access menu path: **Logistics** ▸ **Sales and Distribution** ▸ **Shipping and Transportation** ▸ **Outbound Delivery** ▸ **Change** ▸ **Single Document**.

4 The system proposes the delivery's document number. Click **Post Goods Issue** (Figure 16.11).

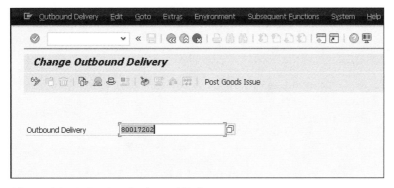

Figure 16.11 *Setting Outbound Delivery*

The stock of the material is reduced accordingly. You can check the stock using Transaction MMBE.

Invoicing

After the goods have been delivered, you can invoice the delivery to the customer. This step is mapped in the SAP system as follows:

1 Call Transaction VF01 by entering the transaction code in the command field or by choosing **Logistics ▸ Sales and Distribution ▸ Billing ▸ Billing Document ▸ Create** in the SAP Easy Access menu. The SAP system automatically proposes the document number of the preceding delivery (Figure 16.12).

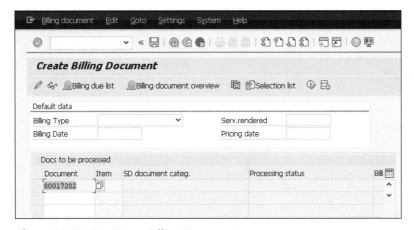

Figure 16.12 *Creating a Billing Document*

2 Save the invoice via the **Save** button (Ctrl+S).

View the print preview of the invoice using Transaction VF03 by following these steps:

1 Select **Billing Document ▸ Output** in the menu bar, or enter Transaction VF03 in the command field.

2 Select the message and click the **Show Invoice** button to generate the print preview.

The customer account, which is determined based on the unique customer number the SAP system, is thus debited (see Chapter 17). You can output the invoice, as shown in Figure 16.13, with Transaction VF31 or via the **Logistics ▸ Sales and Operation ▸ Billing ▸ Output** menu path.

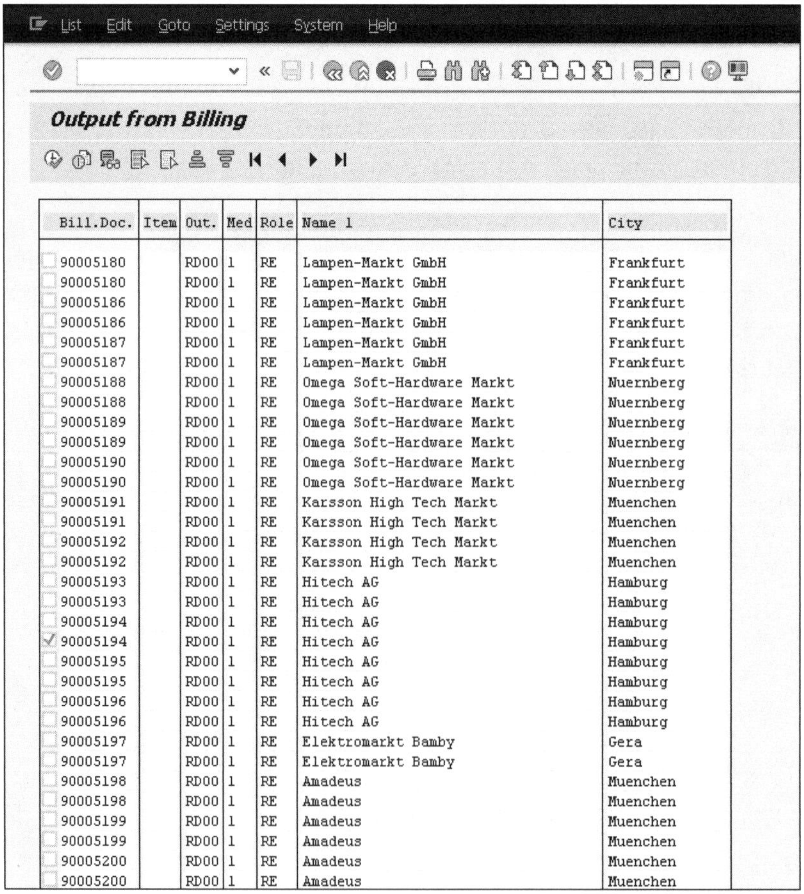

Bill.Doc.	Item	Out.	Med	Role	Name 1	City
90005180		RD00	1	RE	Lampen-Markt GmbH	Frankfurt
90005180		RD00	1	RE	Lampen-Markt GmbH	Frankfurt
90005186		RD00	1	RE	Lampen-Markt GmbH	Frankfurt
90005186		RD00	1	RE	Lampen-Markt GmbH	Frankfurt
90005187		RD00	1	RE	Lampen-Markt GmbH	Frankfurt
90005187		RD00	1	RE	Lampen-Markt GmbH	Frankfurt
90005188		RD00	1	RE	Omega Soft-Hardware Markt	Nuernberg
90005188		RD00	1	RE	Omega Soft-Hardware Markt	Nuernberg
90005189		RD00	1	RE	Omega Soft-Hardware Markt	Nuernberg
90005189		RD00	1	RE	Omega Soft-Hardware Markt	Nuernberg
90005190		RD00	1	RE	Omega Soft-Hardware Markt	Nuernberg
90005190		RD00	1	RE	Omega Soft-Hardware Markt	Nuernberg
90005191		RD00	1	RE	Karsson High Tech Markt	Muenchen
90005191		RD00	1	RE	Karsson High Tech Markt	Muenchen
90005192		RD00	1	RE	Karsson High Tech Markt	Muenchen
90005192		RD00	1	RE	Karsson High Tech Markt	Muenchen
90005193		RD00	1	RE	Hitech AG	Hamburg
90005193		RD00	1	RE	Hitech AG	Hamburg
90005194		RD00	1	RE	Hitech AG	Hamburg
90005194		RD00	1	RE	Hitech AG	Hamburg
90005195		RD00	1	RE	Hitech AG	Hamburg
90005195		RD00	1	RE	Hitech AG	Hamburg
90005196		RD00	1	RE	Hitech AG	Hamburg
90005196		RD00	1	RE	Hitech AG	Hamburg
90005197		RD00	1	RE	Elektromarkt Bamby	Gera
90005197		RD00	1	RE	Elektromarkt Bamby	Gera
90005198		RD00	1	RE	Amadeus	Muenchen
90005198		RD00	1	RE	Amadeus	Muenchen
90005199		RD00	1	RE	Amadeus	Muenchen
90005199		RD00	1	RE	Amadeus	Muenchen
90005200		RD00	1	RE	Amadeus	Muenchen
90005200		RD00	1	RE	Amadeus	Muenchen

Figure 16.13 *Output from Billing*

The basic sales process is complete with the invoice.

As you saw in Section 16.1, the SAP system lets you do an availability check, which we'll cover next.

16.5 Availability Check

Customers care about the price, quality, and availability of goods on the requested delivery date. Remember that during sales order creation, you can check in the SAP system whether the required material is available on the requested date and can thus be delivered on time. For the availability check, SD is closely integrated with Materials Management (MM) and Production Planning (PP) components of SAP so that a delivery date can be confirmed for the customer.

Because the availability check in the SAP system occurs at the plant and storage location level, it's crucial that the storage location be specified in the sales order. You can set various availability check methods in the SAP system (e.g., considering the available warehouse stock and planned receipts and issues, using product allocations for individual customers or regions, or using forecasting).

If the availability check is positive, it's confirmed with a sales order. If it's negative, the desired goods are manufactured (for in-house production) or ordered (for external procurement).

Transaction VA01 (Create Sales Order) includes the **Availability Check** button at the bottom of the screen (not shown in the figure). To familiarize yourself with the function, create a new sales order with the master records you've already created. Don't save it yet, but select the item. Click to run an availability check.

Figure 16.14 shows that the desired quantity can be confirmed for the delivery date. A scheduling agreement delivery schedule arises if, for example, the customer orders 400 pieces and requires 200 pieces in 10 days and the other 200 pieces in two months. You can check these scheduling agreement delivery schedules against the availability check (e.g., whether the delivery can be made on time for the desired point in time).

16

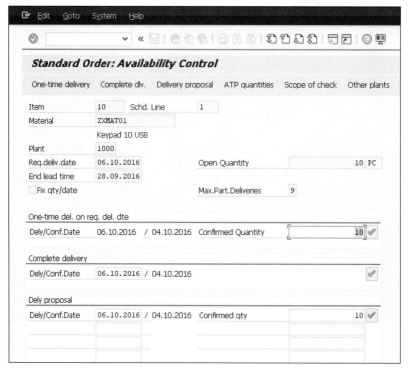

Figure 16.14 *Implementing the Availability Check*

16.6   Complaint Processing (Returns)

If customers receive incorrect or defective goods, or if the invoice is incorrect, they send a complaint. Two methods of responding to these complaints are available to you in complaint processing:

- **Customer returns the goods**
  The customer returns the ordered goods or parts thereof and receives, depending on the agreement, either a substitute delivery or a refund of the entire or partial invoice amount.

- **Customer doesn't return the goods**
  It's possible to refund the paid amount to the customer or replace the goods without their return. For example, if the invoice amount was too high, a credit memo is created based on the complaint. A debit memo is created if the amount invoiced was too low.

This section addresses the complaint processing with returns. For this purpose, you must create returns in the SAP system. If the returned goods reach the warehouse, you must post the goods receipt with reference to the returns you've previously created. After the returns check, you can refund the corresponding amount to the customer by creating a credit memo request or a subsequent delivery that is free of charge (as illustrated in Figure 16.15).

You create complaints or returns in the SAP system with Transaction VA01 (menu path, **Logistics ▸ Sales and Distribution ▸ Sales ▸ Order ▸ Create**). In this example, one piece of the material that you've sold (ZXMAT01) was damaged during transport, so the customer receives a credit memo.

Figure 16.15 *Procurement Process with Returns*

In the initial screen of the transaction, first enter **Order Type** "RE" for returns (Figure 16.16). Then reference the preceding sales order.

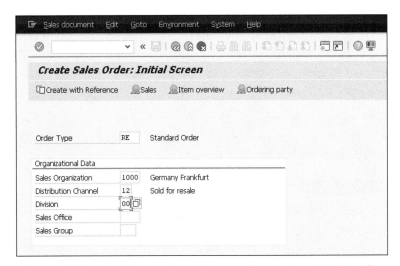

Figure 16.16 *Initial Screen: Create Returns (Transaction VA01) with Order Type RE*

Figure 16.17 shows how to create returns.

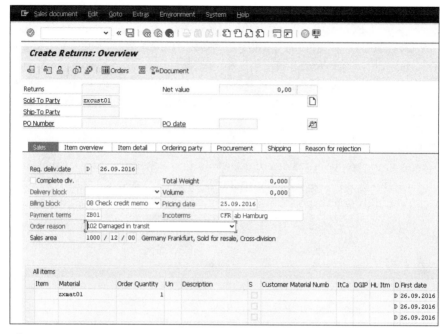

Figure 16.17 *Creating Returns*

16.7   Standard Reporting

The SAP system offers a wide range of standard reports, also found in the SD sales information system (**Logistics ▸ Sales and Distribution ▸ Sales Information System ▸ Standard Analyses**).

If you need an overview of order quantities and sales volumes, you can use the customer analysis (Transaction MCTA), as shown in Figure 16.18. Enter the required selection criteria in the initial screen.

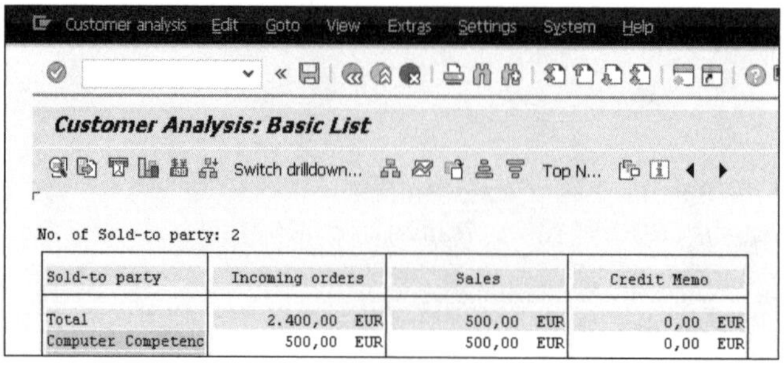

Figure 16.18 *Customer Analysis: Basic List*

Table 16.2 describes the customer analysis transactions.

Transaction	Evaluation
Transaction MCTA	Standard analysis, evaluation by customer
Transaction MCTC	Standard analysis, evaluation by material
Transaction MCTE	Standard analysis, evaluation by sales office

Table 16.2 *Examples of Evaluations in Sales*

Additional Information

Refer to *100 Things You Should Know about Sales and Distribution with SAP* (*www.sap-press.com/2946*) to get more information on the sales process in the SAP system.

17 SAP ERP Financials

Everything started with financial accounting! The SAP ERP Financials (FI) component that was developed in the 1970s is the first and oldest SAP software product. This chapter introduces financial accounting with SAP and the central component.

This chapter discusses the following:

- Primary tasks of FI
- Critical organizational structures
- SAP General Ledger (G/L) accounting functions
- Managing open payables for vendors in accounts payable (AP) accounting
- Managing open receivables of customers in accounts receivable (AR) accounting
- Reports and evaluations available in FI

17.1 Financial Accounting Tasks

Financial accounting includes all information concerning the enterprise. This naturally includes information that directly refers to the financial situation. In addition, logistics and HR processes are also relevant for accounting; the data from these processes are incorporated in FI in real time.

The task of financial accounting is to document all available data and figures (historical values) and map them in accounting. Here, a business's accounts must be kept in such a way that third parties can get an overview of its financial situation (transparency). Transparency and traceability are achieved with the document principle; that is, every business transaction of an enterprise is linked with a document in the IT system. In this context, every process that can be entered with numeric values, for example, goods movements, operating costs, or payments, constitute a business transaction.

17

Document Principle

Because documents are the link between the business transaction and posting, there must be a document for every posting to check each posting for accuracy. Documents include receipts, incoming and outgoing invoices, checks, bank statements, and other items. Because of its important role, the document's structure is defined strictly. Every document is identified by a unique document number in the SAP system and has a document header (which contains the type of business transaction), the date of the document and posting, posting period, reference, currency, and descriptive text.

The information that is gathered in financial accounting isn't only documented transparently but also evaluated and interpreted. This evaluation of historical values takes place at specific points in time, for month-end closing, end-of-quarter closing, and particularly year-end closing, when you create the financial statement. The following questions need to be resolved:

- How much capital does the business have at time of closing?
- Has the enterprise gained profits or suffered losses in the previous period?
- Is the enterprise solvent?

Based on the evaluated historical values, you can derive statements on the enterprise's current status: amount of assets, profits or losses, amount of open receivables, and amount of open payables.

The results of the evaluations are made available by FI to the authorities, creditors, investors, and banks. Because financial accounting presents the business's financial status to the outside world, it's also known as external accounting. Internal accounting, that is, controlling, is discussed in Chapter 18.

External accounting is bound to national and possibly international commercial and tax laws and regulations. The tasks of external accounting include the provision and disclosure of information about capital, financials, and profits, which are used as the basis of taxation. This information is presented in the financial statement as well as the profit and loss (P&L) statement. The financial statement provides information about its existing resources by comparing capital (assets) and debts (liabilities) in account form. The P&L statement gathers a list of all expenses and profits in the course of a fiscal year.

FI is closely integrated with the remaining components of the SAP system because all transactions that are relevant for accounting and come from logistics and human resources management (see Chapter 19) are posted in FI in real time and sometimes forwarded to Controlling (CO).

Financial accounting is responsible for opening accounts at the beginning of the fiscal year, keeping postings current during the year, and preparing the year-end closing. The maintenance of current postings demands the most space and time.

INFO

Double-Entry Accounting

The system of double-entry accounting is usually deployed in the private sector. Double-entry accounting has a long history, as it was invented by Luca Pacioli, an Italian Franciscan monk, at the end of the 15th century. The concept of "double" refers to the fact that every business transaction (posting record) is entered twice—once as a debit and once as a credit—to ensure accuracy (Figure 17.1).

Customer A		Costs	
Debits	Credits	Debits	Credits
	1,000 (1)	(1) 1,000	

Figure 17.1 Sample Posting in Double-Entry Accounting

In accounting, accounts in T form (in which debits are entered on the left side and credits on the right side) are used to keep presentations clear and uncluttered. In addition to that, all postings are shown in the financial statements and the P&L statement.

17

Accounts are the central unit in accounting. Every account has an account number and comprises the two columns for debits and credits.

The general ledger and various subledgers (which represent the business transactions in a more differentiated approach) are kept in double-entry accounting. The general ledger consists of all accounts to which business transactions are posted and that are listed in a chart of accounts. Postings in the subledgers (e.g., AR accounting for customers and AP accounting for vendors) automatically generate a corresponding posting in the SAP General Ledger (G/L), as shown in Figure 17.2.

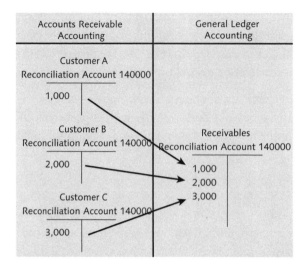

Figure 17.2 *Connection between Subledger and General Ledger Accounting*

The customer in subledger accounting is linked with the receivables account in SAP General Ledger Accounting through the reconciliation account, which you enter in the master record of the customer.

For every complex posting in the SAP system, you must enter the following information at the minimum: document date, posting date, document type, posting key, the account number, and amounts.

FI's most important functions, which are used to map financial accounting in the SAP system, refer to the following areas:

- **SAP General Ledger Accounting (FI-G/L)**
  This records all business transactions relevant for accounting on G/L accounts (accounts in the chart of accounts).

- **Accounts Payable (FI-AP)**
  This area posts all business transactions that refer to vendors and gets its most of its data from purchasing (see Chapter 15).

- **Accounts Receivable (FI-AR)**
  This records all business transactions that refer to customers and receives most of its information from Sales and Distribution (SD) (see Chapter 15).

- **Bank Accounting (FI-BL)**
  This records and manages business transactions that involve banks or the business's payment transactions.

- **Asset Accounting (FI-AA)**

  This records all business transactions that refer to the business's assets. In this context, its assets include all complex fixed assets that are permanently available for value creation (e.g., buildings, machines, or securities). In terms of accounting, the evaluation of assets (asset values, depreciations) is particularly interesting.

Moreover, FI also includes the following two components, which aren't deployed in all enterprises:

- **Funds Management (FI-FM)**

  FM is responsible for creating and controlling budgets and for transferring budgets to user departments.

- **Travel Management (FI-TV)**

  TV supports processes related to business trips, for example, application, planning, posting, and settlement.

In the rest of this chapter, we'll describe AR and AP in detail and explain how to work with these two subledgers. Before you can work with FI, we first describe the foundations that you must lay in financial accounting for this purpose. AA and BL aren't further discussed in this book because these subledgers aren't directly relevant for most users.

17.2 Organizational Structures

You're already familiar with organizational structures from the previous chapters and particularly in Chapter 4. Before you can work with the SAP system, you must first make some basic settings in Customizing and map the business structures in the SAP system. From the FI perspective, the following organizational structures are particularly important. Here again, the client is paramount.

- **Company code**

  The company code is the smallest unit for which complete accounting is possible in the SAP system. Among other things, a chart of accounts and a currency is assigned to the company code, which creates its own financial statement.

- **Business area**

  The business area describes a defined activity area within the enterprise, but the definition and use of business areas aren't mandatory in the SAP system. Following are examples of business areas, including keys, in the SAP system:

- 5000 Energy production
- 6000 Transport engineering
- 7000 Medical engineering

Deploying business areas can help you create evaluations more easily. A business area serves internal purposes because it gets an overview of business-relevant data. This way, you can evaluate results or financial statements separately according to business areas.

- **Chart of accounts**

  The accounts in the G/L are structured according to a chart of accounts that represents a directory of all G/L accounts. The following information must be available for each account:

  - Account number
  - Description
  - G/L account type (P&L account or balance sheet account)

  It's mandatory that a chart of accounts, which can be used by several company codes, be assigned to every company code.

You can map several company codes in a client, even if you use different charts of accounts and must comply with different accounting principles (Figure 17.3).

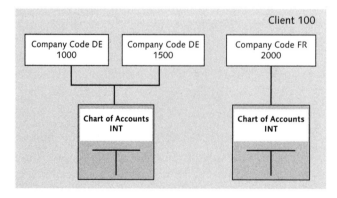

Figure 17.3 *Organizational Structures in Financial Accounting*

Now that you know the most important organizational units in FI, let's discuss SAP General Ledger Accounting.

17.3   Creating the Financial Statement and Profit and Loss Statement

SAP General Ledger Accounting is the central instance of FI because it forms the basis for statutory reporting (financial statement and P&L statement). The FI-GL component is responsible for SAP General Ledger Accounting in the SAP system, which is based on G/L accounts. The G/L accounts, in turn, must be specified in the chart of accounts and must also be created together with the relevant master data so that postings can be made to these accounts. The primary cost element in CO derives from the G/L account (see Chapter 18).

> **Transfer from Subledgers**
>
> In FI, data are available in real time. If a posting is made in a subledger (e.g., in the vendor account), a corresponding posting is also automatically made in the G/L. This is known as automatic entry.

The G/L and the subledgers are linked by a reconciliation account (Figure 17.4). This is a special header account of SAP General Ledger Accounting that guarantees the automatic entry of all items of the subledgers in SAP General Ledger Accounting. You need at least one reconciliation account for customers and one reconciliation account for vendors.

You enter the number of the reconciliation account in the master record or the customer/vendor to link the subledgers (AR and AP) with SAP General Ledger Accounting.

SAP General Ledger Accounting has the following essential tasks:

- Forms the basis for the financial statement
- Used for account management and guarantees a full proof of all business transactions
- Forms the basis for the P&L statement

17

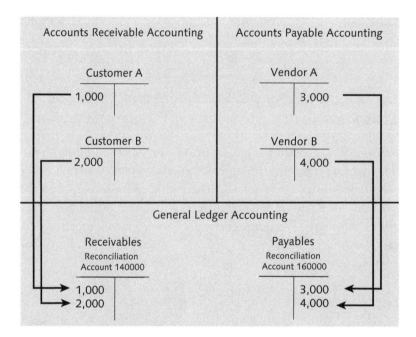

Figure 17.4 *Reconciliation Account Function*

The financial statement is a compact list and evaluation of all assets of a business. An opening financial statement is created when an enterprise is founded, and a closing financial statement is made at the end of each fiscal year. Throughout the fiscal year, all business transactions are posted in G/L accounts that are merged for the closing financial statement at the end of the fiscal year.

A P&L statement is created based on information from the G/L and published at the end of the fiscal year. It compares expenses and gains to indicate the operating income.

Why Financial Statement and Profit and Loss Statement?

When you post every transaction in the P&L statement and the financial statement at the same time, you can determine at any time which resources are available (financial statement) and which path you've already completed (P&L statement). You could compare this with a car: If you travel from Munich to Hamburg, you'll only feel comfortable when you know how much gas is left (financial statement) and what distance you've already covered (P&L statement). Of course, you would

> also reach your destination if you only had a mileage indicator, and you stopped every 100 miles to check with a probe how much gas is left in the tank. This corresponds to an accounting where the expenses and gains are permanently posted, and a review is made once at the end of the year. Modern cars, however, have a mileage indicator and a gas gauge that provide the correct values simultaneously and in real time. This also applies to modern accounting; both the financial statement and P&L statement are updated at the same time.

In the SAP system, you can automatically call the structure of either statement for each or several company codes if you've assigned G/L accounts to the individual, bottom-line financial statement, and P&L statement items in Customizing. The standard version of SAP provides the classic financial statement and P&L statement structures, which you must populate with the G/L accounts from your chart of accounts.

Let's assume your financial statement items are structured as in Figure 17.5.

Assets		Liabilities	
I	Intangible and Financial Assets	I	Equity
		II	Special Reserve with an Equity Portion
II	Current Assets	III	Payables

Figure 17.5 *Items in the Financial Statement Structure*

In this case, you must assign the corresponding accounts to the individual items (e.g., current assets) in Customizing. Follow these steps to call the financial statement:

1 Enter Transaction S_ALR_87012284 in the command field or select the following path in the SAP Easy Access menu: **Accounting ▸ Financial Accounting ▸ General Ledger ▸ Information System ▸ Reports for General Ledger ▸ Financial Statement/Profit and Loss Statement/Cash Flow ▸ General ▸ Actual/Actual Comparisons ▸ S_ALR_87012284 Financial Statement/Profit and Loss Statement**.

2 The system displays the initial screen of the financial statement and the P&L statement (Figure 17.6). Enter the following values:

- Chart of accounts: "CAUS"
- Company code: "1000"
- Financial statement version: "IKR"
- Reporting year: "2016"
- Reporting periods: "1" to "16"
- Comparison year: "2015"
- Comparison periods: "1" to "16"
- List output: Classical list

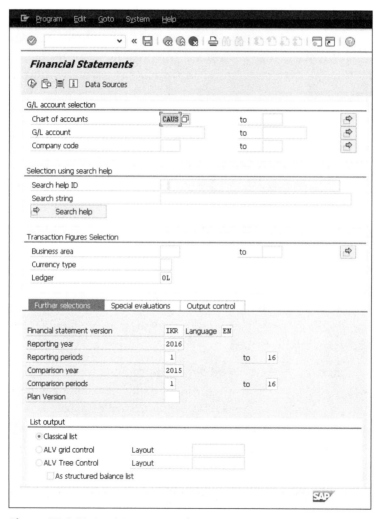

Figure 17.6 *Maintaining Financial Statements*

3 After you've made your entries, press F8 or click the **Execute** button to continue.

4 As you can see in Figure 17.7, the system now displays the financial statement/P&L statement for the selected period and chart of accounts as requested.

The **Financial Statements** report is the most critical report that you can call in SAP General Ledger Accounting. If you made the corresponding settings in Customizing, you can also implement other reports, for example, advance return for tax on sales/purchases within the scope of closing operations.

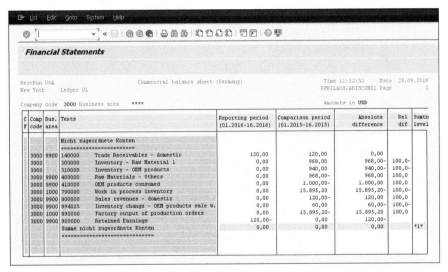

Figure 17.7 *Financial Statements Report*

Now that you know the most important functions of SAP General Ledger Accounting, let's turn our attention to the first subledger.

17.4 Processing Vendor Invoices

AP accounting deals with business transactions that concern vendors and manages the payables of the business. These tasks are primarily associated with the administration and posting of the following business transactions:

- Invoices
- Credit memos
- Outgoing payments

The SAP component used to map AP accounting is FI-AP, and it's closely interlinked with Purchasing (see Chapter 15). Within AP accounting, the Invoice Verification (MM-IV) component (in which you can post incoming invoices) is of particular interest. Outgoing payments are made based on the posted invoice.

Accounts that are kept in AP accounting and AR accounting are known as subledger accounts. The subledger accounts of AP accounting are referred to as vendor accounts. The prerequisites for these are the vendor master records in the vendor account, which you create via Transaction FK01 or the SAP Easy Access menu under **Accounting ▸ Financial Accounting ▸ Accounts Payable ▸ Master Records ▸ Create**. You can change the account via Transaction FK02.

> **NOTE**
>
> **One-time Accounts**
>
> What happens if you post an invoice only once, and a payment must be made to the vendor? In this case, you create and post to a one-time account as a collective account for various one-time vendors.

Let's now consider a sample scenario in AP accounting: You require a spare part for a company car at short notice. This spare part is available at a local dealer. Here, you don't need to trigger a procurement process because the invoice can be entered directly in accounting. Before you buy this spare part from the dealer, you must check if this dealer exists as a vendor in the SAP system.

Follow these steps to check if the master data of the vendor is created in the SAP system:

1. Enter Transaction FK03 in the command field or choose the **Accounting ▸ Financial Accounting ▸ Accounts Payable ▸ Master Data ▸ Master Data ▸ Display** path in the SAP Easy Access menu.

2 Check whether vendor BALTUS30 is created in the system. In the initial screen of Transaction FK03, enter "BALTUS30" in the **Vendor** field and "1000" in the **Company Code** field, and select the **Address** checkbox.

The vendor exists in the Internet Demonstration and Evaluation System (IDES). If this isn't the case, you must create the master record using Transaction FK01. You can use the vendor of Chapter 15 as a template.

3 Enter the following information in the initial screen (Figure 17.8):

- **Vendor:** "BALTUS30"

- **Company Code:** "1000"

4 Activate the **Address, Control,** and **Payment transactions** checkboxes.

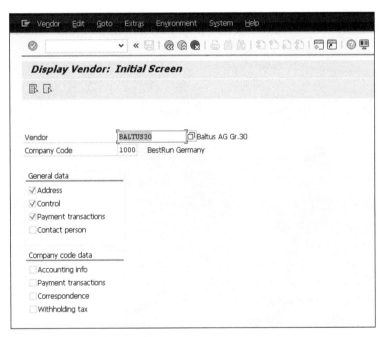

Figure 17.8 *Display Vendor Screen*

5 Press ⌜Enter⌝ or click the **Next** ⊘ button to go to the next screen.

6 The **Display Vendor: Address** screen indicates that the vendor is created in the SAP system (Figure 17.9). If this wasn't the case, you could picked another master record in the IDES and adapt it accordingly.

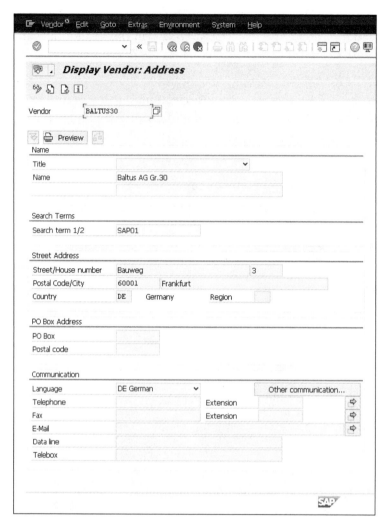

Figure 17.9 *Define Vendor Address*

Because the dealer is created as a vendor in the SAP system, you can purchase the urgently required spare part without any additional work. The vendor sends you the invoice for the spare part (Figure 17.10). You want to enter this invoice in the SAP system.

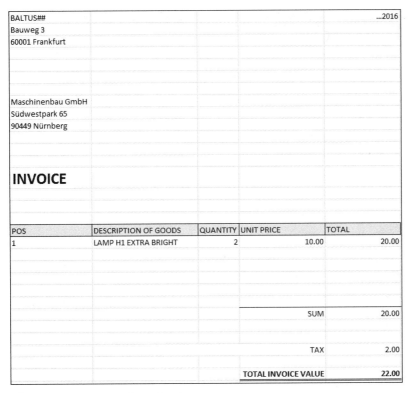

POS	DESCRIPTION OF GOODS	QUANTITY	UNIT PRICE	TOTAL
1	LAMP H1 EXTRA BRIGHT	2	10.00	20.00
			SUM	20.00
			TAX	2.00
			TOTAL INVOICE VALUE	22.00

BALTUS##
Bauweg 3
60001 Frankfurt

...2016

Maschinenbau GmbH
Südwestpark 65
90449 Nürnberg

INVOICE

Figure 17.10 *Invoice from Vendor*

The invoice provides the following information:

- Invoice amount (total net EUR): 20.00 EUR
- Invoice amount (total EUR): 22.00 EUR
- Tax: 10% (input tax), 2.00 EUR
- Vendor: BALTUS30
- Company code: 1000

Follow these steps to enter the invoice in the SAP system:

1 Enter Transaction FB60 in the command field, or choose the **Accounting ▸ Financial Accounting ▸ Accounts Payable ▸ Posting ▸ Invoice ▸ FB60 – Invoice** path in the SAP Easy Access menu.

2 The initial screen for entering the vendor invoice opens. Enter the following information (Figure 17.11):

17

- **Vendor:** "BALTUS30"
- **Reference** (if selected as a mandatory field): any information to refer to the invoice
- **Invoice date:** Information from the invoice (today's date)
- **Amount:** 22.00 EUR
- **Calculate tax** checkbox: Select
- **Tax rate:** 1I 1I (Input tax 10%)
- **Text:** "INVOICE LAMP" (optional)
- **G/L acct:** "890000"
- **Amount (in document currency):** "22.00" EUR
- **Cost center:** "4100"

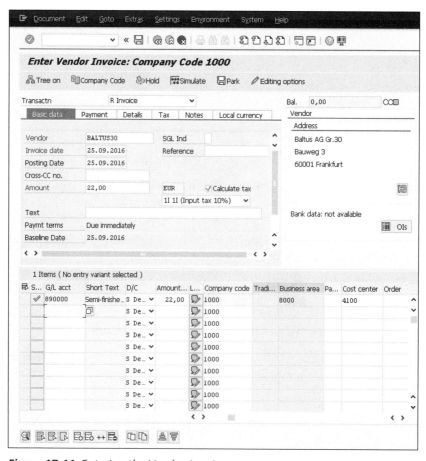

Figure 17.11 *Entering the Vendor Invoice*

3 If all entries are made, click **Save** 💾. The invoice is now entered in the SAP system.

Before you pay the invoice, you may want to check whether any other open invoices exist for this vendor. Follow these steps:

1 To display open invoices for a vendor, enter Transaction FK10N in the command field, or select **Accounting ▸ Financial Accounting ▸ Accounts Payable ▸ Account ▸ Display Balances** in the SAP Easy Access menu.

2 The system opens the balances of AP where you enter the following information in the open fields (Figure 17.12):

- **Vendor**: "BALTUS30"

- **Company code**: "1000"

- **Fiscal year**: "2016"

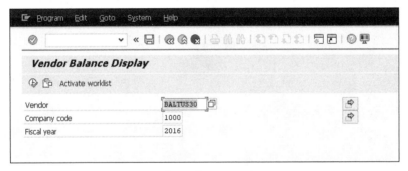

Figure 17.12 Creating a Vendor Balance Display

3 After you've entered the data in the initial screen, click the **Next** 🔃 button or press F8. The system then displays the balances for the selected vendor (Figure 17.13). The balance display shows the vendor's open or settled receivables in an account presentation.

17

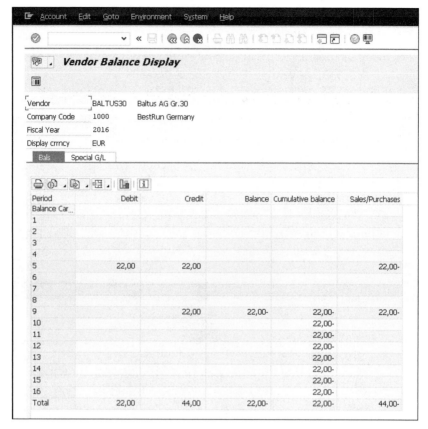

Figure 17.13 Vendor Balance

You now need to post the outgoing payment by following these steps:

1. Enter Transaction F-58 in the command field, or choose the **Accounting ▸ Financial Accounting ▸ Accounts Payable ▸ Posting ▸ Outgoing Payment ▸ Posting+Form Printout** path in the SAP Easy Access menu. Transaction F-58 provides the option to print a check form.

2. Populate the following fields in the initial screen that now opens (Figure 17.14):

   - **Company Code:** "1000"

   - **Payment method:** "C" (check)

   - **House Bank:** "1000"

- Check lot number: "1"
- Printer for forms: "LP01"

3 Activate the **Calculate pmnt amnt** checkbox.

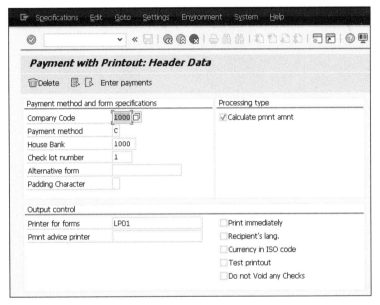

Figure 17.14 Creating Outgoing Payment

4 After you've entered all necessary information in the initial screen, click **Enter payments**.

5 Enter the following data in the next screen (Figure 17.15):

- **Vendor**: "BALTUS30"
- **Amount**: "22.00" EUR

6 Click the **Save** button to confirm your entries and implement the posting. The fields highlighted in blue don't need to be processed because this is only required for an alternative payee.

7 Finally, you want to check the balances for the vendor using Transaction FK10N. Populate the fields **Vendor** ("BALTUS30"), **Company Code** ("1000"), and **Fiscal Year** ("2016").

In Figure 17.16, you can see that the balances are now cleared.

17

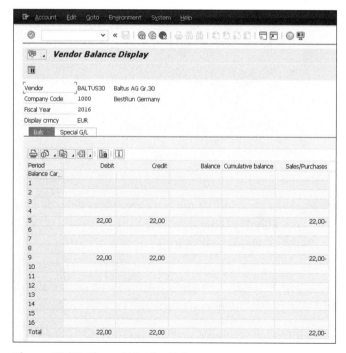

Figure 17.15 Entering Payments

Figure 17.16 Cleared Vendor Balance

Now that you know the most critical functions in AP accounting, we'll now use similar examples to described AR accounting.

17.5 Processing Customer Invoices

AR accounting in the SAP system deals with business transactions that concern the enterprise's customers. These primarily involve the management of receivables from the customer. The relevant invoices are posted in SD and forwarded to FI. Customers are managed in both SD and FI-AR.

The day-to-day activities in AR accounting comprises the following areas:

- Management of customer master records (payment targets, delivery blocks, dunning levels, etc.)
- Receivables management
- Monitoring and recording incoming payments
- Closing operations and dunnings

The business transactions in AR accounting are posted in the customer account.

Let's take a look a sample scenario: At a trade fair, you sold material directly to a customer. You can use Transaction FD03 to check quickly whether this customer already exists in the SAP system. The customer purchases material for 100.00 EUR. Follow these steps:

1. To check the customer master record, choose Transaction FD03 or **Accounting ▸ Financial Accounting ▸ Accounts Receivable ▸ Master Data ▸ FD03 – Display** in the SAP Easy Access menu. Check whether customer CUSTOMER00 is entered in the SAP system.

2. Enter the following information on the required customer in the **Display Customer: General Data** screen (Figure 17.17):

   - **Customer:** "CUSTOMER00"

3. A data record is found, so you now know that the customer is already entered in the SAP system. Exit the transaction by clicking the **Exit** button.

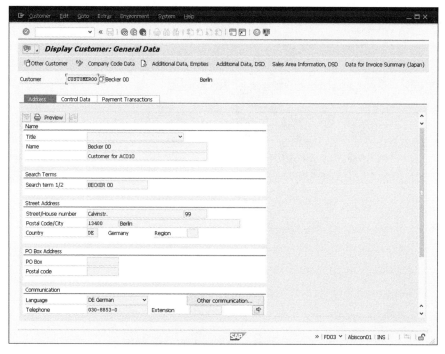

Figure 17.17 *General Data Screen*

Next, you need to post the invoice by following these steps:

1 Enter Transaction FB70 in the command field, or choose the **Accounting ▸ Financial Accounting ▸ Accounts Receivable ▸ Posting ▸ FB70 – Invoice** path in the SAP Easy Access menu.

2 Enter the following data in the screen that now opens (Figure 17.18):

- **Customer:** "CUSTOMER00"

- **Invoice date:** Current date

- **Amount:** "100" EUR

- **In items:** 00 00 (Output tax 0 ..

3 Select the **Calculate tax** checkbox.

4 Select the **Payment** tab, and enter "0.00" (EUR) in the **Discount** field.

5 Click **Save** 💾 to enter the invoice in the SAP system.

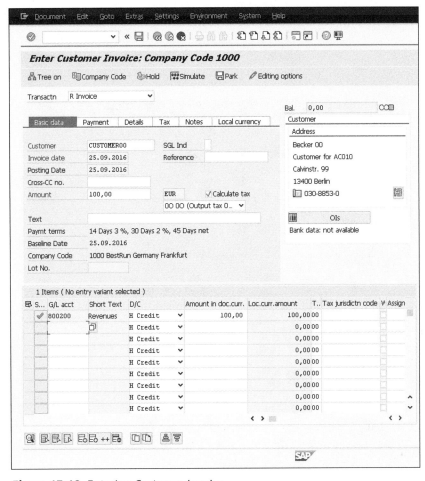

Figure 17.18 *Entering Customer Invoice*

To now post the incoming payment, follow these steps:

1. Choose Transaction F-28 or **Accounting ▸ Financial Accounting ▸ Accounts Receivable ▸ Posting ▸ F-28 Incoming Payment** in the SAP Easy Access menu.

2. Enter the following information in the screen that now opens (Figure 17.19):

   – **Document Date:** "25.09.2016"

   – **Company Code:** "1000"

3 In the **Bank data** area, enter "113108" in the **Account** field, and enter "100" in the **Amount** field.

4 In the **Open item selection** area, enter "CUSTOMER00" in the **Account** field.

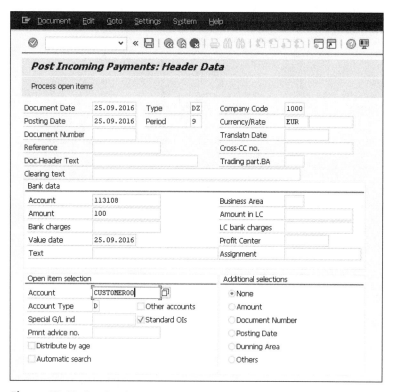

Figure 17.19 *Posting Incoming Payments*

5 Click Process open items and remove the cash discount Figure 17.20.

6 Click **Save** to post the incoming payment.

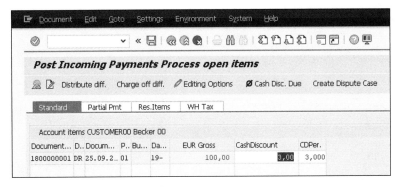

Figure 17.20 *Removing Cash Discount*

Now check the incoming payment on the customer account by following these steps:

1 To display all the customer's open items, check the customer account using Transaction FBL5N or via the SAP Easy Access menu path: **Accounting ▸ Financial Accounting ▸ Accounts Receivable ▸ Account ▸ FBL5N – Display/Change Line Items**.

2 Enter the following data in the open item list (Figure 17.21):

- **Customer account:** "CUSTOMER00"

- **Company code:** "1000"

3 Select the **Open items** radio button, and then enter today's date in the **Open at key date** field.

4 Click **Execute** to display open items. Because the account is balanced, no open items were selected.

You now also know the most critical functions in AR accounting. To complete our descriptions of FI, we now want to present some important evaluations.

17

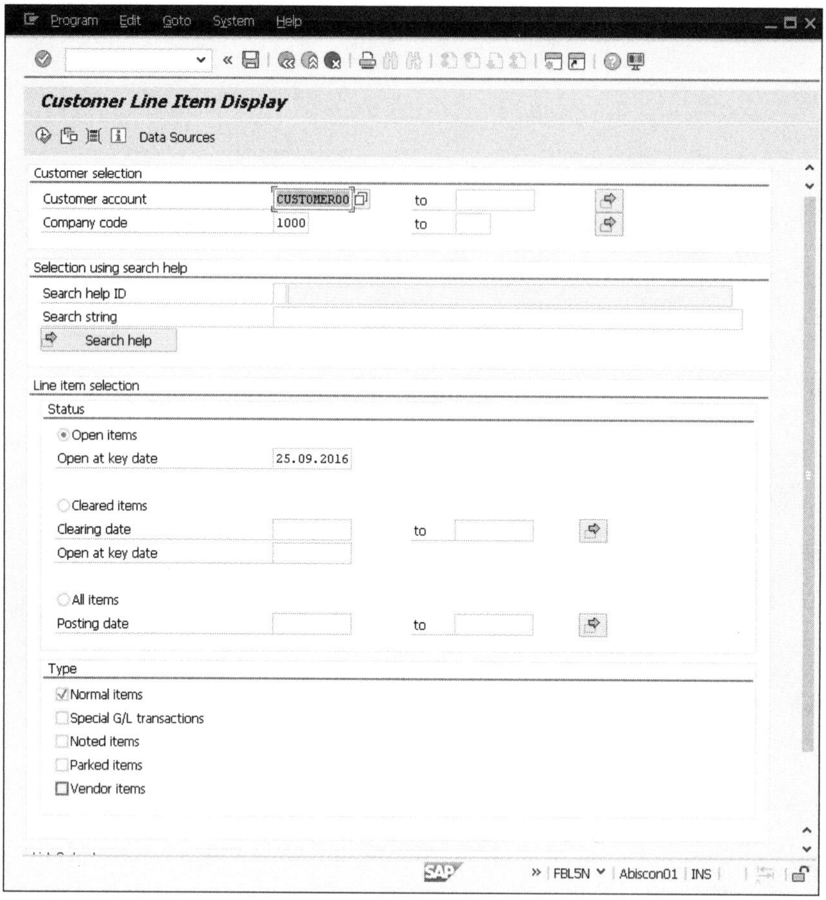

Figure 17.21 Checking Incoming Payment

17.6   Evaluation

This chapter concludes with the representation of some standard reports for
FI. You can find the FI standard reports in the information system in the SAP
Easy Access menu under **Information Systems ▸ Accounting ▸ Financial
Accounting**. Our example shows how to evaluate how much turnover was
achieved with the sales orders of the last fiscal year. Follow these steps:

1 Start Transaction S_ALR_87012186 via the command field, or choose
the **Information Systems ▸ Accounting ▸ Financial Accounting ▸ Accounts
Payable ▸ Reports for Accounts Payable Accounting ▸ Vendor Balances ▸
S_ALR_87012186 Customer Sales** path in the SAP Easy Access menu.

282

2 Enter the following values in the fields (Figure 17.22):

- – **Company code**: "1000"
- – **Fiscal Year**: "2016"
- – **Reporting Periods**: "01" **to** "16"

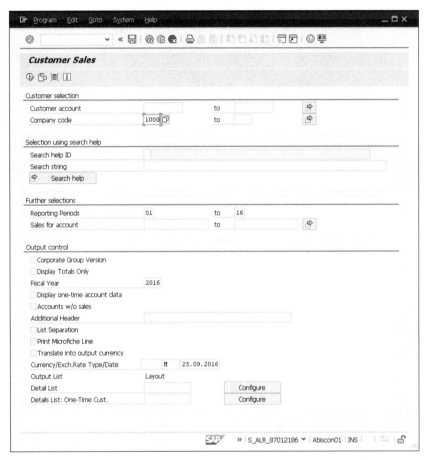

Figure 17.22 *Evaluating Turnover*

3 Start the report by pressing F8 or clicking **Next** ⬚.

The report is displayed (Figure 17.23). This example displays the sales of all customers of the current fiscal year in company code 1000.

Figure 17.23 Customer Sales Report

Table 17.1 lists some examples for reports in FI.

Transaction	Function
Transaction S_PL0_86000030	G/L accounts balances (new)
Transaction F.08	Balances list
Transaction S_ALR_87012093	Vendor sales
Transaction F0.01	Financial statement
Transaction S_ALR_87012186	Customer sales
Transaction S_ALR_87012172	Customer balances

Table 17.1 Examples of Standard Reports in Financial Accounting

From this chapter, you learned about the tasks and functions associated with external accounting. Chapter 18 describes managerial accounting, known as Controlling (CO).

Additional Information

Get more information about FI from *Financial Accounting in SAP: Business User Guide* (*www.sap-press.com/3978*).

18 Controlling

Chapter 17 provided a brief overview of the accounting tasks through which business transactions are posted according to legal regulations. Controlling lays the foundations for strategic and operational corporate decisions. These decision-making processes require deep insights into corporate figures (mainly costs and revenues) from all areas of the enterprise. As its name implies, the task of controlling is to control the enterprise rather than monitor it.

> **This chapter describes the following:**
> - Tasks of controlling
> - Organizational units used in controlling
> - Settling overhead costs and product costs
> - Profitability analysis
> - Controlling reports in SAP

18.1 Controlling Tasks

To implement corporate governance and make strategic decisions, the business's management requires information from all areas of the organization (e.g., sales and distribution, production, purchasing, etc.).The figures from financial accounting don't provide sufficient information for this purpose because information that is required from managerial accounting (another name for controlling) has to be more detailed than in external accounting. Financial accounting is closely integrated with controlling because it's the source of much of the latter's data. Nevertheless, financial accounting can't answer the following questions, as controlling can:

- How can costs be assigned to individual departments and products in the business?
- How can revenue/profit and costs be assigned to customers and products?
- Which revenues/profits and costs will be incurred in the future?

18

Information in controlling is usually monitored with the help of Key Performance Indicators (KPIs). KPIs are prepared in compressed (aggregated) form and reflect the success or failure of an enterprise. KPIs are determined from figures that exist in the SAP system and are provided by the individual user departments.

EXAMPLE

Key Performance Indicators

KPIs are critical to controlling. They provide information about a business situation in a quantifiable and aggregated form, help keep the business objective transparent, and ensure that the standard of success is measurable. The following are examples of KPIs from various areas of the business:

- **Sales volume per customer**: What is the average sales volume per customer?
- **Absence ratio**: What percentage of the planned working time is lost due to employee absences?
- **Storage duration**: How long are the goods or raw materials (and thus capital) stored in the warehouse on average?
- **Service level**: How many sales orders were delivered on the requested delivery date minus all returns?
- **Total Cost of Ownership (TCO)**: What are the costs for operating a device or facility (e.g., an IT system like SAP) in a specific period?

KPIs can be either absolute (e.g., the number of employees) or relative (e.g., price per piece).

Controlling can be divided into two areas: operational and strategic controlling.

In operational controlling, costs and revenues are collected, and variances against the predefined plan are calculated and analyzed. One example of the question answered by operational controlling might be the following: Why did the production costs for a product increase?

The main tasks of operational controlling include the following:

- Ensuring cost transparency
- Identifying and taking countermeasures against bottlenecks
- Monitoring the ratio of costs and revenues

The core task of strategic controlling is to identify opportunities and risks for a business. In this context, the data lays the foundation for early warning systems in enterprises. If variances between actual and planned costs are identified, effective countermeasures and actions can be taken in the future.

The main tasks of strategic controlling include the following:

- Planning all business factors
- Ensuring the existence of the enterprise in the long term
- Implementing strategic plans in operational processes

The costs that a business incurs can be examined from various perspectives:

- **What costs have been incurred?**
  This question is answered in cost-element accounting by linking the cost elements with the accounts.
- **Where have the costs been incurred?**
  Cost Center Accounting deals with this question by associating the costs with cost centers (departments).
- **Why (for which products) have the costs been incurred?**
  This is answered in cost object accounting by associating the costs with work orders, sales orders, or projects.
- **Which results are achieved per product, customer, or sales order, for example?**
  These questions are critical for Profitability Analysis where costs and revenues are associated with individual market segments.

The following sections describe these concepts in detail.

When you examine costs, you're either assessing records from past transactions or projected (future) transactions. Costs from the actual consumption of goods and services are called actual costs, whereas costs of the future are planned costs. You additionally differentiate between full costs and variable costs. In full absorption costing, all costs—including the fixed costs (overhead costs)—from a specific period are allocated to the corresponding cost objects, which gives rise to the term fully loaded cost. In variable costing, in contrast, only the decision-relevant costs (strictly speaking, the variable part) are allocated.

18

Planned/Actual Costs

Table 18.1 illustrates how planned and actual costs are determined. You've planned your costs per cost element; the actual values are set based on those in SAP ERP Financials (FI) and compared to the planned values, and then possible variances are analyzed.

Cost Element	Planned (in $)	Actual (in $)	Planned/ Actual Comparison (in $)
Energy Costs	10,000	12,000	2,000
Rental Costs	20,000	21,000	1,000
Telephone Costs	3,000	2,500	−500

Table 18.1 Planned and Actual Cost Determination

You might also want to make similar planned/actual comparisons for different windows of time (e.g., a fiscal quarter or a year).

Full and Variable Costing

What's the difference between variable costing and absorption costing? To answer this question, let's assume you manufacture two products and generate sales volumes in dollars per product.

Variable costing (contribution margin accounting) only takes the variable costs, such as material consumption, into account. These costs depend on the production quantity in the sense that the material input will vary with the volume of goods produced. Table 18.2 provides an example that illustrates variable costing.

	Product 1 (in $)	Product 2 (in $)	Total (in $)
Sales Volume	10,000	16,000	26,000
Variable Costs	6,000	11,000	17,000
Variable costing	4,000	5,000	9,000

Table 18.2 Full and Variable Costing

Absorption costing takes both the fixed costs and the variable costs into account (Table 18.3). Fixed costs are incurred regardless of the production quantity (e.g., heating costs for a warehouse).

	Product 1 (in $)	Product 2 (in $)	Total (in $)
Sales Volume	10,000	16,000	26,000
Variable Costs	6,000	11,000	17,000
Variable Costing	4,000	5,000	9,000
Fixed Costs	2,000	4,000	5,000
Profit	2,000	1,000	4,000

Table 18.3 Absorption Costing

The profit can be determined only after you've considered all costs (both fixed and variable).

In the SAP system, the Controlling (CO) component answers questions concerning costs and revenues in enterprises. The following are the most important subcomponents in CO:

- **Overhead Cost Controlling**
  Overhead costs are costs that can't be directly allocated to products or services. This component mainly manages cost centers and internal orders. In the SAP system, Overhead Cost Controlling is especially closely integrated with FI. This means that any overhead costs recorded in FI are mapped in the SAP system to the cost elements and cost centers.

- **Product Cost Controlling**
  This area deals with product costing. Consequently, Product Cost Controlling retrieves a lot of data from Production Planning (PP) and Purchasing (MM). Cost object accounting is used to record the product costs in the SAP system, capturing the material usage and work performed per product.

- **Profitability Analysis (CO-PA)**
  This area matches revenues from sales and distribution with costs from overhead cost and product cost accounting, so it receives critical data from

18

291

Sales and Distribution (SD). This interaction provides information on the profitability or on the contribution margin.

These three main areas of controlling are introduced in this chapter. As in the previous chapters, however, let's first take a look at the structures on which CO of SAP ERP are based.

18.2 Organizational Structures

You've already learned about organizational structures in the previous chapters (particularly in Chapter 4). This section discusses the organizational units that are relevant for CO (Figure 18.1). Though client and company code also play a role in CO, they aren't explained again.

- **Controlling area**
  The controlling area is a self-contained unit; it's at this level that cost accounting (as part of CO) is implemented. One or more company codes can be assigned to a controlling area. In turn, one or more controlling areas can be assigned to an operating concern.

- **Operating concern**
  The operating concern is a part of the business that is used to structure the sales market. It provides a complete view of the business's operating profits.

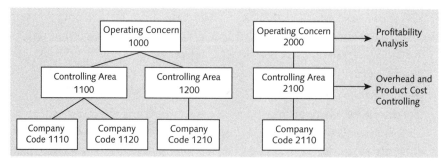

Figure 18.1 *Organizational Units in Controlling*

In CO, further organizational units play a role but are maintained in other SAP components: plant and storage location (in MM), company code (in FI), and sales area (in SD).

The following sections discuss the critical areas of CO. We start with Overhead Cost Controlling, which also covers the largest part of this chapter, because overhead costs represent a large part (often the majority) of the costs incurred in an enterprise.

18.3   Overhead Cost Controlling

In contrast to direct costs, overhead costs are those costs that can't be directly assigned to products or services (e.g., rental costs, wages and salaries, general energy costs). This distinction may sound simple, but overhead cost accounting is very demanding because the correct entry, analysis, and settlement of overhead costs are very complex. The Overhead Management component (CO-OM) enables you to plan, control, and monitor overhead costs for corresponding cost centers.

Before illustrating how Overhead Cost Controlling works in the SAP system, we'll first explain the most important concepts from this area:

- True and designated overhead costs
- Cost centers
- Activity types
- Internal orders
- Primary and secondary cost elements

It's important to distinguish between direct and indirect overhead costs. True overhead costs can't be directly assigned to an account assignment object, such as a cost center. Examples include salaries, energy costs, or facility costs. Designated overhead costs can be assigned to an account assignment object, but this process involves a disproportional amount of effort. Theoretically, you can record them as direct costs and allocate them to an individual product. However, this procedure can be relatively time-consuming, so overhead costs are often distributed to the cost centers using a percentage-based allocation (Figure 18.2). Depending on the type of overhead costs, the basis for this distribution can be the number of employees, the space requirements of the department, the number of computers in the department, and so on.

18

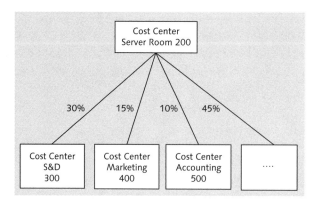

Figure 18.2 *Example of Cost Distribution to Cost Centers by Percentage*

The most important areas of Overhead Cost Controlling are Cost Center Accounting and internal orders.

A cost center is a business-specific account assignment object to which expenses are posted. Cost Center Accounting lets you implement precise cost planning and allocation in the SAP system so you can track the costs back to their origin. Cost centers help assign costs within the business.

In most cases, cost centers are set up to correspond to the functional areas in the business, such as sales and distribution, marketing, human resources, IT, and financials. Accordingly, in the SAP system, a cost center is assigned to a department or production plant. In very small businesses, however, departments often encompass multiple cost centers to ensure transparent cost records and cost accounting. The reason for the assignment is to ensure that the actual costs in the cost centers don't exceed the planned costs or budget costs.

Cost centers belong to central master data in CO. In the SAP system, you can create cost centers via Transaction KS01 or the SAP Easy Access menu path: **Accounting ▸ Controlling ▸ Cost Center Accounting ▸ Master Data ▸ Cost Center ▸ Individual Processing ▸ Create**. Here, you can enter key data, such as the person responsible for the cost center, controlling area, business area, and so on. Cost centers can be linked hierarchically (i.e., a cost center group for a department can contain several cost centers). In this case, however, you can make a posting only to the cost centers at the lowest level.

EXAMPLE

Cost Centers in the IT Department

The cost centers for the IT department could be subdivided into cost centers for hardware, software, support, or consulting:

- K100 IT
- K1001 IT hardware
- K1002 IT software
- K1003 IT support
- K1004 IT consulting

Cost center K100 is used for reporting purposes only; individual postings are made to cost centers K1001–K1004.

In the SAP system, you can create and maintain cost center groups (Figure 18.3) via the following menu path: **Accounting ▸ Controlling ▸ Cost Center Accounting ▸ Master Data ▸ Cost Center Group ▸ Create/Change/Display.**

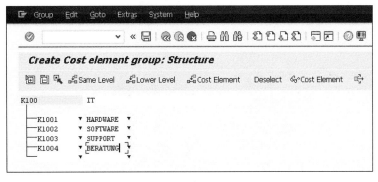

Figure 18.3 *Cost Center Group in the SAP System*

Activity types are used for comprehensive cost center management. An activity type assigns performed activities to cost centers; they are then valuated using prices (output price).

Activity Types

Let's assume a cutting machine is mapped by a cost center. To perform an activity with the cutting machine, you need both the machine and an employee to operate it. This example involves machine activities and person activities. If you map these activities in time units, the two activity types are defined as machine time and person time, in which certain

18

> activities are performed simultaneously at the cutting machine in a spe-
> cific period. Activity types are illustrated in Figure 18.4.

A critical process within Cost Center Accounting is variance analysis, which compares actual and planned costs.

| List | Edit | Goto | Settings | Extras | System | Help |

Display Activity Types: Basic Screen

Create Group...

Controlling Area 1000
Date   01.01.2016 to 31.12.9999
Activity Type   1000 to 999999

ActTyp	Name	CCtr cat.	AUn	Alloc. CElem	A	Lock ind.	COAr
1000	Internal Transport	*	D	614000	1	✓	1000
1123	Energy Base Costs	*	M3	617000	1	✓	1000
1231	Energy Consumpt. kWh	*	K...	617000	1	☐	1000
1232	Energy Consumpt. kWh	*	K...	617000	1	☐	1000
1410	Repair Hours	*	H	615000	1	☐	1000
1411	Repair Hours Overt.	*	H	615000	1	☐	1000
1412	IT Services	*	H	618000	1	☐	1000
1413	Drive Hours	*	H	615000	1	☐	1000
1414	CPU Minutes	*	MIN	639100	2	☐	1000
1420	Machine Hours	*	H	620000	1	☐	1000

Figure 18.4 *Activity Types in the SAP System (Transaction KL13)*

Internal orders provide an additional option for determining actual costs. They are monitored to provide a permanent comparison of actual costs and revenues with planned costs and revenues. As you can with cost centers, you can compare the actual costs of an internal order with its planned costs. However, internal orders for internal projects (e.g., an SAP implementation) provide more transparency because the costs are listed for individual tasks and not for the entire cost center. Internal orders are activated for a certain period, such as for the duration of the project; after the project has been completed, they are locked. Cost centers, by comparison, have a longer life-cycle, although they, too, can change their assignments or managers over time.

In the SAP system, you can create an internal order (Figure 18.5) via Transaction KO01 or the following menu path: **Accounting ▸ Controlling ▸ Internal Orders ▸ Master Data ▸ Special Functions ▸ Order ▸ Create.**

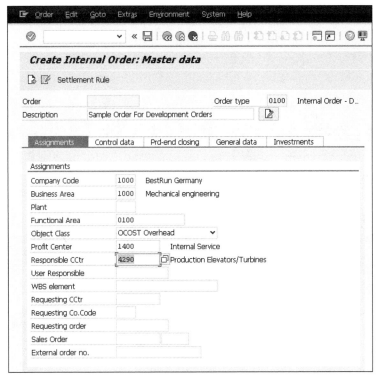

Figure 18.5 *Creating an Internal Order*

In CO, all postings are recorded using cost elements in the controlling area. Cost elements are SAP General Ledger (G/L) accounts (see Chapter 17), which are relevant for CO. The following are examples of cost elements:

- Material costs
- Personnel costs
- Service costs
- Costing-based costs (depreciations, interests, etc.)
- Taxes and fees

If you've defined a G/L account as a cost element in CO, you have to check that the costs for the cost element are assigned to a CO account assignment for every posting. Usually the account assignment is a cost center or internal order. If you don't enter a CO account assignment (initiating object), you can't complete the posting, and the system issues an error message.

18

Cost Elements

If you post a vendor invoice of $100 travel expenses in G/L account 474240, CO automatically implements a parallel posting of the same amount for cost element 474240 (Figure 18.6). This must be associated with a cost center or order.

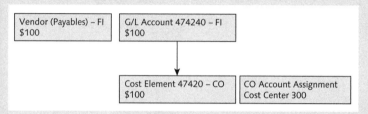

Figure 18.6 *Example of a Parallel Posting of Cost Elements in Controlling*

This way you can separate the costs from SAP General Ledger Accounting at a later stage.

Cost elements are divided into primary and secondary cost elements. Primary costs are directly transferred to CO as actual costs if the primary cost element has been defined as a G/L account in the chart of accounts. Secondary cost elements, by comparison, are only used for cost management within CO and aren't mapped in FI. That is, no G/L accounts are created for secondary cost elements in the chart of accounts. Secondary cost elements are assigned to a different number range from the one used for primary cost elements. This way, you can quickly determine in CO which posting was recorded as a primary posting (invoice entry) and which posting was made as the result of cost allocation.

Primary and Secondary Cost Elements

A business has a cafeteria that incurs costs. However, the cafeteria doesn't provide services for itself but instead for two departments—administration and production. So at the end of the month, the cafeteria costs are charged to the respective departments by creating a transfer posting. The transfer posting is made using the secondary cost element (Figure 18.7).

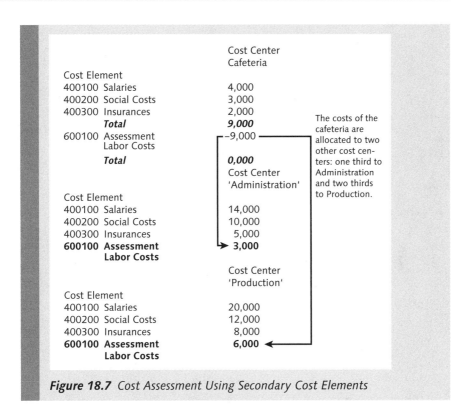

Figure 18.7 *Cost Assessment Using Secondary Cost Elements*

18.4   Product Cost Controlling

It's critical for every business that sells a product to have the product costs under control. If the production or procurement costs increase, the profitability can be directly and seriously affected. Consequently, the SAP component for Product Cost Controlling provides options for calculating and recording product and service costs. Product Costing (CO-PC) focuses on the following tasks:

- Product costing
- Inventory valuation
- Simultaneous costing
- Variance calculation

Product Cost Controlling is based on the use of a standard cost estimate that sets the standard price for internally produced materials based on the bill of

18

material (BOM) and routing. CO-PC is closely integrated with PP, in which you create the BOMs and routings. These are then used to calculate costs in CO-PC.

> **INFO**
>
> **The Production Planning Component**
>
> PP handles the planning and control processes for the manufacture of goods (production processes).

Here, you distinguish between material costs and activity costs.

- **Material costs**
  These include all goods that are purchased, produced, or sold in the business (e.g., raw materials, intermediate products, finished products, trading goods, supplies, assemblies, packaging material, and even services). Material prices are used to determine the costs of materials. They are calculated using the consumption quantity (from the BOM) and the material price (from the material master). The relevant information is stored in the material master in the SAP system (see Chapter 15). The material master is created in the MM component and contains information about all materials that a company procures, produces, stores, or sells.

- **Activity costs**
  These are charged when a direct activity allocation takes place within Overhead Cost Controlling and uses activity types that are valuated with a price. The individual production steps are listed in the routing or recipe.

> **EXAMPLE**
>
> **Bill of Material and Routing**
>
> The BOM lists the quantities and materials that are required to produce something. A BOM for a book in DIN A5 format with 16 pages can include the following:
>
> - 8 pages A4
> - 1 cover
> - 2 clips
>
> The routing defines which steps are necessary to produce a product. For our book, the following steps are necessary:
>
> - Printing
> - Cutting
> - Folding

- Stapling
- Binding

CO-PC determines the standard price that will be used to valuate the inventory of the respective material. A product cost estimate is usually performed for products manufactured in-house, and it sets the standard price while purchased materials are valuated with a moving average price (MAP).

> **Moving Average Price**
>
> The MAP is used for the valuation of items that have been purchased at different prices over time. With each goods movement case, the system automatically adjusts the material prices to include the price variances caused by the goods movements and invoices. You can find an example for the determination of a MAP in Chapter 15.

In cost object accounting, the costs are planned for every production order on the basis of the BOM of the material to be manufactured and the routing. This cost is then used for simultaneous costing. Because the exact costs for the production of a product can only be determined retroactively using the SAP Material Ledger (ML), simultaneous costing is used in the interim to determine the financial effects of price reductions and additional expenses. Any variances between actual costs and planned costs (e.g., price changes for purchased materials or the additional consumption of materials) can be analyzed in detail to detect the cause of the difference.

The following is an example of Product Cost Controlling in the SAP system: CO-PC with quantity structure is normally carried out per material. A quantity structure is a detailed representation of all material components (from the BOM) and services that are required to manufacture a product. Costing without quantity structure excludes BOMs and routings and is usually used if the quantity structure data from PP is incomplete or unavailable. If you use a quantity structure, the system implements the costing automatically. For this reason, BOMs and routings need to be available in the SAP system. In the SAP system, follow these steps:

 Start Transaction CK11N, or navigate in the SAP Easy Access menu. Create a material cost estimate with quantity structure in the application menu via **Controlling ▶ Product Cost Controlling ▶ Product Cost Planning ▶ Material Costing ▶ Cost Estimate with Quantity Structure ▶ Create**.

18

2 In the initial material cost estimate screen (Figure 18.8), enter the **Plant**
("1000" in the example) in which the material will be manufactured, the
Material number ("T-AS801"), and the **Costing Variant** ("PPC1"). Then
click **Execute** ✅.

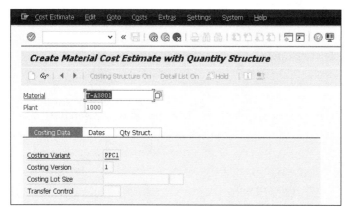

Figure 18.8 *Create Material Cost Estimate with Quantity Structure:*
Costing Data

The screen in the SAP system that appears displays the material's components to the left. To the right, you can view the costing for the selected material (Figure 18.9).

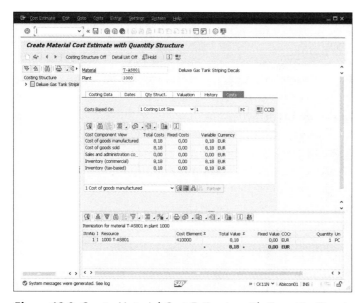

Figure 18.9 *Create Material Cost Estimate with Quantity Structure: Costs*

After this overview of product cost accounting, the next section focuses on Profitability Analysis.

18.5   Profitability Analysis

One of the key reasons to implement CO is to understand profitability. Here, the focus is on with which product or customer the highest profit is made. *Profitability Analysis* (CO-PA) answers this question.

CO-PA is used, for example, for variable costing (contribution margin accounting) or absorption costing in combination with specific criteria such as customer, product, or region. Businesses incur costs for wages, salaries, energy, materials, and so on. Selling the manufactured goods leads to revenues. At its simplest, the difference between revenues and costs is the profit. The contribution margin is the difference between the earned revenues and the variable costs, and thus refers to the amount that is available to cover fixed costs. In full absorption costing, in turn, all costs are allocated to cost objects. That is the business perspective.

In addition, it can be important to know the difference between costs and revenue per product, customer, market segment, and so on. To determine this, you have to integrate data from other SAP components. Because these data are mainly related to sales, the central information is provided by SD. In the Customizing of CO-PA, you define which information from SD you want to copy as a characteristic to CO-PA (e.g., division, article, customer, or material group) and which numeric values you want to transfer from SD to CO-PA (e.g., sales quantity or gross revenue).

INFO

Characteristics and Value Fields

The data structure in CO-PA consists of characteristics and value fields that let you structure, select, and sort your data. You can copy the characteristics from SD or directly from the article or customer master. For example:

- Division (SD)
- Product (SD sales order)
- Customer (SD sales order)
- Material group (article master)

18

> Alternatively, you can derive your characteristics from an existing characteristic. For example, you can derive the continent from the country of the customer and thus sort your evaluations by country and continent.
>
> Value fields represent values or quantities, for example:
>
> - Sales quantity (SD sales order)
> - Gross revenue (SD conditions)

The advantage of the data structure in CO-PA is its flexibility. Because there is no defined structure, you can develop the structure according to your specific requirements. You decide whether you want to have the bill-to party or ship-to party as a characteristic in addition to the customer, or whether you need discounts from the SD conditions in addition to the level of detail already being transferred from CO-PC to cover the product costs. Figure 18.10 shows an example of profitability analysis.

	Sales Revenues
./.	Variable Costs
=	Contribution Margin I
./.	Product-Dependent Fixed Costs
=	Contribution Margin II
./.	Product-Group-Dependent Fixed Costs
=	Contribution Margin III
./.	Department Fixed Costs
=	Contribution Margin IV
./.	Corporate Fixed Costs
=	**Operating Profit**

Figure 18.10 *Example of Profitability Analysis*

The operating profit for a product is calculated using the sales revenue minus all variable and fixed costs. The individual contribution margins are calculated as subtotals. To give you an overview of how you can call your CO-PA data, the following example displays a profitability report for the individual divisions. Follow these steps:

1 Call Transaction KE30 via the command field, or navigate via the SAP Easy Access menu path: **Accounting ▶ Controlling ▶ Profitability Analysis ▶ Information System ▶ Execute Report.**

2 If the system prompts you to, set the **Operating concern** (in this example, "IDEA") before the system takes you to the initial screen (Figure 18.11).

3 Press ⌨Enter or click the **Next** ✅ button..

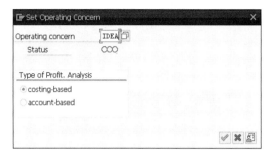

Figure 18.11 *Setting the Operating Concern*

4 In the next screen, you have to select the profitability report (in this example, **IDES-010**) that you want to view (Figure 18.12). Select the report, and press ⌨Enter.

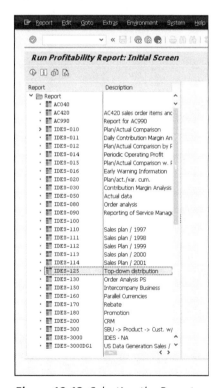

Figure 18.12 *Selecting the Report*

5 In the **Report selections** area, make the following specifications: **Period from** "001.2002", **Period to** "012.2002", and **Version** "100" (Figure 18.13). The version is used to differentiate the various costing variants for one material.

6 Under **Output Type**, you can select the graphical report output (not displayed here).

7 Click the **Execute** button, or press [F8].

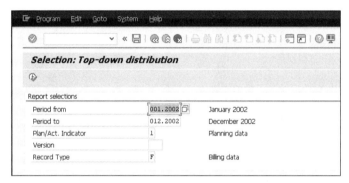

Figure 18.13 *Selection for the Profitability Report*

The next screen displays the profitability report for the individual divisions (Figure 18.14).

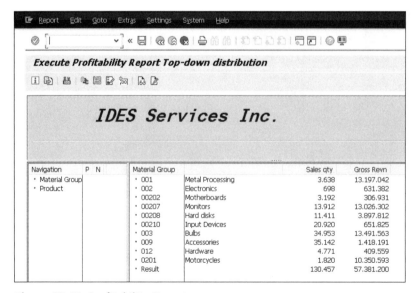

Figure 18.14 *Profitability Report*

In the lower part of the screen, you can now see your sales quantity and gross revenues (value fields) as planned and actual data, absolute variances, and variances in percentages as the total. By double-clicking this navigation area, you get detailed information about division, article, customer, or material group characteristics.

18.6   Evaluations

Now you know some of the tasks and transactions of CO. Especially in CO, evaluation of the various data from a business's various departments is critical for making decisions and planning processes. The SAP system also provides a range of standard reports for CO (e.g., planned/actual comparisons, line item reports, and business unit analyses).

This section provides an overview of some evaluations that are available in the SAP system. The following report, for example, provides information on planned and actual costs of a sales order: Logistics ▸ Production ▸ Shop Floor Control ▸ Information System ▸ Controlling Reports ▸ Product Cost by Sales Order ▸ Detailed Reports ▸ For Sales-Order Cost Estimate and Order BOM Cost Estimate (Figure 18.15).

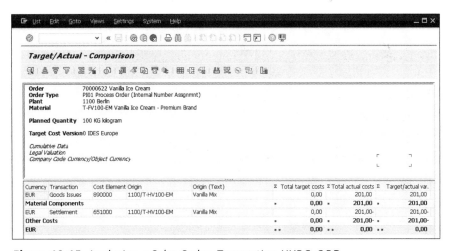

Figure 18.15 *Analyzing a Sales Order: Transaction KKBC_ORD*

Table 18.4 lists some standard reports for CO in SAP ERP 6.0.

Transaction	Evaluation
Transaction KKBC_ORD	Analysis of sales orders
Transaction KE30	Profitability analysis
Transaction S_ALR_87010779	Comparison between current and previous year
Transaction S_ALR_87012082	Vendor balances
Transaction S_ALR_87012173	Open customer items
Transaction S_ALR_87012186	Customer sales

Table 18.4 *Sample Reports in CO*

Because complex report requirements are common in CO, reporting tools that can be used to create individual evaluations are more important here than in other areas of the enterprise. This includes the Report Painter and Drilldown Reporting tools that were introduced in Chapter 8.

Additional Information

If you want to access additional information on CO, refer to *Controlling with SAP—Practical Guide* (*www.sap-press.com/3625*).

This chapter gave you a brief overview of the functions of CO. Chapter 19 deals with human resources in SAP ERP Human Capital Management (SAP ERP HCM).

19 Human Resources

Because employees are the key asset of any enterprise, effectively cultivating and managing an employee base is highly important. The significance of employees in an enterprise is also reflected in the name of SAP's latest component for human resources, SAP ERP Human Capital Management (SAP ERP HCM). In earlier SAP releases, the component had been called SAP Human Resources (SAP HR) but was renamed with the release of mySAP ERP 2004.

This chapter describes the following:
- Managing a business's structural organization
- Searching for new employees
- Maintaining HR master data
- Training employees
- Recording working times
- Implementing payroll for salaries and wages

19.1 Tasks in Human Resources

The tasks of SAP ERP HCM encompass much more than just managing a business's employees. In fact, the tasks of the HR department are versatile: For example, if a new position needs to be filled, the position—which was created first in the organizational structure through Organizational Management—must be advertised. Recruitment helps you manage applicant data and thus search for and select the appropriate candidate for the job. After an appropriate applicant is hired, important HR master data (address, date of birth, marital status, etc.) needs to be entered into the system. This data that is managed in Personnel Administration is mandatory for nearly all HR processes.

Perhaps a new colleague recently started working for your company. The payroll department is now responsible for transferring the salary to the

19

employee's account and for making the payroll results available to SAP ERP Financials (FI) and Controlling (CO). (Due to deviations in regulations on taxes and Social Security contributions, payroll is highly country-specific.) Time management is closely tied to payroll. Here, employees' working times, vacation days, and sick days are recorded and evaluated. The management of business trips also falls into the realm of the HR department. For this purpose, you can use Travel Management. An additional task of the HR department is personnel development. Because employees have to develop their skills to master changing business requirements, "employee lifelong learning" ceases to be a meaningless buzzword and becomes a business necessity. Trainings are planned, implemented, and processed with Training and Event Management.

The smooth execution of HR business processes saves time and money because employees in this department should deal with administrative tasks as infrequently as necessary.

The following are the central elements of SAP ERP HCM that support businesses in meeting these requirements:

- **Personnel Administration**
  You use Personnel Administration to enter and edit employee-related data. The SAP system checks the data for plausibility, and the processing history of the data remains transparent in the system. The information on each employee is stored in infotypes that structure the data, facilitate its entry, and enable time-based data storage. The infotypes for a process are combined in personnel actions.

- **Recruitment**
  Recruitment is everything that falls between creating applicant data and filling vacant positions. The SAP system supports the management of applicants as well as the selection process and communication with applicants.

- **Talent Management**
  This SAP subcomponent supports enterprises in training employees. You can implement continuing education and trainings both to motivate employees and to respond to organizational and structural changes in the business.

- **Payroll**
  Payroll ensures that the remuneration for performed work is determined and paid to an employee; it includes the preparation, settlement, and

transfer of the remuneration and takes tax specifications and Social Security contributions into consideration. That is why payroll is highly country-specific.

- **Time Management**
  With Time Management, you can manage time accounts and provide information to payroll. This subcomponent lets you enter time data and integrates with time recording tools.

- **Organizational Management**
  This subcomponent enables you to map the business structure (e.g., the department hierarchy) and the reporting structure in a structural organization. You can use it to implement Talent Management and to recruit efficiently.

- **Training and Event Management**
  This SAP subcomponent helps you plan, implement, postprocess, and settle events. You can maintain the information that is required for the event (rooms, materials, etc.), determine the requirements for the event, schedule dates, manage participants, and allocate costs.

- **Travel Management**
  Use this to enter and allocate employees' travel costs.

Due to its versatile usage areas, SAP ERP HCM is closely connected to other SAP components. This is specifically discussed in later sections of this chapter.

The following sections give you a detailed overview of the essential HR tasks with SAP with emphasis on organizational management, recruitment, personnel administration, time management, and payroll. The first section deals with a component in which numerous prerequisites are met and structures are defined. In this context, it also briefly explains the organizational structures in SAP ERP HCM.

19.2 Organizational Management

In the Organizational Management component in SAP ERP HCM, you maintain data that maps the business structure or structural organization. This data is used, for example, to create organization charts, job descriptions, job indexes, and evaluations. Organizational Management is also useful when you want to develop an authorization concept (see Chapter 14), but it isn't required by all businesses that deploy SAP ERP HCM.

Organizational structures map the business's structural organization in the SAP system from the HR perspective. The structural organization reflects the task-related (i.e., functional) organizational structures of the company, such as positions, which are filled by employees and linked to each other. You can also define further links (e.g., to tasks or jobs). The various structural organizations are known as plan versions in the SAP system. These let you reproduce different scenarios (e.g., a reorganization of the company) with different plans.

The organizational structure is made up of the individual organizational units so that the hierarchies of the existing business structure are transferred to the SAP system. In contrast to the logistics or accounting organizational structures, the SAP ERP HCM organizational structures aren't defined in Customizing but in Organizational Management.

Organizational Management also lets you integrate organizational units that are created in other SAP components, such as cost centers. A cost center is an internal account assignment object in the business and is usually sorted by functional area. Cost centers are maintained in FI and assigned to the organizational units in Organizational Management.

The following objects or organizational units play a central role in Organizational Management:

- **Organizational units**
  Organizational units describe the business's structural organization according to business, regional, and responsibility aspects.

- **Jobs**
  Jobs classify tasks in the business. Accordingly, the respective task areas and employee requirements are assigned to jobs. Jobs have general descriptions, such as *Head of Financial Accounting* or *Agent for Accounts Payable Accounting*.

- **Positions**
  Positions are concrete jobs in a business that are filled by employees. The company defines the respective number of positions. Therefore, a job is kind of a template for the position.

- **Persons**

  Persons are objects that fill positions. Examples include the following:

  - J. Doe fills the *System Administrator* position.
  - H. Smith fills the *Personnel Consultant* position.

- **Infotypes**

  An infotype is a summary of a data record's fields (HR master record). In SAP, you enter master data using infotypes. More information on infotypes can be found later in this section.

Figure 19.1 shows a typical business structure. Sales and Distribution and Financial Accounting report directly to management. Sales and Distribution is subdivided into enterprise customers and private customers. Financial Accounting is subdivided into accounts payable accounting and accounts receivable accounting.

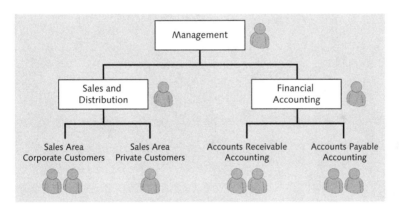

Figure 19.1 *Example of an Enterprise Structure*

To create an organizational unit (e.g., a position) in SAP ERP HCM, follow these steps:

1. In the SAP Easy Access menu, select **Human Resources ▶ Organizational Management ▶ Organizational Plan ▶ Organization and Staffing** (Transaction PPOCE).

2. The initial screen for creating a root organizational unit opens (Figure 19.2). Define the validity period and confirm it by pressing Enter.

19

Figure 19.2 *Confirming the Validity Period*

3 Double-click the organizational unit you want to create in the left screen
area to select it, and then create it by clicking the **Create** 🗋 button
(Figure 19.3).

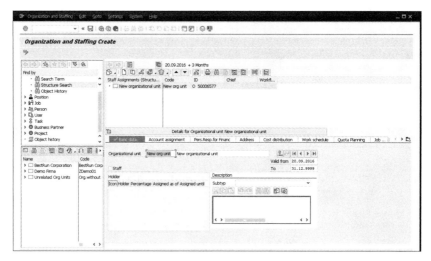

Figure 19.3 *Creating Organization and Staffing (Transaction PPOCE)*

After this overview of the organizational structures in SAP ERP HCM, the
next section deals with recruitment.

19.3   Recruitment

It's very important for businesses to meet changing requirements in terms of
employees, especially as the enterprise grows. For applicants, too, a potential
employer is very attractive if its HR department responds quickly and profes-
sionally to their job applications. The SAP component for Recruitment helps
you determine workforce requirements, advertise open positions, manage
applicant information, and select the appropriate applicants.

After the workforce requirements are determined and defined, the process of searching for a new employee is usually as follows (Figure 19.4):

1 A job is advertised inside or outside the business.

2 Applicant data are entered into the system and evaluated.

3 The applicants are contacted, and interviews are carried out for the selection process.

4 An employment contract is generated after an applicant is hired.

5 Finally, the applicant data are entered in the HR master.

Figure 19.4 *Recruitment Process Steps*

In the SAP system, you can create a requirements profile for the job you want to fill (Figure 19.5). In this profile, you can select the qualifications that you'll look for in applicants (Transaction PBAP).

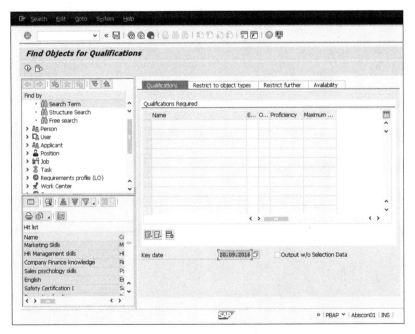

Figure 19.5 *Searching for Applicants with Defined Qualifications (Transaction PBAP)*

Information about applications can be entered either by HR department employees or by applicants themselves via a portal for job-seekers.

Applicant Portals

More and more businesses provide specific portals for online applications on their websites. Another common option is using commercial job exchanges. In both cases, the applicant himself enters his information, which is transferred to the SAP system and processed there. Not all businesses that deploy SAP ERP HCM use this option, but it does mean that employees from the HR department don't have to enter the applicant data manually into the system.

You can call the applicant data via Transaction PB20 or through the SAP Easy Access menu path, **Human Resources ▶ Personnel Management ▶ Recruitment ▶ Appl.master data.**

The infotypes that are maintained in the applicant master record are selected with a green checkmark [✓]. To view an infotype, select the line and click **Display** [🔍] (Figure 19.6).

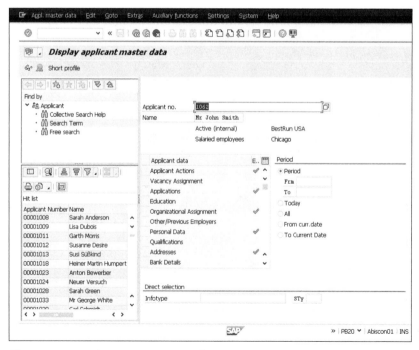

Figure 19.6 *Applicant Master Record*

The short profile provides a summary of the applicant profile (Figure 19.7). Click the **Short profile** button to display the applicant's short profile.

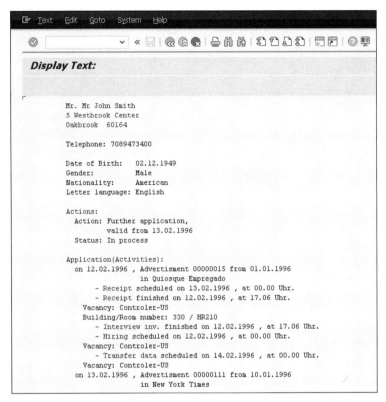

Figure 19.7 *Short Profile of the Applicant*

In addition to helping users select the best applicants, SAP ERP HCM aids in corresponding with them during the recruitment process. This correspondence includes the generation of acknowledgments of receipts, invitations for interviews, and letters of rejection. If an applicant is hired, his data are transferred to the HR master record and maintained in Personal Administration.

The next section discusses the SAP ERP HCM Personnel Administration component.

19

19.4   Personnel Administration

The Personnel Administration area covers all business activities that are carried out within the scope of employee management, including the creation, maintenance, and assignment of HR master data. Maintaining quality HR master data is critical to performing personnel activities effectively.

> **TIP**
>
> **Good Master Data Maintenance**
>
> HR department employees are responsible for keeping the master data complete, up-to-date, and correct. Changes should always be implemented immediately. In addition, in SAP ERP HCM, it's very important to not delete historical data but keep it in the SAP system.

Examples of central master data in Personnel Administration include the personnel number by which you uniquely identify an employee and the employment status that indicates whether an individual is currently employed by the business.

> **NOTE**
>
> **Human Resources and Data Protection**
>
> Master data in SAP ERP HCM is highly sensitive personal data that must be treated with due diligence by the business and responsible employees. Violating the legal requirements that regulate data protection can lead to legal consequences for the business and the involved HR department employee.
>
> Of course, this not only applies to the information stored in SAP ERP HCM but also to general personal data. In the SAP system, a role concept ensures that only authorized employees can access the data and transactions. Chapter 14 provides more information on roles and authorizations.

The management of employee data is based on predefined processes called personnel actions. The HR data maintenance processes include each employee's employment (or reentry), organizational change (when employees change departments), or leave (e.g., due to termination or retirement).

Employee data are stored in infotypes, which play a central role in your work with SAP ERP HCM. A personnel action consists of the infotypes for which you have to enter data during the personnel action. For example, if a new employee is hired, you subsequently process all fields that are necessary for this personnel action.

Infotypes consequently refer to a logically related area of data. Table 19.1 lists the infotypes that must be maintained for the *Employment* personnel action in Personnel Administration.

Infotype	Name
0000	Actions
0003	Payroll Status
0001	Organizational Assignment
0002	Personal Data
0006	Addresses
0007	Planned Working Time
0008	Basic Pay
0009	Bank Details
0012	Tax Data
0013	Social Security Data
0020	Pensions
0016	Integral Parts of the Contract
0019	Monitoring of Tasks
2006	Absence Quotas

Table 19.1 Infotypes for the "Employment" Personnel Action

All of this master data needs to be entered when a new employee is hired. To call personnel actions, enter Transaction PA40 in the command field, or select **Human Resources** ▶ **Personnel Management** ▶ **Administration** ▶ **HR Master Data** from the SAP Easy Access menu. The system displays the initial screen for personnel actions (Figure 19.8). Enter the entry date, along with the hired employee's **Personnel No.**. Then select the **Hire** action type, and click **Execute** 🔄. Processing the **Termination** action type (when an employee leaves the business) is similar.

19

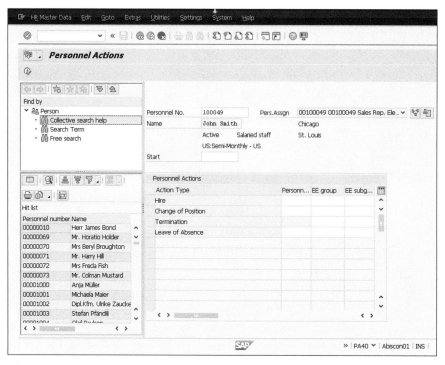

Figure 19.8 *Personnel Action: Employment*

Proceed with the infotypes that are necessary for each action and which were already listed in the table. Maintain the respective fields for each infotype. After entering all data, click **Save** 🖫. The SAP system then prompts the next infotype that needs to be maintained for the action's completion.

A lot of the infotypes already contain default values. In addition, the SAP system checks the plausibility of the entries and questions anything unlikely.

Every infotype has a time constraint. The time constraint defines whether it can contain several records. There are four types of time constraints:

- **Time constraint 0**
  One infotype record exists and doesn't change throughout the entire period of validity of the HR master.

- **Time constraint 1**
  One valid infotype record must exist.

- **Time constraint 2**
  Either no or exactly one valid infotype record exists.

- **Time constraint 3**
Either no or multiple valid infotype records exist in parallel.

Time Constraint

Let's take Infotype 0021 (Family/Related Person) as an example of the different time constraint types:

- **Time constraint 0**: The employee must always have the same spouse.
- **Time constraint 1**: The employee must always be married but not necessarily to the same spouse.
- **Time constraint 2**: The employee can have a spouse but doesn't have to.
- **Time constraint 3**: The employee can have no, one, or several spouses.

If you want to have the system display an infotype for your work, you can call the infotype by entering the number, for example, in Transaction PA20 (Display HR Master). In the SAP Easy Access menu, the path is **Human Resources ▸ Personnel Management ▸ Administration ▸ HR Master Data**. You can determine and view the HR master record by entering the personnel number. If you don't know someone's personnel number, you can search for the master record in the SAP system using search criteria. Call the search window with the **Input Help** button ▣. In the **Personnel Number** field, enter the personnel number, and press ⌜Enter⌟. Alternatively, use the search window of the input help to find the person.

Enter the required infotype number into the **Infotype** field, and then click the **Display** ◈ button.

The next section discusses personnel planning and development.

19.5   Talent Management

Qualified and motivated employees contribute to the success of every enterprise. The personnel development area in SAP ERP HCM, today known as Talent Management, enables strategic HR work to train and motivate employees. In combination with Training and Event Management, Talent Management provides options for planning and implementing measures to

19

further educate and train employees. The requirement for personnel development can be derived from the job description and the employee's existing qualifications.

Employees' qualifications are managed in a qualification catalog that lists the skills and knowledge necessary for each job in the enterprise. This catalog helps the HR department manage the required qualifications of employees (and applicants) and compare them with the requirements of the individual tasks.

In SAP ERP HCM, you store the qualifications that are required for a specific job in requirements profiles. The qualifications of individual employees are also stored in profiles. In addition to qualifications, you also assign interests, dislikes, assessments, and so on to the employee. These qualifications not only include specific certifications or language skills but also soft skills, such as leadership qualities and organizational skills. You can compare the requirements profile with the employee's qualification profile and derive measures for further training based on deviations.

EXAMPLE	**Measures for Further Training** The employee Jane Doe is supposed to become the assistant to the head of production in the next fiscal year. The job description for this position says that SAP ERP HCM knowledge is a requirement for management tasks. Currently, the employee only has knowledge of SAP Supply Chain Management (SAP SCM), so Jane Doe will attend further training sessions. An external SAP trainer will support the employee for three days during her first days with SAP ERP HCM.

19.6 Time Management

On one hand, Time Management is used to enter attendance times (including the duration and length of attendance times and breaks), information on working times outside the usual workplace (e.g., business trips), and activities performed during the time recorded. On the other hand, it's also used to maintain deviations from the original work schedule, such as overtime, extra shifts, reduced hours, or reintegration. You can also document absences (e.g., sick days and leave days) in the system.

You can only evaluate this information if the planned working times of an employee are specified in a work schedule that documents the agreed number of hours per week and which days the employee doesn't work (e.g., public holidays), as shown in Figure 19.9. As in the other SAP ERP HCM components, the time data is stored in infotypes.

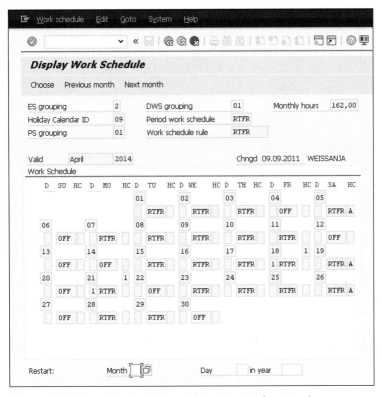

Figure 19.9 *Annual Calendar (Working Days) of an Employee*

The time recording process can be automated in the time recording system by HR employee deemed responsible for the task or by the employee himself. The time can be recorded using both positive recording and negative recording. (Combinations of the two recording types are also possible.) With positive recording, the times when the employee arrives and leaves are recorded, usually via time-recording terminals (e.g., time cards). In negative recording, defined working times are presumed, and only the deviations are documented.

> **EXAMPLE**
>
> **Integration with Other SAP ERP HCM Components**
> An employee requests leave for a week in August during which he is registered for a training session on the new IT system. The SAP system sends a message that indicates the time conflict to the HR department.

The following might be considered deviations from the planned working schedule:

- Extra shifts
- Reintegration after illness
- Parental leave

> **INFO**
>
> **Cross-Application Time Sheet**
> SAP provides a user-friendly time recording tool for employees called Cross-Application Time Sheet (CATS). CATS lets you record working times that can be assigned to a Work Breakdown Structure (WBS) element and a cost center. (WBS refers to the model that hierarchically maps the activities to be carried out in a project.)
> CATS is an Employee Self-Service (ESS) application that is made available to the employees as a web application in an Internet browser (and not in the SAP GUI).

Time Management data provide critical information for Payroll, which is described in the next section.

19.7   Payroll

Payroll calculates the remuneration for employees. It consists of the preparation, settlement, transfer, Social Security contributions, and transport of the data to FI. Payroll processes are very country-specific because they take into consideration numerous legal requirements that govern taxes and Social Security contributions. If the business has subsidiaries abroad, it's possible that you need to take into account both your own country's special requirements and those of foreign countries. SAP ERP HCM considers the legal requirements from more than 50 countries.

The Payroll component is closely integrated with FI. The remunerations are paid to the employee via Data Medium Exchange (DME) from SAP ERP HCM, and then the totals from Payroll are posted in FI. The data from Time Management and Personnel Administration are processed for settlement, and finally the results are transferred to FI and CO.

> **INFO**
>
> **Retroactive Accounting**
>
> Section 19.4 already taught you that SAP ERP HCM always also stores historical data. Because this also applies to information from Payroll, settlements from the past can be corrected. If relevant infotypes are changed retroactively, the system automatically triggers retroactive accounting. To document the changed settlement results, the SAP system creates a history.

The settlement process occurs as follows:

1. The settlement is prepared after the relevant data are maintained in SAP ERP HCM. This includes information on taxes and Social Security as well as variable salary components, such as paid extra shifts, end-of-year bonus, and so on.

2. Next, payroll is implemented. The gross and net amounts of the remuneration are determined. The net amount is derived from legal deductions (taxes, pension insurance, unemployment insurance, health insurance) and optional deductions, such as retirement plans. Before the settlement can start, it must be released.

3. After the results are checked, and if no corrections are necessary, the amount is paid to the employees, and the corresponding remuneration statement is created.

4. Social Security contributions, taxes, and so on are calculated and transferred to the respective tax offices and Social Security carriers at defined intervals (usually monthly).

5. At this time, various evaluations are carried out as required.

6. Finally, the results from the settlement are posted in FI, and the cost centers to which the costs are allocated are recorded in CO.

Before you start the actual settlement process, you can simulate a settlement to check if the master data have been maintained correctly.

19

Figure 19.10 illustrates the payroll process for an employee. The settlement simulation creates the payroll for any period. Start the settlement simulation via Transaction PC00_M99_CALC_SIMU or via the SAP Easy Access menu path, **Human Resources ▶ Payroll ▶ International ▶ Payroll**.

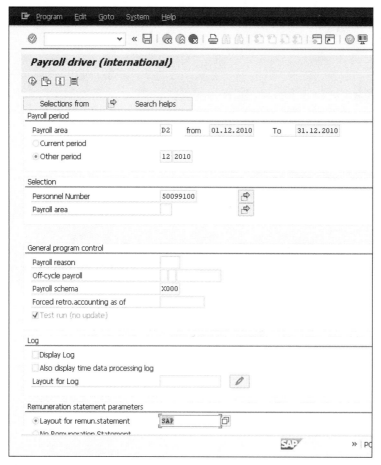

Figure 19.10 *Selection Screen for the Payroll Simulation*

19.8   Standard Reporting

The standard version of the information system in HR already provides you with numerous reports and evaluations. You can find them via the SAP Easy Access menu path, **Human Resources ▶ Information System ▶ Reports**. For a list of ecaluations in HR, see Table 19.2.

Transaction	Function
Transaction S_AHR_61015509	Applicants by Names
Transaction S_AHR_61015512	Applications
Transaction S_AHR_61015513	Applicant Statistics
Transaction S_PH9_46000223	Entered and Left
Transaction S_PH9_46000221	Birthday List
Transaction S_AHR_61016354	Telephone Directory

Table 19.2 *Examples of Evaluations in HR*

TIP

Additional Information

For additional information on SAP ERP HCM, refer to *Discover SAP ERP HCM* (*www.sap-press.com/1846*).

This chapter introduced you to human resources in SAP ERP HCM. Chapter 20 combines the information from the previous five chapters in a case study, which you can reproduce in the SAP IDES.

19

20 Case Study

This chapter will help you reinforce your knowledge and deploy it with a real-life case study. As an exercise, you'll implement a case study by carrying out various tasks and processes in the system.

> **In this case study, you'll perform the following:**
> - Create a material master record
> - Create a vendor master record
> - Create a purchasing info record
> - Create a purchase order
> - Receive goods
> - Verify an invoice
> - Display open items
> - Post an outgoing payment
> - Create a customer master
> - Add customer data to the material master record
> - Create a condition
> - Enter a sales order
> - Deliver and issue goods
> - Create an invoice
> - Post an incoming payment

Our case study consists of a list of tasks from different areas that can be processed by you or your team. Among these areas are Materials Management (MM), Sales and Distribution (SD), and SAP ERP Financials (FI).

You can use limitless resources to aid you during this case study; in fact, use all means that are available to you if they are available to you in real-world situations. Cooperating with colleagues and sharing your experiences with them will also solidify your understanding of these concepts.

Table 20.1 lists the transactions needed for this case study.

Transaction	Transaction Code
Create/Change/Display a Material Master Record	MM01, MM02, MM03
Create/Change/Display a Vendor	XK01, XK02, XK03
Create/Change/Display a Purchase Info Record	ME11, ME12, ME13
List Display of the Purchasing Info Records	ME1L
Create/Change/Display a Purchase Order	ME21N, ME22N, ME23N
Goods Receipt	MIGO
Invoice Verification	MIRO
Display an Invoice Document	MIR4
Release a Blocked Invoice	MRBR
Display Open Items	FK10N
Outgoing Payments	F-53
Create/Change/Display a Customer	XD01, XD02, XD03
Expand Material Master Record	MM01
Create/Change/Display Sales Conditions	VK11, VK12, VK13
Create/Change/Display a Sales Order	VA01, VA02, VA03
Create a Delivery/Goods Issue	VL01N, VL02
Create/Change/Display an Invoice	VF01/VF02/VF03
Post an Incoming Payment	ZD-A-10
Display the Material Stock	MMBE

Table 20.1 *Overview of Relevant Transactions for the Case Study*

To implement the complete case study, you require an SAP Internet Demonstration and Evaluation System (IDES). SAP provides IDES as a test environment to its customers.

> **TIP**
>
> **Documentation**
>
> Document your work. In a real-world scenario, you might have to present your progress to a project team. Good documentation also makes repeating individual steps at a later stage much easier. You should also document how and why you perform certain steps.

Carry out these tasks in the sequence they are presented because the individual process steps are based on each other. Tasks that have the *optional* addition aren't relevant for subsequent processes, so you don't have to perform them.

Remember to always implement the case study in a training environment and never in a live SAP system! If you're unsure, ask your SAP administrator, supervisor, key user, or trainer. Good luck!

20.1   The Sample Business

You're an employee of a business called Sportbikes International, which produces and sells road bikes and mountain bikes. These bikes are distributed to resellers and directly to customers. The company is headquartered in Germany but has plans to start subsidiaries in Great Britain and the United States in the medium term. Currently, 200 employees work for the business. The bikes are manufactured in-house but are also procured from a supplier and resold. Sportbikes International recently decided to implement SAP to support logistics and financial accounting. It plans to use the following components: FI, CO, SD, and MM.

As an experienced user, you're a member in the project team for the SAP implementation, and you're provided with work packages with various tasks for testing functions and processes in the system.

20.2   The Enterprise Structure

In this case study, you work in the preconfigured IDES enterprise structure (i.e., in the SAP training environment), so you don't have to make specific Customizing settings.

First, get to know the business's structure and its presentation in the SAP system. Table 20.2 lists relevant information on the business structure.

System	Your training system
Client	(Your client)
Company Code	1000
Plant	1000 Hamburg
Storage Location	0001
Storage Location	0002
Purchasing Organization	1000
Purchasing Group	000

Table 20.2 *Organizational Units for the Case Study*

Check that you have the necessary authorizations and logon information.

Table 20.3, enter your logon information.

System	
Client	
Logon Name	
Password	

Table 20.3 *Your Logon Information*

Complete the following task and answer the following questions associated with the business structure:

1 Outline the enterprise structure in an organization chart.

2 To how many company codes can a plant be assigned?

3 Which information is mandatory for logging on to an SAP system?

4 Can the key of a plant (e.g., 1000) be assigned several times in a client if the plant is located in another company code?

5 What's the purpose of storage locations?

20.3 Creating a Material Master Record

Your company sells two kinds of bikes: road bikes and mountain bikes. For these products, which are called materials in the SAP system, you require the respective material master records, which you must first create.

Complete the following tasks associated with material master records: Create the material master records for the two bikes in the SAP system using the data listed in Table 20.4. Use the transaction in the SAP Easy Access menu under **General Create**. Make sure that you select the correct organizational units and views.

	Road Bike	Mountain Bike
Material Number	ZYM-BIKE10	ZYM-BIKE20
Industry	Mechanical engineering	Mechanical engineering
Material Type	Finished good	Finished good
Required Views	Basic Data 1	Basic Data 1
	Purchasing	Purchasing
	Purchase Order Text	Purchase Order Text
	Plant Data/ Warehouse 1	Plant Data/ Warehouse 1
	Accounting 1	Accounting 1
Organizational Units	Plant 1000	Plant 1000
	Storage location 0001	Storage location 0001
	Purchasing org. 1000	Purchasing org. 1000
Material Short Text	Roadbike Speed XL	Mountainbike Alpine XL

Table 20.4 *Material Master Data Sheet: Sample Data for Materials*

	Road Bike	Mountain Bike
Base Unit of Measure	Piece	Piece
Gross Weight	25	25
Net Weight	10	13
Weight Unit	kg	kg
Material Group	ZT00	ZT00
Purchasing Group	000	000
Purchase order text	Roadbike Speed XL, RH 56, aluminum	Mountainbike Alpine XL, RH 54, steel
Valuation Class	7920	7920
Price Control	MAP	MAP
Moving Average Price	400.00 EUR	300.00 EUR

Table 20.4 *Material Master Data Sheet: Sample Data for Materials (Cont.)*

Complete the following task and answer the following questions associated with creating a material master record:

1. Use Transaction MM01 to create the materials ZYM-BIKE10 and ZYM-BIKE20.

2. Test the functioning of the material master records after creation. How could you do this?

3. What are the views used for in material master records?

4. What is the Moving Average Price (MAP)?

5. Determine the MAP for the following scenario:
   - Opening stock: 10 pieces, price per piece €400.00
   - Purchase: 20 pieces, price per piece €300.00

6. Can you also procure material ZYM-BIKE10 for another plant (e.g., 1200)?

20.4 Creating Vendor Master Records

Your business purchases materials from several vendors. This time, you'll create master records for the vendors. Table 20.5 contains the required field content for two vendors.

	Vendor 1	Vendor 2
Vendor Number	ZYK-A10	ZYK-A20
Name and Address	Any name and address	Any name and address
Organizational Units	Company code 1000 Purchasing org. 1000	Company code 1000 Purchasing org. 1000
Account Group	ZTMM	ZTMM
Search Term	ZYK-A10	ZYK-A20
Country	Germany	Germany
Language	German	German
Reconciliation Account	160000	160000
Purchase Order Currency	EUR	EUR
Term of Payment Purchase	0002	0002

Table 20.5 Vendor Master Data Sheet: Sample Data for Vendors

Complete the following tasks associated with vendor master records:

1 Create the two vendor master records for vendor A and vendor B in the system using the data in the table. Use Transaction XK01 for this purpose.

2 Test the two vendor master records by creating (but not saving) a purchase order.

3 Add the transaction to your favorites.

20.5   Creating Purchasing Info Records

The purchasing department notifies you that prices for the road bikes and mountain bikes have already been negotiated with the vendors. Enter these conditions into the SAP system using purchasing info records.

Complete the following tasks associated with purchasing info records:

1 Use Transaction MMME11 to create the corresponding info records. Use the agreed-upon conditions from Table 20.6.

	Vendor 1	Vendor 2
Material	ZYK-A10	ZYK-A20
Purchasing Organization	1000	1000
Plant	1000	1000
Net Price for ZYM-BIKE10	€400.00/1 PC	€410.00/1 PC
Net Price for ZYM-BIKE20	€320.00/1 PC	€300.00/1 PC
Planned Delivery Time	1 day	1 day
Incoterms	EXW (ex works)	EXW (ex works)
Purchasing Group	000	000
Standard Quantity	1 piece	1 piece
Validity	Unlimited (12/31/9999)	Unlimited (12/31/9999)

Table 20.6 Sample Data for Purchasing Info Records

2 After creating the info records, check them using Transaction ME1L or via the SAP Easy Access menu path, **Logistics ▸ Materials Management ▸ Purchasing ▸ RRF/Quotation ▸ Request for Quotation ▸ Reporting ▸ Purchasing Information System ▸ Environment ▸ Master Data ▸ Info Record**.

Transaction ME1L lets you display an overview of all info records of vendors that are stored in the SAP system (Figure 20.1). This transaction can also be used for price simulations using the corresponding material/vendor combinations.

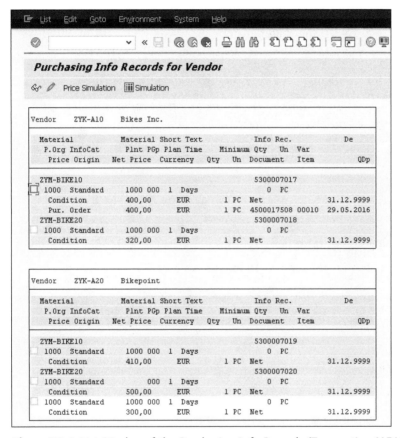

Figure 20.1 *List Display of the Purchasing Info Records (Transaction ME1L)*

20.6   Creating a Purchase Order

With this task, you start the procurement process (Figure 20.2). In the subprocess of the example, you procure finished bikes (the finished goods) from the vendors.

Figure 20.2 *First Step in the Procurement Process: Purchase Order*

Ten road bikes with the material number ZYM-BIKE10 are required for a trade show. Your task is to procure them from vendor ZYK-A10.

Complete the following tasks associated with the purchase order:

1. Use Transaction ME21N to create the purchase order. Check it for accuracy before you save it (Figure 20.3).

    Use the data from Table 20.7 for the purchase order.

Vendor	ZYK-A10
Purchasing Group	000 (boss)
Purchasing Organization	1000
Company Code	1000
Material	ZYM-BIKE10
Quantity	10
Plant	1000 Hamburg
Storage Location	0001

Table 20.7 *Sample Data for the Purchase Order*

2. Which price does the system propose?

3. Write down the document number.

4. Check the stock quantity of material ZYM-BIKE10 in the Hamburg plant. You can check the material stock using Transaction MMBE or via the SAP Easy Access menu path, **Logistics ▸ Materials Management ▸ Material Master ▸ Others ▸ Stock Overview**.

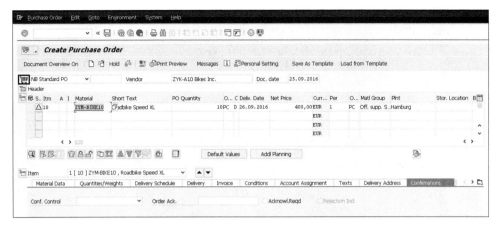

Figure 20.3 *Creating a Purchase Order (Transaction ME21N)*

20.7   Receiving Goods

You now receive the goods for the previously made purchase order (Figure 20.4). Assume that the purchase order you created in the previous section has been implemented and that the goods have been delivered accordingly.

Figure 20.4 *Second Step in the Procurement Process: Goods Receipt*

Complete the following tasks associated with goods receipt:

1 Post the goods receipt of the ordered road bikes. Refer to the purchase order number from the previous step. Select **OK** for the item, and store the road bikes in storage location 0001. Use Transaction MIGO (Figure 20.5).

2 Write down the number of the material document.

3 Check the stock quantity of material ZYM-BIKE10 in the Hamburg plant (Figure 20.6). What is the stock quantity now?

Figure 20.5 *Goods Receipt (Transaction MIGO)*

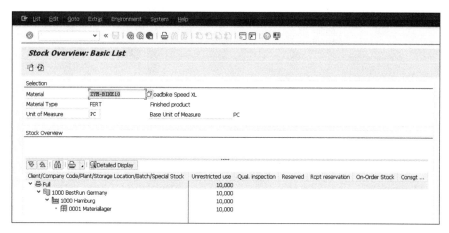

Figure 20.6 *Stock Overview (Transaction MMBE)*

20.8 Verifying an Invoice

After the goods have been delivered, the vendor sends the invoice. You now have to verify the invoice to initiate its payment (Figure 20.7). Verify the invoice for the previously made purchase order and for the received goods.

Figure 20.7 *Third Step in the Procurement Process: Invoice Verification*

Vendor ZYK-A10 provides the invoice for the ordered and stored road bikes.

Complete the following tasks associated with invoice verification:

1 Verify the invoice in the SAP system using Transaction MIRO (Figure 20.8). Refer to the document number of the purchase order that you've already created. The invoice contains the information listed in Table 20.8.

Vendor	ZYK-A10
Date	Today
Net Amount	4,000.00 EUR
Tax Rate	1I (Input tax 10%)
Gross Amount	4,400.00 EUR

Table 20.8 *Sample Data for the Invoice Verification*

2 Using Transaction MIR4, you can display the invoice document again. Blocked invoices can be released using Transaction MRBR.

How does the transaction indicate whether the goods receipt has been carried out after the purchase order?

Figure 20.8 *Invoice Verification (Transaction MIRO)*

20.9 Displaying Open Items (Optional)

Before you post the incoming payment, you want to get an overview of the open items (i.e., of outstanding payments to the vendor).

To display open items for vendor ZYK-A10, use the data from Table 20.9 for this example (Transaction FK10N), as shown in Figure 20.9.

Vendor	ZYK-A10
Company Code	1000
Fiscal Year	Current year

Table 20.9 *Sample Data for Selecting the Open Items*

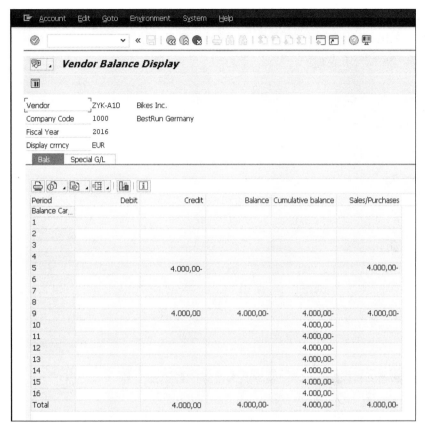

Figure 20.9 *SAP General Ledger Account Balance Display (Open Items) (Transaction FK10N)*

20.10   Posting Outgoing Payments

The purchasing process is now completed, and it's time to pay the invoice (Figure 20.10). This task is performed in FI. For this process, refer to the previous documents that exist in the system and were generated in the previous procurement steps.

Figure 20.10 *Fourth Step in the Procurement Process: Outgoing Payments*

Complete the following tasks associated with outgoing payments:

1 Post the outgoing payments using Transaction F-53 (Figure 20.11) and the data from Table 20.10.

Document Date	Today
Posting Date	Today
Bank data Area	
Account	113100
Amount	4,000.00 EUR
Value date	Today
Open item selection Area	
Account	ZYK-A10
Discount	None

Table 20.10 Sample Data for Outgoing Payments

Figure 20.11 Posting Outgoing Payments (Transaction F-53)

2 Again, check the open items of the vendor using the data from Table 20.11.

Vendor	ZYK-A10
Company Code	1000
Fiscal Year	Current year

Table 20.11 Sample Data for Selecting the Open Items

20.11 Creating a Customer Master

Your business sells the bikes to end customers and resellers. For the sales and distribution process, create the necessary customer master records in the SAP system.

Complete the following tasks associated with the customer master record:

1 Create the customer master record using the data from Table 20.12 (Transaction XD01).

Account Group	ZK10 sold-to party group 10
Customer	ZYD-A10
Sales Organization	1000
Distribution Channel	12 reseller
Division	00 cross-division
General Data, Address	
Name and Address	Hans Muller, Sample Rd 23, 91325 Adelsdorf
Country	DE
Region	Bavaria
Transport Zone	Region Nuremberg
General Data, Tax Data	
Tax Number 1	DE47110815

Table 20.12 Sample Data for the Customer Master Record

Company Code Data	
Reconciliation Account	140000
Terms of Payment	Immediately without discount
Sales Area Data	
Shipping Condition	Immediately
Delivering Plant	Hamburg
Tax Classification	Subject to tax
Incoterms	Free delivered

Table 20.12 Sample Data for the Customer Master Record (Cont.)

2 Test the customer master record that you created. How could you do this?

20.12   Adding Sales Data to the Material Master Record

The **Sales and Distribution: SalesOrgData 1** and **Sales and Distribution: General/Plant Data** views must be added to the existing material master records. Currently, the existing materials can be procured but not sold. Although you don't have to create the material master records again, you do have to add the sales data to the existing master records.

Complete the following tasks associated with adding sales data to material master records (Figure 20.12):

1 Select the transaction for creating a material (Transaction MM01). In the **Material Number** field, enter the preexisting material number.

2 Select the **Sales: Sales Org. Data 1** and **Sales: General/Plant Data** views. Enter the required sales data and save the master record. Carry out these steps for both master records.

3 Add the data from Table 20.13 to the master records.

	Road Bike	Mountain Bike (Optional)
Material Number	ZYM-BIKE10	ZYM-BIKE20
Plant	1000	1000
Sales Organization	1000	1000
Distribution Channel	End customer sales	End customer sales
Sales: Sales Org. Data 1 View		
Sales Unit	Piece	Piece
Delivering Plant	Hamburg	Hamburg
Storage Location	0001	0001
Tax Data	Full tax	Full tax
Sales: General/Plant Data View		
Transport Group	0001 Pallets	0001 Pallets
Loading Group	0003 Manual	0003 Manual

Table 20.13 *Material Master Data Sheet: Sample Data for Adding Sales Data to the Material Master Record*

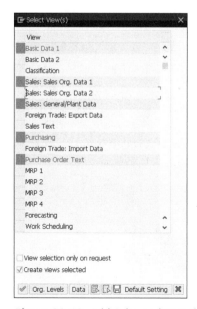

Figure 20.12 *Add Sales and Distribution Views to a Material (Transaction MM01)*

20.13 Creating Conditions

Define conditions in the system for sales organization 1000 and distribution channel 12. When a customer orders goods within the organizational units, the system prompts the conditions that you defined.

Carry out the following tasks regarding the conditions:

1 Create the conditions in the SAP system using Transaction VK11 (Figure 20.13) and the data from Table 20.14.

Condition Type	PR00
Sales Organization	1000
Key Combination	Customer/material with release status
Distribution Channel	End customers
Customer	ZYD-A10
Material	ZYM-BIKE10
Amount	€800.00/1 piece
Validity	Unlimited (today through 12/31/9999)

Table 20.14 Sample Data for Conditions

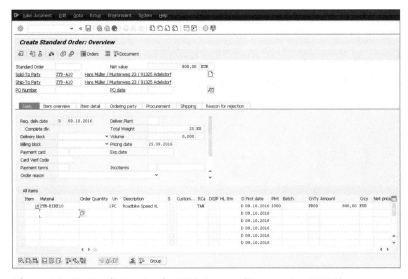

Figure 20.13 Conditions in the SAP System (Transaction VK11)

20.14   Creating a Standard Order

In this case, the actual sales process starts with the sales (standard) order. Again, use the data that has been created for this case study.

One of your customers now orders mountain bikes via telephone.

Figure 20.14 *First Step in the Sales Process: Order*

Complete the following tasks associated with the sales order:

1 Enter the standard order in the system using Transaction VA01 and the data from Table 20.15.

Order Type	TA
Sales Organization	1000
Distribution Channel	10
Division	00
Sold-To Party	ZYD-A10
Ship-To Party	ZYD-A10
Purchase Order Number	Any
Requested Delivery Date	2 weeks from today
Material	ZYM-BIKE10
Order Quantity	1 piece
Incoterms	Ex works
Terms of Payment	Cash without discount

Table 20.15 *Sample Data for the Standard Order*

2 Save the standard order, and write down the document number.

20.15   Delivering and Issuing Goods

Create the delivery, referring to the sales order that you created in the previous section. Then post the goods issue and deliver the goods to the customer according to that standard order (Figure 20.15).

Figure 20.15 *Second Step in the Sales Process: Delivery and Goods Issue*

Complete the following tasks associated with goods issue:

1 Create the delivery for the previous sales (standard) order using Transaction VL01N (Figure 20.16), and write down the document number. Use the sample data in Table 20.16.

Shipping Point	Hamburg
Selection Date	2 weeks from today
Order Number	Your order number

Table 20.16 *Sample Data for the Delivery*

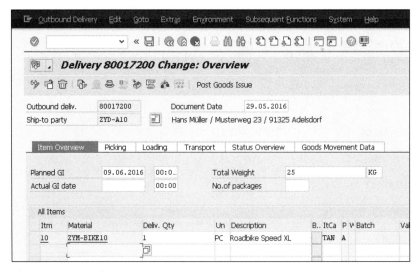

Figure 20.16 *Delivery (Transaction VL01N)*

2 Post the goods issue (Figure 20.17).

Figure 20.17 *Goods Issue (Transaction VLO2)*

20.16 Creating an Invoice

Now invoice the delivered bikes to the customer (Figure 20.18).

Figure 20.18 *Third Step in the Sales Process: Invoice*

Complete the following tasks associated with invoicing:

1 Create an invoice for the sales order using Transaction VF01 (Figure 20.19), and write down the document number.

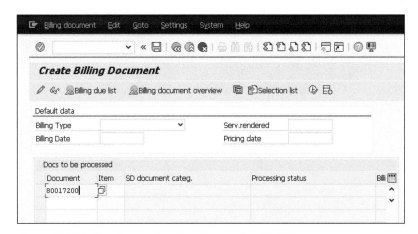

Figure 20.19 *Creating an Invoice (Transaction VF01)*

After invoicing your delivery, you can post the incoming payment.

20.17 Posting Incoming Payments

The customer has transferred the complete invoice amount, which corresponds to the already performed sales order, and you can post the incoming payment (Figure 20.20).

Figure 20.20 *Fourth Step in the Sales Process: Incoming Payments*

Complete the following tasks associated with incoming payment:

1 Post the incoming payment of the customer using Transaction F-28 (Figure 20.21) and the data from Table 20.17.

Document Date	Today
Bank Data	
Account	113100
Amount	880.00 EUR
Selection of Open Items	
Account	ZYD-A10

Table 20.17 *Sample Data for Incoming Payments*

2 Now check the current stock quantity of material ZYM-BIKE10 (Figure 20.22).

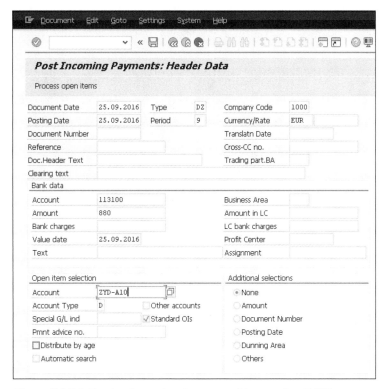

Figure 20.21 *Posting Incoming Payments (Transaction F-28)*

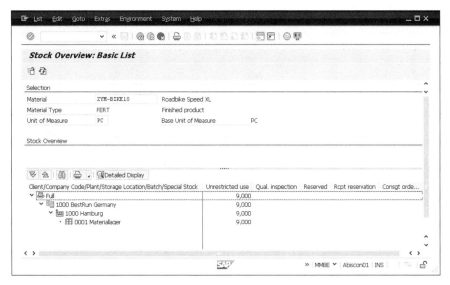

Figure 20.22 *Stock Overview (Transaction MMBE)*

Congratulations! You've successfully implemented numerous processes in the SAP system. If you had any difficulty performing the tasks, you can find solution notes for the exercises on the SAP PRESS website at *https://www.sap-press.com/using-sap_4155/*.

Appendices

A   Abbreviations

Abbreviation	Long Form	Explanation
ABAP	Advanced Business Application Programming	SAP programming language; see Chapter 3
AP	Accounts Payable (FI-AP)	Accounts payable accounting; see Chapter 17
AR	Accounts Receivable (FI-AR)	Accounts receivable accounting; see Chapter 17
CATS	Cross-Application Time Sheet	See Chapter 18
CO	Controlling	Controlling component from SAP ERP; see Chapter 18
EDI	Electronic Data Interchange	See Chapter 12
ERP	Enterprise Resource Planning	See Chapter 3
ESS	Employee Self-Service	See Chapter 19
FI	SAP ERP Financials	See Chapter 17
G/L	SAP General Ledger (FI-G/L)	Financial accounting; see Chapter 17
GUI	Graphical User Interface	See Chapter 5
HR	Human Resources	See Chapter 19
IDES	Internet Demonstration and Education System	See Introduction
IMG	Implementation Guide	See Chapter 2
IS	Industry Solution	See Chapter 3
IV	Invoice Verification (MM-IV)	See Chapter 15
LO	Logistics	Logistics (general); see Chapter 3

Abbreviation	Long Form	Explanation
MM	Materials Management	See Chapter 15
OM	Overhead Management (CO-OM)	Overhead cost controlling; see Chapter 18
P&L	Profit and loss statement	See Chapter 17
PA	Profitability Analysis (CO-PA)	See Chapter 18
PA	Personnel Administration (HCM-PA)	See Chapter 19
PM	Plant Maintenance	See Chapter 3
PP	Production Planning	See Chapter 3
PReq	Purchase Order Requisition	See Chapter 15
PT	Personnel Time Planning (HCM-PT)	Time management; see Chapter 19
PY	Payroll (HCM-PY)	See Chapter 19
SAP CRM	SAP Customer Relationship Management	See Chapter 3
SAP ERP HCM	SAP ERP Human Capital Management	Human resources; see Chapter 19
SAP PLM	SAP Product Lifecycle Management	See Chapter 3
SAP SCM	SAP Supply Chain Management	See Chapter 3
SAP SRM	SAP Supplier Relationship Management	See Chapter 3
SD	Sales and Distribution	See Chapter 16

B Glossary

ABAP Advanced Business Application Programming. SAP-specific programming language.

accounts payable accounting Posts all business transactions that refer to vendors and receives its data from purchasing. Supported by the FI-AP component from SAP ERP Financials (FI).

accounts receivable accounting Records all customer-related business transactions. A lot of this information originates from Sales and Distribution (SD). In the SAP system, accounts receivable accounting is supported by the Accounts Receivable (FI-AR).

activity type Categorizes the activities that are rendered within a controlling area (in time or quantity units).

Asset Accounting Records all business transactions that refer to a business's assets. The Asset Accounting (FI-AA) component is used for the management of assets with regard to accounting (e.g., for their evaluation).

authentication Process that checks the identity of a computer user to allow access to the system or data.

authorization The user's right to carry out a specific action in the SAP system.

background job Task that runs via background processing in the SAP system without user intervention.

Business Add-In (BAdI) SAP enhancement technology; locations predefined by SAP where you can link custom developments (your own program code). See *user exit.*

Business Application Programming Interface (BAPI) Interface in the SAP system to which specific business rules are linked.

business area Organizational unit in the SAP system; in SAP ERP Financials (FI), it corresponds to a defined area of responsibility to which the recorded value movement can be assigned.

business intelligence (BI) Collective term for processes that evaluate data that are available across the enterprise. These evaluations are provided to users to support them in decision-making processes. BI data are often stored in a data warehouse. See *data warehouse.*

business partner Natural or legal person or a group of persons outside the business with which the enterprise collaborates at a business level.

business process Sequence of linked steps that are supposed to have a defined result and are carried out in a business environment. SAP applications support typical business processes, such as invoicing.

Business Workplace A work environment within the SAP system that supports the user with functions for managing messages, documents, and appointments.

chart of accounts List of all accounts of an enterprise and an integral part of double-entry accounting in which the accounts are systematically structured. Usually, a standard chart of accounts is used in the business.

client Topmost organizational unit in the SAP system; an entire enterprise can be mapped by client, for example. All organizational units within a client (e.g., company codes) follow a standard chart of accounts and are managed together. You always log on to a SAP system in a specific client.

client-server architecture   System architecture that enables you to distribute tasks across clients and servers within a network. The server provides services that the clients (user PCs) use. SAP ERP is based on a three-layer concept: database, server, and client.

company code   Part of the organizational structure in the SAP system; the smallest organizational unit for which a complete, self-contained set of accounts can be drawn up for the purposes of financial accounting.

compliance   Procedure for compliance with laws and guidelines, such as the Sarbanes-Oxley Act (SOX) or the Occupational Safety and Health Act (OSHA).

consolidation   In financial accounting, merging individual financial statements of various subsidiary companies into a consolidated financial statement. In the general context, consolidation refers to merging data, information, and so on.

Controlling (CO)   The Controlling (CO) component in SAP ERP Financials (FI) serves to monitor, plan, and control business costs and revenues.

controlling area   Organizational unit in the SAP system for controlling. Expenses and revenues are managed and allocated at this level. One or more company codes can be assigned to a controlling area.

cost center   Enterprise-specific account assignment object to which costs are posted. In the SAP system, the cost center is an organizational unit within a controlling area that presents a defined location of cost incurrence.

cost element   Cost elements are SAP General Ledger (G/L) accounts that are relevant for Controlling (CO). Primary cost elements have the respective G/L accounts in FI and are directly transferred to CO as actual costs. Secondary cost elements are only used for cost management in CO and don't have any effects on SAP ERP Financials (FI).

Cross-Application Time Sheet (CATS) SAP self-service application for employees and external service providers that enable time recording using the time sheet.

Customer Relationship Management (CRM)   See *SAP Customer Relationship Management (SAP CRM)*.

Customer Service   Component in SAP ERP that supports the processes in service processing (e.g., the processing of returns, spare part deliveries, repair processing, and installation of devices) as well as the management of service contracts and maintenance.

Customizing   Customization of standard SAP software to fit the customer's requirements. In Customizing (in contrast to custom developments), the software is adapted to the business's processes without programming. See *Implementation Guide (IMG)*.

data warehouse   A centralized database whose data come from various sources (e.g., SAP ERP) and can be provided for analysis and reporting. It also contains historical data. The data warehouse in the SAP system is SAP Business Warehouse (SAP BW).

database   System for electronic data management in which large data volumes are stored and required data are made available in the appropriate display format for users and application programs. The most commonly used databases for SAP systems are MaxDB by SAP, Oracle, and DB2 by IBM.

debits and credits   Basic principle of double-entry accounting in which expenses (debits = disposition of funds) and revenues (credits = source of funds) are posted separately. Every business transaction is posted on the debit and on the credit side to different accounts.

distribution channel   Organizational unit in the SAP system in which various sales channels (e.g., wholesale) are mapped in Sales and Distribution (SD). You can assign any number of distribution channels to a sales organization.

division   Organizational unit in the SAP system that is mainly used for Sales and Distribution (SD). The products of a business are assigned to a division to map the responsibility in sales or the responsibility for profits from products.

document principle   Financial accounting principle that there must be a document for every posting.

double-entry accounting   Accounting procedure that lists value changes in two different locations: debits and credits are posted in the posting record. See *debits and credits*.

Electronic Data Interchange (EDI) Electronic data exchange procedure.

Employee Self-Service (ESS)   SAP function that enables employees to access data and execute processes using their user roles (e.g., to submit leave requests or register for employee training). See *Manager Self-Service (MSS)*.

Enterprise Controlling (EC)   SAP ERP component for business controlling; contains functions for consolidation and profit center accounting.

Enterprise Resource Planning (ERP) Solution for human resources, logistics, and accounting that supports all core business transactions in an enterprise. See *SAP ERP*.

ERP Central Component (ECC)   Technical core of SAP ERP.

financial statement   Maps the payables (outside capital) and net assets (stockholders' equity) of an enterprise at a specific time. See *profit and loss statement*.

Financial Supply Chain Management (FSCM)   Deals with the optimization of cash flows within the business to improve liquidity. FSCM includes SAP Receivables Management, for example.

Governance, Risk, and Compliance (GRC)   Guiding principles for responsible and successful business management in which risks are identified and avoided, and internal standards are met.

Graphical User Interface (GUI)   The application interface on the computer screen that the user uses to communicate with the computer.

HR area   Organizational unit in SAP ERP Human Capital Management (SAP ERP HCM) that helps to generate default values during the entry of data, serves as a selection criterion for evaluations, and is critical for authorization checks.

human capital management   See *SAP ERP Human Capital Management (SAP ERP HCM)*.

human resources   See *SAP ERP Human Capital Management (SAP ERP HCM)*.

IDES   Internet Demonstration and Education System; model enterprise whose business processes are implemented in the SAP system for training purposes.

All business areas are already configured and mapped in an integrative manner.

Implementation Guide (IMG)   Menu for the Customizing of the SAP system. The IMG has a hierarchical structure based on the hierarchy of the SAP components.

industry solution (IS)   SAP software solution tailored to a specific industry (e.g., utilities, retail, automotive, banking, etc.). Currently, 24 ISs are available.

infotype   Information unit in SAP ERP HCM. Groups of related data fields are joined in infotypes to structure information, facilitate its entry, and enable time-dependent data storage.

integration   Linking various applications and merging data in one software application with the aim of making processes more efficient and improving data quality.

internal order   Enables the planning, collection, and monitoring of costs regarding specific transactions and tasks in the SAP system.

inventory management   Deals with the quantity-based and value-based management of material stocks, the management of goods movements, and the physical inventory. In the SAP system, inventory management is supported by the Inventory Management (MM-IM) component.

Investment Management   The Investment Management component in SAP ERP supports the planning and financing of tangible assets, investments in research and development, further training, and maintenance tasks in your business. For financial assets, see *Treasury*.

invoice verification   Comparison of vendor invoices with purchase order and goods receipt. In the Materials Management (MM) component of SAP ERP, Invoice Verification (MM-IV) is used for invoice verification.

Key Performance Indicator (KPI)   Quantitative information that is mapped in compressed (aggregated) form and reflects the success or failure of a business.

Knowledge Management   SAP solution that enables you to create, classify, and present information as well as distribute it across the entire business.

ledger   In accounting, framework for the recording of value or quantity transactions for a specific subarea of financial accounting. See *SAP General Ledger Accounting*.

Logistics Execution System (LES)   SAP ERP component that supports transport and distribution. This includes the transport of goods of all kinds using various means of transport.

Logistics Information System (LIS)   Tool in SAP ERP for the evaluation of data from purchasing, production, sales and distribution, warehouse, plant maintenance, quality management, and transport management.

Manager Self-Service (MSS)   Lets managers access data and carry out tasks in the SAP system using their roles in the enterprise (e.g., hiring employees or planning budgets). See *Employee Self-Service (ESS)*.

master data   Information that remains unchanged over a longer period of time and is repeatedly required in business processes. Examples of master data include name, address, and date of birth of an employee.

Master Data Management   See *SAP NetWeaver Master Data Management (SAP NetWeaver MDM)*.

Material Requirements Planning (MRP)   Umbrella term for the planning and distribution of orders as well as for the assignment/provision of resources in order processing.

Materials Management (MM)   The MM component in SAP ERP supports the entire purchasing process from purchasing management, to inventory management, to invoice verification. See *Purchasing*.

one-time account   Collective account for various vendors in financial accounting that is used for one-time invoices and payments.

operating concern   Central element in Profitability Analysis (PA).

organizational structure   Mapping of the enterprise structure in the SAP system in which every enterprise area (e.g., FI) is structured via organizational units.

overhead cost controlling   Overhead Management (CO-OM) in SAP ERP Financials (FI), encompasses all tasks that support the coordination, monitoring, and optimization of indirect costs (costs that cannot be directly assigned to a product or service).

Payroll   Component in SAP ERP HCM that determines the remuneration for an employee. This includes preparation, settlement, transfer, Social Security contributions, and the transport of the data to FI. Payroll processes are subject to numerous legal regulations, such as taxes.

Personnel Administration   SAP ERP HCM component that supports all activities to be carried out within the scope of employee management in the business. Particularly critical are the creation, maintenance, and assignment of employee data.

Personnel Development   Component in SAP ERP HCM for strategic HR work to train and motivate employees. Today, it's known as Talent Management.

Personnel Time Management   Component in SAP ERP HCM for recording working times (attendance times, breaks, business trips, extra shifts, reduced hours, absences, etc.).

plant   Organizational unit of the SAP system in logistics; structures the business from the production, MRP, and plant maintenance perspective. Each plant is assigned to a company code, which can contain multiple plants.

Plant Maintenance (PM)   PM supports the planning, implementation, and settlement of maintenance tasks. SAP now markets this component as SAP Enterprise Asset Management (EAM).

product cost controlling   Product Costing (CO-PC) component in SAP ERP Financials (FI) supports product cost planning and basically uses data from Production Planning (PP) and Materials Management (MM).

Production Planning (PP)   PP component from SAP ERP covers the planning and control of the logistics processes within production (i.e., the provision of raw materials and supplies, production processes, and transport of the manufactured products).

Profit and loss (P&L) statement   Part of the year-end closing, which has to be created according to country-specific legal requirements. The P&L statement includes a list of all expenses and revenues for the fiscal year.

profit center accounting   A separate period result is determined for a part of an enterprise, for example, a subsidiary or branch store. Profit centers collect revenues and costs for the cost center for which they are responsible, like an independent business. In the SAP system, profit center accounting is supported by the Profit Center Accounting (CO-PCA) component.

Profitability Analysis (PA)   Controlling approach. The Profitability Analysis (CO-PA) component from SAP ERP Financials (FI) relates revenues from Sales and Distribution (SD) with costs from overhead cost controlling and product cost controlling.

purchase   Procuring goods and services at an optimum cost/performance ratio with the goods being available at the right place at the right time. In contrast to procurement, which consists of strategic tasks, purchasing mainly deals with operational tasks. The purchase process is managed with Materials Management (MM). See *Materials Management (MM)*.

purchase requisition (PReq)   PReq initiates the procurement process. The user department creates a purchase requisition based on a requirement for goods or services and forwards it to the purchasing department.

purchasing group   Organizational unit in the Materials Management (MM) component. The purchasing group is responsible for the procurement of specific materials or service providers and is the point of contact for certain vendors.

purchasing organization   Organizational unit in Materials Management (MM). The purchasing organization is responsible for all purchasing processes. In legal terms, it's the procuring unit. Purchasing organizations are assigned to company codes and plants, and they determine the purchase type (group-

related, enterprise-related, or plant-related).

Quality Management (QM)   The SAP QM component controls quality planning and checks and supports problem management and issue quality certificates. It meets the requirements for QM systems according to ISO 9000.

Real Estate Management   SAP ERP RE consists of the management of real estate, contract and area management, and financial mapping (control of cash flows, postings and evaluations, controlling, etc.).

reconciliation account   SAP General Ledger (G/L) account that can be used to update the subledger accounts in parallel to the G/L. There is a reconciliation account for every subledger.

Recruitment   Component in SAP ERP HCM that is used to manage applicant data and thus facilitate the search for and selection of appropriate candidates.

Return on investment (ROI)   Key figure that enables you to measure the yield of the capital employed.

sales and distribution   Refers to all processes that are necessary for selling a product or service to a customer. The Sales and Distribution (SD) component in SAP ERP supports sales processes as well as delivery and transport processes.

sales organization   Organizational unit in the SAP system that is the most critical element in sales and distribution. In legal terms, it refers to a selling unit. Complete sales business transactions are managed here. A company code can have several sales organizations, but a sales organization can only belong to one company code.

SAP Advanced Planning and Optimization (SAP APO)   Part of SAP Supply Chain Management (SAP SCM); software for the management and integration of sales, distribution, and production planning; production control and external procurement; and vendor cooperation.

SAP Business All-in-One   Integrated software system by SAP that is based on SAP Best Practices for small- and medium-sized enterprises.

SAP Business ByDesign   On-demand solution for customers in medium-sized businesses; a completely integrated solution with an easy configuration hosted at SAP.

SAP Business Explorer (SAP BEx)   Part of SAP Business Warehouse (SAP BW), contains reporting tools that you can use to map data from the data warehouse in various reports. See *SAP Business Warehouse (SAP BW)* and *data warehouse*.

SAP Business One   SAP software for small- and medium-sized businesses; like SAP ERP, it covers all core business requirements.

SAP Business Suite   Comprehensive enterprise solution by SAP containing the following solutions: SAP ERP, SAP Customer Relationship Management (SAP CRM), SAP Product Lifecycle Management (SAP PLM), SAP Supply Chain Management (SAP SCM), and SAP Supplier Relationship Management (SAP SRM). See these entries.

SAP Business Warehouse (SAP BW)   See *data warehouse*.

SAP Business Workflow   SAP component that is used to facilitate business processes. In the SAP system, a workflow controls the flow of documents, which are usually processed by several

people and have to be handled according to a defined pattern.

SAP Customer Relationship Management (SAP CRM)   SAP solution for the management of business contacts and customer relationships; contains functions for marketing, sales and distribution, and customer service.

SAP Easy Access menu   User menu in the SAP system that is displayed as a tree structure on the left side of the screen after you have logged on to the system. It can be used for the user-specific navigation in the SAP system.

SAP Enterprise Portal   Component of SAP NetWeaver (old name: SAP NetWeaver Portal); can be used to merge information and applications centrally in an enterprise portal and provide them in a uniform way.

SAP ERP   Software solution that covers the core business requirements of medium-sized and large businesses. Among other things, it includes human resources (SAP ERP HCM), financial accounting (SAP ERP Financials), Sales and Distribution (SD), and logistics (SAP ERP Operations). See *Enterprise Resource Planning*.

SAP ERP Financials (FI)   External accounting. FI is used to manage and map all accounting data according to the document principle. It covers SAP General Ledger Accounting as well as accounts payable accounting, accounts receivable accounting, Asset Accounting (AA), and Bank Accounting.

SAP ERP Human Capital Management (SAP ERP HCM)   Part of SAP ERP for the management of human resources, such as personnel administration, time management, payroll, travel management.

SAP Fiori   New user interface technology that allows role-based usage independent of the devices used (e.g., smartphones or tablets). Functions are provided in the form of SAP Fiori apps. See *SAP S/4HANA*.

SAP General Ledger (G/L) account
Account in the G/L that is directly included in the financial statement or profit and loss (P&L) statement.

SAP General Ledger Accounting
Records all accounting-relevant business transactions using G/L accounts (accounts in the chart of accounts). In SAP ERP Financials (FI), it's mapped by the FI-G/L component.

SAP HANA   In-memory database from SAP that is the basis of SAP S/4HANA.

SAP NetWeaver   SAP technology platform; technical basis for most of the SAP solutions.

SAP NetWeaver Application Server
Formerly SAP Web Application Server; technical basis for most of the SAP products. It consists of an ABAP application server (formerly SAP R/3 Basis) and a Java EE application server that can be used together or separately.

SAP NetWeaver Exchange Infrastructure (SAP NetWeaver XI)   Obsolete name for SAP Process Integration (SAP PI). See *SAP Process Integration (SAP PI)*.

SAP NetWeaver Master Data Management (SAP NetWeaver MDM)   Component for master data management.

SAP Process Integration (SAP PI)   SAP NetWeaver component that enables the integration of processes and thus the communication between applications.

SAP Product Lifecycle Management (SAP PLM)   SAP software solution that provides support for product development, project management, product plan management, and quality management.

SAP Project System (PS)   The PS component supports the technical and commercial part of a project and ensures the structuring, workflow planning, and cost accounting of a complex project.

SAP R/3   Software that is based on the client-server architecture by SAP. It was introduced in 1992 and was the predecessor of SAP ERP.

SAP S/4HANA   The new software generation of SAP. The new SAP Business Suite is based on the database SAP HANA and leverages the new SAP Fiori intuitive interface technology.

SAP Service Marketplace   Online help system by SAP in which customers can enter error messages that are then processed by SAP employees (*http://www.service.sap.com*, logon required). SAP Notes (formerly OSS notes) provide support for various topics.

SAP Solution Manager   An SAP support tool that supports SAP customers in the implementation and operation of SAP software.

SAP Strategic Enterprise Management (SAP SEM)   Part of SAP ERP Financials (FI) that contains functions for enterprise planning and consolidation.

SAP Supplier Relationship Management (SAP SRM)   SAP solution from the logistics area that supports businesses in managing procurement processes and vendor communication.

SAP Supply Chain Management (SAP SCM) SAP solution from the logistics area; used to coordinate supply and demand; monitor the supply chain, manage distribution, transport, and other logistics tasks; and provide collaboration and analysis tools.

scalability The system's ability to be enhanced and extended.

Service-Oriented Architecture (SOA) A software architecture that enables the use of exchangeable web services for the creation of business processes.

Solution Manager See *SAP Solution Manager*.

storage location Organizational unit for logistics in the SAP system that allows for the differentiation of stocks within a plant. A plant can have several storage locations. In a complex warehouse, storage locations can be further divided into warehouse numbers, storage types, and storage bins.

Supply Chain Management See *SAP Supply Chain Management (SAP SCM)*.

Time Management Personnel Time Planning; is used to record and manage time data in human resources (PT component in SAP ERP HCM).

Training and Event Management Component in SAP ERP HCM for planning, implementing, and managing events, such as trainings.

transaction code Alphanumeric code that is used to navigate via the command field in the SAP system. It lets you enter the required functions directly.

transaction data Data that can be changed and is usually valid for a defined period of time for a specific transaction only. It's created during business processes and is edited by users or other applications for a limited period of time. See *master data*.

Treasury Manages financial transactions on the money and capital market. The Treasury functions in SAP ERP Financials (FI) support analyzing and monitoring financial risks on the money and capital market.

user exit Predefined points in the SAP system for custom developments (custom program code), similar to Business Add-Ins (BAdIs).

Warehouse Management (WM) The WM component in SAP ERP controls and manages internal goods movements, goods receipt, and goods issue as well as all warehouse processes.

web service Module that consists of program code that provides a business function and is made available via the Internet. Usually, together with other web services, it forms a business process and can, once created, be reused in other business processes.

C Buttons, Key Combinations, and Function Keys

C.1 Key Combinations

Action	Key combination
Cancel actions step by step	`Esc`
Select all	`Ctrl`+`A`
Activate selected element	`Enter` or space
Cut	`Ctrl`+`X`
Insert	`Ctrl`+`V`
Activate entry in list	`Enter`
Replace	`Ctrl`+`H`
Navigate in list of entries which can be selected	`←`
Copy	`Ctrl`+`C`
Delete	`Del` (numeric keypad)
Search	`Ctrl`+`F`
Repeat	`Ctrl`+`Y`
Cut line	`Ctrl`+`Shift`+`X`
Duplicate line	`Ctrl`+`D`
Copy line	`Ctrl`+`Shift`+`T`
Delete line	`Ctrl`+`Shift`+`1`
Move line upward	`Ctrl`+`Alt`+`8` (numeric key pad)
Move line downward	`Ctrl`+`Alt`+`2` (numeric key pad)
Change lines	`Ctrl`+`Alt`+`T`
Go to menu	`Alt`
Navigate to next element	`Tab`

Action	Key combination
Navigate to previous element	Shift + Tab
Navigate to next group	Ctrl + Tab
Navigate to previous group	Shift + Ctrl + Tab
Undo	Ctrl + Z
Refresh SAP Easy Access menu	Ctrl + F1

C.2 Function Keys

Function Key	Explanation
F1	Help
F3	Back
F4	Display search list
F5	Overview
F6	Copy to personal value list
F12	Cancel

C.3 Buttons

Standard Toolbar

Button	Key Combination	Function
	Enter	Enter
	Ctrl + S	Save
	F3	Back
	Shift + F3	Exit

Button	Key Combination	Function
🔳	F12	Cancel
🔳	Ctrl + P	Print
🔳	–	New session
🔳	F1	(F1) help
🔳	Ctrl + F	Search
🔳	Ctrl + G	Find next
🔳	Ctrl + Page ↑	First page
🔳	Ctrl + Page ↓	Last page
🔳	Page ↑	Next page
🔳	Page ↓	Previous page
🔳	–	Desktop link
🔳	Alt + F1	Customize local layout

General Functions

Button	Key Combination	Function
🔳	F8	Execute
🔳	F6	Create
🔳	–	Copy
🔳	Ctrl + Shift + F3	Change favorites
🔳	Ctrl + F6	Display
🔳	F7	Switch: display/change
🔳	F7	Select all lines
🔳	F8	Deselect
🔳	–	Retrieve variant
🔳	F5	Display document overview
🔳	Shift + F6	Screen help

Button	Key Combination	Function
⇨	–	Multiple selection
⟳	–	Refresh
🗑	Shift + F2	Delete
🔒	–	Lock
🔓	–	Unlock
⚑	Ctrl + Shift + F6	Released
⊠	F12	Cancel
⭐	Ctrl + Shift + F6	Add favorite
⭐	Shift + F2	Delete favorite
▣		Object services
📄	Shift + F5	Display next document
🖱	F6	Display document header
⬥	–	Selection variants

F4 Help

Button	Function
✓	Execute search
✕	Close
⬥	Multiple selection
ⓘ	Documentation
🖨	Print hit list
⭐	Copy value to personal hit list
⭐	Delete value from personal hit list
🔖	Change to personal value list
🌐	Display all values

Reports

Button	Key Combination	Function
	Ctrl + F4	Sort in ascending order
	Ctrl + Shift + F4	Sort in descending order
	Ctrl + F5	Set filter
	Ctrl + F6	Total
	Ctrl + Shift + F6	Subtotals
	Ctrl + F8	Change layout
	Ctrl + Shift + F11	Create diagram
	–	Mass change
	Ctrl + F7	Send message
	Ctrl + Shift + F9	Local file
	Ctrl + Shift + F7 / F8	Export to Word processing/spread-sheet
	Ctrl + F1	ABC analysis
	Ctrl + Shift + F3	Display details

D   The Author

 **Olaf Schulz** works as an SAP consultant. In addition, he has been working as a trainer for SAP education partners for several years. Since 1995, Olaf has worked in the field of IT and organization where he has gained profound insight into implementation, development, and maintenance of business systems; planning and execution of trainings; and designing IT infrastructures. In cooperation with user departments, he has analyzed their requirements, implemented them in SAP systems, and launched them in the enterprise. In this book, Olaf wants to provide SAP users and seminar participants with a structured, easily comprehensible, and complete book to familiarize them with this complex topic. This book is based on experience obtained from system and user support and numerous trainings he has conducted.

Index

Q

R

- ▶ Learn how SAP S/4HANA enables digital transformation
- ▶ Explore innovative financials and logistics functionality
- ▶ Understand the technical foundation underlying SAP S/4HANA advances

Baumgartl, Chaadaev, Choi, Dudgeon, Lahiri, Meijerink, and Worsley-Tonks

SAP S/4HANA

An Introduction

Looking to make the jump to SAP S/4HANA? Learn what SAP S/4HANA offers, from the Universal Journal in SAP S/4HANA Finance to supply chain management in SAP S/4HANA Materials Management and Operations. Understand your deployment options—on-premise, cloud, and hybrid—and explore SAP Activate's implementation approach. Get an overview of how SAP HANA architecture supports digital transformation, and see what tools can help extend your SAP S/4HANA functionality!

449 pages, pub. 12/2016
E-Book: $59.99 | **Print:** $69.95 | **Bundle:** $79.99

www.sap-press.com/4153

▶ Explore SAP HANA in all its forms: as database, as application platform, as driver for SAP S/4HANA

▶ Learn about data modeling, data provisioning, and administration

▶ Get the basics you need to speed into the world of SAP HANA

Silvia, Frye, Berg

SAP HANA

An Introduction

What does SAP HANA mean for you? This book is your introduction to all the essentials, from implementation options to the basics of data modeling and administration. With cutting-edge coverage of SAP HANA smart data access, SAP HANA Vora, and more, this bestseller has everything you need to take your first steps with SAP HANA.

549 pages, 4th edition, pub. 11/2016
E-Book: $59.99 | **Print:** $69.95 | **Bundle:** $79.99

www.sap-press.com/4160